Praise for *Stealing Water*

'Tim Ecott's *Stealing Water* is the greatest memoir to come out of white Africa since Rian Malan's *My Traitor's Heart* – and what is remarkable about it is that it reads like *Angela's Ashes* rewritten by Nick Hornby under a baking Johannesburg sun – ultimately it is the story of a family fighting to survive, and a tale told with warmth, humanity and humour to burn.'

– Tony Parsons

'Tim Ecott's story of growing up in Ireland and Africa is both haunting and funny. He writes with compassion and honesty to give us a truly memorable account of an extraordinary upbringing.'

– Fergal Keane

'*Stealing Water* clearly demonstrates how much we have to forgive our parents and by the same token, how much our children will eventually have to forgive us. This is a truthful story brilliantly told – both funny and moving. I often had to lay the book aside to recover from laughter, or to think through the stories revealed. Tim Ecott cleverly captures the feeling of an extraordinary life lived in two wildly dissimilar countries.'

– Lynne Reid Banks

'*Stealing Water* is a simultaneously hilarious and heartbreaking portrait of poor-white family life in the twilight of apartheid'

– Richard E. Grant

'There are belly laughs enough, and some serious criminality to boot, but Ecott's outstanding talent as an author is for pathos. His mother's scorn of logic, fate and the laws of probability, carrying on her shoulders a whole world of worry, debt, misfortune and illness, and all her family's fortunes, moved me more than once to tears.'

– Matthew Parris, *The Times*

STEALING WATER
Tim Ecott

SCEPTRE

First published in Great Britain in 2008 by Sceptre

An imprint of Hodder & Stoughton
An Hachette Livre UK company

First published in paperback in 2009

2

A CIP catalogue record for this title is available from the British Library

ISBN 978 0 340 93664 1
Expot ISBN 978 0 340 92486 0

Typeset in Sabon by Hewer Text UK Ltd, Edinburgh
Printed and bound in the UK by CPI Mackays, Chatham ME5 8TD

Hodder & Stoughton policy is to use papers that are natural, renewable
and recyclable products and made from wood grown in sustainable forests.
The logging and manufacturing processes are expected to conform
to the environmental regulations of the country of origin.

Hodder & Stoughton Ltd
338 Euston Road
London NW1 3BH

www.hodder.co.uk

For
S.H.E. and P.M.E.

Tarts and Bullets

Babette kept a monkey called François in her bra. Babette's breasts were large, and François was a very small squirrel monkey, but a monkey all the same. It didn't seem possible, but once that monkey got down inside the bra he was invisible. Whenever François got bored with the great outdoors he would scamper from Babette's shoulder, down her décolleté and disappear into her cushion-plump bosom. François wasn't the friendliest monkey you could meet, nor was he the cleanest.

Babette was a short woman with a thick waist and hair dyed so blonde it was translucent. She piled her hair up into an improbable beehive that doubled the size of her head. Maybe she wanted to look taller, but in combination with her large breasts it just made her top-heavy. She also wore very high heels, her little chubby feet bursting their flesh at the margins of the leather. Up-close Babette always smelled very slightly of monkey-piss. Her dress had brown stains on it too, although the good thing about squirrel monkeys is that they crap in tiny quantities.

The real mystery about Babette was that she was a tart. We knew a lot of full-time girls but Babette only worked when money was short. I always wondered where the monkey went when Babette had a customer to entertain. Or if it watched.

Apart from keeping the monkey in her bra, we knew that Babette had a temper. Jarek, her Polish boyfriend, was a dealer who made a precarious living by selling pieces of jewellery, loose gemstones and antique porcelain to shops in the city. He went off travelling for weeks at a time and came back with more stones. Sometimes he said he'd been in Zambia, sometimes Zimbabwe or even Angola. Babette was always scared he would get caught, either for smuggling or just for dealing in uncut stones, because at that time all uncut diamonds in South Africa belonged to De Beers. The papers often ran stories about people being arrested for 'illicit diamond buying', a crime so common they used the acronym 'IDB'. And the sentences they reported were harsh: seven to ten years was common.

Jarek was short and lean with a big fleshy nose and a badly pock-marked face. He barely spoke above a whisper, and carried a gun in a brown leather holster under his jacket. Jarek had a short wiry body and extra white skin, and didn't strike me as the type to inspire passion. One day he took off his shirt and showed us a network of horrendous scars, keloid lines that criss-crossed his skinny stomach and pale chest. Even as he told us what had happened he didn't raise his voice or show much emotion, except to smile slightly when he talked about the pain he had felt on the way to hospital. Two years earlier Babette had found out that he had been sleeping with another woman. She didn't confront him with the news straight away, but waited a few weeks to see if he was serious about her rival. Then, she crept out of bed one night and retrieved Jarek's gun from the bedside cabinet. He said he was awoken by a loud noise, and the sensation that someone was standing on his chest. Jarek thought it was all part of a dream until he saw Babette at the foot of the bed. She was holding his gun and pointing it at his heart. Without speaking, she fired twice more, but then decided to call an ambulance when she realised he was still breathing. Jarek didn't press charges, and told us that the incident had brought them closer together. None of us ever asked him what he made of Babette being on the game. Or whether he was turned on by the smell of monkey piss.

———————

We arrived in South Africa during a drought. It was January, the middle of the summer when the highveldt around Johannesburg should have been green and lush after the rains. Now, years later, I love it when the great thunderstorms light up the sky all the way to the horizon. The African rain is more satisfying than English drizzle, and more welcome. Towering graphite-tinted clouds threaten to cover the world and grand electrical pulses make the air tremble so much only God could send them. You can smell the water too, long before it hits. It comes in sweeping sheets that scrub the air of all the heat and dust and dirt and stops the earth from suffocating.

But that year the rain didn't come. Dad had told us it was the wet season, but like a lot of what he told us about Africa, it wasn't true. In that hard summer the grass was bright yellow and the earth was red and so coarse it felt like sand. We lived on the edge of the city where the veldt was an endless canvas of open plains striped with gold and ochre. The air was so dry that you got nose-bleeds.

Underground at The Whatnot

Babette, François the monkey and Jarek were regulars at The Whatnot. That was the name above the door, but we just called it the Shop. Jarek was one of a dozen small-time dealers that came through the door, and often stayed until well after official closing time. Sometimes Babette was there too, with the monkey. She didn't like Jarek talking to other women, so he generally wouldn't stay long if they were together. If she had made good money that day, Pamela, the shop owner, kept enough gin and tonic in the back room to keep a party going, and quite often, usually on Friday nights, The Whatnot turned into a drinking club. The dealers stayed until the gin was gone, but they also stayed because they were all in love with Pamela. I loved her too: she was my mother.

To her customers, Mum was a sympathetic ear, someone who listened to their woes and didn't judge them for their mistakes. She laughed a lot, and they liked the fact that she rebelled against any sort of bureaucracy or official authority. But I hated the way the dealers and customers doted on her.

'These people aren't my friends,' she explained when I got jealous. 'They're just people I do business with.'

'Having a shop is like having a baby,' Mum would remind me, if I complained about how much time she spent at The Whatnot. 'You can never leave it with someone else for very long. And it doesn't grow unless you look after it very carefully.'

Buying and selling, swapping and haggling, that was what Mum had learned to do. She sold furniture and jewellery, porcelain and ornaments. She bought at auction, at house clearances, and from pawn dealers and scrap metal shops, or just from people who wandered in off the street in need of money. And sometimes she bought things from thieves who had hot loot to fence. Mum said you never knew who was coming through the door next: bargain hunters, collectors, guilty husbands appeasing their wives with a surprise gift or desperate old ladies reduced to selling their jewellery to pay the rent. The Whatnot stayed open after most other shops closed, and Mum sold anything that would make a profit. For her special customers, she knew a man who could supply false passports, and people who could get you over the border if you were evading military service under the apartheid regime. Those kinds of deals earned her a healthy commission.

Over the years, Mum refined her skills as a merchant. When she spoke to Jewish customers I would see her absent-mindedly fondle a gold Star of David pendant she wore around her neck. 'Didn't you know your mother was Jewish?' she mocked when I asked her why she was wearing it. Having been born in a British military hospital near Cairo, I once heard her telling Zakhi the Lebanese that she had Arabian blood. 'After all,' she lied, 'my mother was half-Egyptian.' A small number of clients, the customers who thought they were her special friends, found out that she could read fortunes from tea leaves, and would beg her for a reading. To them, her Irish heritage (which was far more genuine than her Egyptian) was the all-important qualification.

Going in to The Whatnot was like entering a secret universe. The shop was one of twenty in an underground arcade in Hillbrow, the high-rise district of Johannesburg close to the city centre. There were no houses in Hillbrow, just apartment blocks, and Joburgers liked to claim that it was the most densely populated suburb in the world. To anyone who had seen pictures of Hong Kong or Bangkok it was clearly untrue, but it was an urban legend that people repeated. To reach the arcade from street level you went down a stairwell next to Babu's Indian gift shop, following a sign that said 'Village Flea Market'. It felt like we were hiding from the real world when we went down there.

The good thing about being underground was that noise from the traffic on Pretoria Street didn't penetrate into the arcade, but it could get very cold in winter and stuffy in summer. Ventilation came from a system of metal ducts that snaked around the basement roof space bringing in air from street level, complete with traffic fumes. It was usually dark by the time Mum shut up shop and, in the afternoons, while it was still light, she sometimes insisted we went upstairs to the Wimpy Bar next door just for a change of scene, or to warm up with a toasted cheese sandwich. In winter Mum lived in her old sheepskin, the only coat she possessed. Back in 1969 it had been an expensive purchase from Moss Bros. in Regent's

Street, a great hunk of animal skin and fleece she said she needed to see her through the Irish winters. It was a bulky thing that needed its own seat in the cinema. By the time she ran the shop it was past its best, the matted fleece was squished down to a thin ghost of its original thickness, and the leather exterior was stained and scuffed. I never liked that coat, and as it deteriorated the front hem developed a curl so that it flared outwards above the knees like dried-up orange peel. The sheepskin made her look like a down-at-heel bookie, but Mum said she would die without it. It was true that she always felt the cold, and one of the rituals of a visit to a restaurant or the cinema with Mum was that she would complain about the temperature. Inevitably, one of us would have to go and find the manager or a waiter and ask for the air-conditioning to be turned down or the heating to be turned up. Often we had to change seats several times looking for a place that wasn't in a draft.

Usually we only bought a cup of tea in the Wimpy, but it was enough to allow us to sit on the stools by the plate glass window and thaw out. She could watch the entrance to the arcade from there, and if she spotted a dealer or a potential customer going downstairs she could hurry back to the shop using a fire-escape near the rear of the Wimpy. The tea came in indestructibly thick white cups with the Wimpy logo in red on the sides, and the glaze on the saucers was always crackled and stained brown. From inside the restaurant you could still hear lonely big city sounds like the whining of the brakes on the double-decker buses as they stopped at the lights on the corner of Banket Street, and the high-pitched buzzing of the messenger boys' mopeds as they weaved in and out of the slower moving cars. Behind the driver's seat the bikes had metal pannier boxes that were painted with company names. The drivers mainly worked for law firms that used them to deliver important documents in thick manila envelopes, or for pharmacies that sent them out with people's medicines in wax-paper bags stapled down to keep the pills inside. On the other side of the Wimpy window we could watch office workers jostling along the pavement, and legions of elderly ladies from the surrounding flats out for their daily stroll. Many of them were escorted by their maids, African women in uniforms who did their shopping and cleaning and acted as their general companions. Often the old dears held onto leads attached to wheezing lap dogs, that took their chance to shit beside the scrawny trees struggling to bloom in the shadow of the apartment blocks that made Hillbrow a miniature New York.

'If only the Whatnot was up here,' Mum complained. 'Look at all these customers walking past, they don't even notice that there are shops downstairs. More passing trade, that's what we need.'

We all knew she couldn't afford to rent a shop up on the street. All of the shopkeepers in the arcade were in the same position. Being constantly short of cash was one their common bonds. Over the years, one or two traders did well enough to move their businesses to street level, but many more went out of business. The Whatnot, precarious as it was, became one of the longest survivors.

I hated the Wimpy. There were plenty of other cafés in Hillbrow. The smart ones were the Café Wien and the Café Zurich, both of them modelled on more famous European originals. Their crockery wasn't chipped and they had thick carpets and big comfortable armchairs and waiters in crisp white jackets. They even had white waiters, whereas the Wimpy employed only Africans. Enoch was our favourite; he would refill our teapot with hot water without charging us extra. At Café Zurich there were chess and backgammon sets for the customers to use, and newspapers mounted on those long wooden sticks that allowed them to be hung up on a stand ready for the next reader. But the tea cost four times as much as it did at the Wimpy. Plenty of the shopkeepers in the Market used the Wimpy, and I didn't care about being seen there by people we knew. It was the stranger's eyes I wanted to avoid. I didn't want the office workers in their smart suits, or the businessmen in their big cars, looking in at Mum and me. They didn't know our names, but they would know we were the kind of people who could only afford to eat at the Wimpy Bar.

Up on Pretoria Street we had another refuge. It was a movie theatre called the Mini-Cine. The Mini-Cine opened at odd hours, and showed mostly old films, not so much vintage classics as things that weren't commercially successful. Because the owner was French, it was also one of the few places in Johannesburg where you could see a foreign language film. One day we could watch Marcello Mastroianni in *Una Giornata Particolare* (1977), and the next day it would be a low-budget comedy like *Even Angels Eat Beans* (Bud Spencer, 1973). Sometimes we went up to the Mini-Cine after the shop closed and, like the Wimpy, in winter it was a warmer alternative to going home. We were usually the only customers, so that made it easier when we went through the inevitable temperature-tweaking routine. Marcel, the owner, was unpredictably moody but he would do it for Mum. Everyone knew that Marcel had a short fuse. One day a Coca-Cola delivery truck for the Wimpy Bar parked across the entrance to the arcade and blocked access to the escalator leading up to the Mini-Cine. It had happened before, and there had been words between Marcel and several of the deliverymen. This time he stormed down the escalator with his pistol and shot out all the tyres on the truck. Then he shot at the drinks crates until the floor was awash with glass and gloopy dark syrup. The police took him away in handcuffs.

Above the Mini-Cine was the Litchi Inn, a dimly lit Chinese restaurant with thick red velour curtains blotting out all natural light. From Tuesday to Saturday they sent takeaway meals out on their own messenger bikes to the flats in Hillbrow, but hardly anyone ate sit-down meals inside. On Sundays the Litchi Inn was officially closed. That was when they made their real money, by operating as an illegal gambling den. You needed an appointment to get inside, but if you knocked very persistently on the door a little peephole would slide open and they asked what you wanted. Because they knew Mum, we were allowed in to buy takeaway portions of the meals they were providing for the gamblers.

The smell of joss sticks hit you as you went down stairs to the arcade, a cloying sickly sweet aroma that emanated from Frank's, an emporium of batiks and cheap tie-dyed clothing, silver toe-rings and brass incense burners. Frank was a regular at the gin parties in the Whatnot, though he usually preferred to stick to his own supply of whiskey. Before he opened up his shop each morning, Frank called in at Solly Kramer's Liquor

Store further down the street to collect his daily ration, a bottle of White Horse. Frank was always very polite, and a stickler for manners. For appearance's sake he would decant the whiskey into an empty Coke can and sip it through a straw. By the end of a day's trading he was propped up against his shop counter like a puppet, barely able to speak. Frank rarely had anyone to help him in the shop which meant that he couldn't easily leave the counter to go to the toilet, and after a few hours he was generally too drunk to bother. It was my brother who noticed that he always had a plastic carrier-bag full of piss to dispose of when he locked up at night. Up the stairs he would go, clasping the iron banister like a crutch and with the knotted bag bouncing and squishing against his knee.

Frank, whose surname was Patel, lived just outside the borders of Lenasia, the township reserved for Indians on the outskirts of Johannesburg. Strictly speaking he was in a 'White area' and he lived in fear of the authorities finding out. The apartheid system was brutally unfair, but around Johannesburg it was also notoriously inefficient. We had friends who were officially classified as 'Coloured' but who lived in so-called 'White areas' because they were relatively pale skinned and then simply lied about their ethnic origins. Mum was fond of Frank, and he trusted her so much that she was registered as the official owner of his family home. At that time, Indians weren't allowed to own property outside designated areas but Frank was optimistic that apartheid would end in his own lifetime. One day, when he was comparatively sober, he asked Mum if she would sign the lease and mortgage papers on a house so that he could buy it. She did, and we often used to joke that when times were hard we could always go and live in

Frank's house. In fact we never even visited his house, nor did he ever come to ours. But, whether it was near Lenasia or not, at times the idea of owning that little house – or any house – seemed to us like paradise.

Frank's shop was popular with kids from Wits University, who bought incense to disguise the smell of dope in their college rooms. South Africa always seemed to me to be at least twenty years behind the times, and the girls were still wearing tie-dye long after the worst fashion crimes of Hippiedom had died out in the rest of the world. However, anyone in Johannesburg who considered themselves even slightly bohemian eventually found their way to the Market. In the uptight moral maze of apartheid South Africa it was definitely different. Nowhere else in the country could you find a sex shop.

Sex shops were illegal, but The Velvet Heart slipped through the net because it was run by a former policeman. There were red satin heart-shaped cushions in the window, pocket-sized canisters of something called 'Stallion Spray', packets of novelty condoms and a few pieces of 'sexy' scarlet silk underwear. Markus, the owner, had been invalided out of the police force after an incident when he was shot during a bank robbery in the centre of town. His physical injuries were compounded by some psychological problems which may or may not have stemmed from the fact that he had shot all three of the robbers dead. We never knew how much money he actually made from the Velvet Heart, but he survived because he used the shop as a way of collecting information on all kinds of people, and passing it onto his former colleagues in uniform. Buying condoms and vibrators wasn't exactly illegal, but the porno tapes he kept in the back room definitely were. Of course, plenty of his customers were policemen anyway.

As well as keeping the races apart, South Africa's ruling National Party were also the guardians of public morals, and they did their very best to keep the country pure. This, it should be remembered, was the government who had kept South Africa free from the evils of television until 1976. And those who opposed its introduction persisted in calling it 'the Devil's Box'. I'll never forget watching an art history programme one Sunday night which featured Botticelli's painting, *Birth of Venus*. There was the familiar figure of the curvaceous goddess emerging from the giant clam shell with her hair cascading down one alabaster shoulder, but where her nipples should have been the producers had inserted two little black strips, blotting out the offending anatomy. The nipples of her friend the wind nymph had received the same treatment. Botticelli or not, nipples could not be shown, especially on a Sunday.

We knew that Frank pissed into a bag behind his counter, and we knew that Markus sold porn. We knew that the two men in the shop next to the Whatnot were gay (also illegal), and that Dannie, the older of the two partners lived in fear of blackmail. Vintage Vinyl specialised in hard-to-find LPs. Dannie had a weakness for records featuring compilations of show-tunes from old musicals and films. There was always a lot of Judy Garland on offer. Dannie liked talking to me because if he mentioned the name of an old musical the chances were I had seen it, and knew the songs. He got most of his stock while abroad thanks to his job as a flight steward for South African Airways and Stefan, his boyfriend, ran the shop when he was overseas.

We were fond of Stefan, who looked very like a Hobbit. He had a small pointed skull and vast ears that stuck out wildly from the side of his head. Stefan was extremely thickset, short but strong with almost no visible neck. He suffered from various birth defects which included a pronounced lisp and webbed feet. Stefan was also extremely hairy, and when parties were in full swing he would start taking off his clothes. If Dannie wasn't watching him closely, and Stefan saw a young man he fancied he pursued them around the corridors of the market, usually with the stated intention of licking them. We used to impersonate Stefan and his fractured English, especially his scant grasp of grammar.

As a traditional working class Afrikaner, Stefan made no secret of his hatred of the English. Seemingly unaware of the irony, he would confide in Mum: 'I does do 'ate ve English. Vey vos verree, verree krew-el to us b'eeple in the War.' He was referring to the Boer War of course. My mother's name came out as 'Bam' when he said it, and his conversation usually consisted of a set of stock phrases that rarely went beyond discussing the weather. 'Bam,' he would intone slowly as if each word was unfamiliar territory. 'It does do be veree, veree g'old do-day. And I doesn't 'ave a winter g'oat to g'eep me warrum.'

Stefan and Dannie sometimes invited us back to their home to watch videos after the shops closed. Thanks to Dannie's frequent trips abroad they always had new additions to their collection. He also had a network of other flight stewards who acquired records for him, and then for a small fee carried them back in their own baggage.

Although they were lovers, Stefan and Dannie kept separate bedrooms in their little cottage a few blocks away from the Market, just in case they were raided by the police, something that happened on more than one occasion. Stefan and Dannie had terrible fights; once Dannie returned from an overseas trip and found that Stefan had been arrested for cruising in the public toilets at Johannesburg railway station. Mum had to go down and post bail for him because Dannie had to keep their relationship secret. Dannie confided to Mum that his boy-friend was something of a liability, but that the record business was registered in Stefan's name. It wasn't an ideal situation for Dannie, but airline regulations forbade employees to run their own companies. Stefan knew that he was registered as the owner of the shop but, conveniently for Dannie, he didn't understand the intricacies of the company accounts.

Babette, Frank, Markus, Dannie and the other characters we met at The Whatnot became part of our lives. We called them the Market People. Like us, many of the traders and their customers lived at the margins of legality, and crossed over the boundary when they were forced to. Some of them had been in prison, and some were on their way. Some had killed, and others would be killed. They were different from the kinds of people we had known before Mum had a shop, and part of the secret world I couldn't talk about when I left Africa. But Market People stuck together, and when times were hard they became my mother's true friends. But they were always the people I was ashamed to admit I knew.

How to Scare the Enemy

We had lodgers in Africa, and the Russian stayed longer than any of the others. He was a brooding presence in the back bedroom of the house, so quiet that we never knew if he was in or out. Mum respected him because he was a medical doctor, a Jewish Russian who had worked in a prison camp in Siberia. He spoke English very slowly and when he got drunk he sang mournful Russian folk songs. His name was Michael, and she always pronounced it the Russian way. '*Meek-ay-eel* has had a very sad life. He left his girlfriend behind in Russia and they knew they could never see each other again. Every New Year's Eve they drink a silent toast, because they promised they would never forget each other.'

I never quite saw the romantic Dr Zhivago side of Michael, but he behaved nicely and sometimes took afternoon tea with us at weekends. 'You should take advice from Michael,' Mum would say when she wanted to annoy me. '*He* was going bald before he started doing his yoga exercises every night. You should do them too.'

Michael's exercises weren't very complicated. He simply stood on his head with his feet resting against the bedroom wall for fifteen minutes every night before he went to bed. When Mum wasn't listening I asked him how they could help stop hair loss.

'Balud supply must areach scelp,' he explained solemnly. 'When myen valking upright all-time, balud is falling away from hayed. Hair is hungary for nutri-shone from balud. Must feed yit.'

Michael said he was looking for a job, but in the two years he lived with us he never even got an interview. Mum didn't mind, as he paid his rent and provided free medical advice, coming to the rescue several times when she had palpitations and what she called 'stress attacks'. And if any of us had ever been to our own doctor, Mum always liked Michael to give a second opinion. Michael had moved in while Dad was working in Saudi Arabia on one of his foreign contracts, and he was initially suspicious of the new lodger: a professional man who seemingly needed to stay in our ramshackle house. When they actually met, they got on well and would sit up at night talking about places they both knew in Europe. Dad surprised us all by interjecting Russian phrases into his conversation. This led to the revelation that he'd been sent on an intensive course at LSE when he'd been in the Army, something he needed to do 'because of the Cold War'. Once he had decided that Michael was some kind of a spy, Dad felt more comfortable.

Michael rarely talked about Russia, but no matter how cold the winter nights became he was happy to wander from his bedroom into the unheated bathroom in his boxer shorts and a cotton T-shirt. We assumed his experiences in Siberia made highveldt winters seem mild. Whether it was because he was Russian and knew something about suffering, or whether it was because he really was something more than just a doctor, Michael could be relied on when things got tough.

The house he shared with us was old. Some aspects of the building had a certain charm, like the pressed metal ceilings with ornate ceiling roses at their centre which gave it a Victorian feel. The wiring was certainly ancient, and the switches were all made of shiny brown Bakelite. It had a tin roof and metal Crittal-style frames in the windows, though thanks to the dry Johannesburg air they hadn't rusted. The front door had stained glass leaded lights and two classical columns supported the outside porch, although in daylight you could see the plaster was badly chipped and cracked. As far as we could tell the house hadn't been renovated or modernised since the 1940s. But the landlord kept putting the rent up. In desperation, Mum decided she would appeal to the city authorities and managed to get someone from the municipality to come and assess its value. They not only opposed the rental increases, they made the landlord reduce his rent to a minimal amount. Even better, they ruled that she had been overpaying for at least a year and was entitled to deduct the surplus from the monthly total. Unsurprisingly Ivan Goldstein, our landlord, wasn't pleased and started looking for ways to get us out. Legally, Mum had established herself as a sitting tenant and couldn't be evicted unless she defaulted on the rent. The reprieve didn't last long. Mr Goldstein found out that Mum rented a shop, and he knew who the landlord was. She got a letter threatening a big rise in the rent of the shop and a verbal message that it could be avoided if she stopped causing trouble for Goldstein. Without the shop we would starve.

Dad happened to be visiting when Mum got the bad news about the shop. He regarded it as an escalation of hostilities that deserved radical action. And he knew where the landlord lived. 'We'll have to kill him,' he announced at dinner one night. 'It's the only way to stop him.'

'Don't be stupid,' Mum replied with a withering glance. 'With your luck you'll be caught. You'll end up on death row and I'll be even worse off.'

Like us, she knew that when Dad talked about killing people in that way, he wasn't making an idle threat. Eventually, Dad's murderous idea was toned down and Mum made him agree that he would simply give Mr Goldstein a fright

That was how Michael happened to come home one night and find Dad in the kitchen making petrol bombs. Far from being horrified, he offered to help. Despite his army career during which he had served for many years in Northern Ireland, I don't think Dad had ever actually made a petrol bomb before. Michael was happy to contribute his own expertise. 'Ah yes,' he exclaimed, 'but this is Molotov cocktail, no?'

They had the basic materials: Coke bottles, petrol, and some sugar to make the incendiary liquid adhere to its target. Initial experiments in the back yard revealed problems with the wicks. They tried newspaper, but found it didn't survive being thrown very well without extinguishing. Cotton wool burned too quickly. Eventually my brother lost patience with the Anglo-Russian experts and contributed his own advice on how they should construct the wick, using a combination of cotton wool and strips of shredded linen. He also pointed out that they needed to keep the bottle only half-full to give the flames space to breathe, and advocated adding some washing-up liquid as well as the sugar to the potion. At this point, Mum, who had been ignoring the sounds of breaking glass and the smell of petrol coming from the back yard, decreed that her ten-year-old son was not to be included in the enterprise.

Once Dad and Michael had perfected the petrol bombs there was another problem to be overcome – transport. We had no car, and taking a taxi with a load of petrol bombs didn't seem like a good idea. But John the Hippie had a car. John was English and had had his own brushes with the law. We never found out exactly what he'd done but he often made vague references to having had to leave England in a hurry. He had no official residency permit for South Africa and lived in fear of being asked for his ID papers. Sometimes he talked about time spent as a minicab driver in London, but because he had smoked so much dope, his memory wasn't reliable. John even found it difficult to finish a sentence, and often had no recall of recent events. For the job in hand, Dad thought that might be an advantage. The disadvantage was that John the Hippie didn't approve of violence. But he had a car, a very rickety VW Beetle. All he had to do was drive.

The plan was to use the petrol bombs to damage Mr Goldstein's new Mercedes. Late one night they set off to the suburb where Mr Goldstein lived in comparative splendour. After a couple of circuits of the neighbourhood, checking for police patrols or neighbours who might still be awake, John parked the Beetle in the road parallel to the landlord's house while Dad and Michael carried out the raid.

VW Beetles are not ideal vehicles for covert operations. John's car was extremely noisy and had only two doors, so it didn't allow for a fast getaway if you had to pick up more than one passenger. It had another flaw: it usually needed a long push-start and, for that reason, John never liked to turn off the engine unless he was parked on a good steep hill. But it was the only car they had.

With John waiting in the next street, Michael and Dad walked around the block to Goldstein's house. The Mercedes was parked in the front drive, close to the road. They placed a couple of petrol bombs under the car and retired a few yards to light another. Dad threw it, and there was a satisfying *whoompf* noise as the bomb hit the ground close to the car. A fierce blaze immediately engulfed the Mercedes. Unfortunately, Dad managed to slop petrol onto his hand and arm as he threw the last bomb and he also caught fire. Michael attempted to smother the flames as they raced back around the block to find John. As they clambered into the Beetle a loud explosion announced the end of the Merc, a car that was probably worth more than ten years rent on our house.

'Jesus Christ! Jesus Christ!' was all John could say as he sat paralysed by fear at the wheel of the Beetle.

'Shut up and drive!' Dad ordered.

On the journey home John's vocabulary expanded a bit. 'We'll all go down for this. I know it. I've got a bad feeling about this. Jesus Christ. Jesus Christ.'

Michael sat up until the early hours applying first aid to Dad's arm and discussing the raid. They convinced John that he should be more afraid of them than the police. And Mum never heard from Mr Goldstein again.

Damp

Dad's army career meant that I went to seven different primary schools in all, a collection that included Bangor, Gutersloh, Taiping, Kuala Lumpur and Towyn. At school, the teachers often reminded me that I was English. It was because of the way I talked. They didn't seem interested in hearing that I had never lived in England. It didn't matter that I had been born in Ireland, or that my closest relatives were all from the island. I didn't sound Irish and that was what counted, even though, to me, Northern Ireland was always home. School was just a nuisance, something I'd hated from the first day I spent there at the age of five. Those early childhood experiences stay with us, and colour our onward journey. Places and people embed themselves in our personality, forever remaining symbols of good or bad times which can be impossible to eradicate. Try as I might, I find it impossible to think fondly of Wales. I can't apologise for it, the country remains for me the place where I began school.

I remember that first day at school very clearly. Because Dad was in the Army, we were stationed in a place called

Towyn, in between Rhyl and Abergele in north Wales. I was already five, and I don't think Mum had ever explained what would happen when the time came for me to go to school. That day, she took me into the classroom and told me she would be back later to collect me. I remember standing there horrified by the sight of so many children. The classroom was huge and there were about eighty children in it, divided into two classes separated by a curtain. Even at five, I think the arrangement struck me as uncivilised. I wouldn't remove my coat.

'Now, take that off or you'll be too hot,' said Mrs Morgan, the teacher. 'And go and sit with the other pupils.'

'No. I'm not staying,' I said. 'My mother is coming back for me.'

That was the first time I ever felt let down by my mother. The next time was when she stepped backwards after getting something out of the fridge and broke the wings off a metal fighter plane I was skimming across the floor. I was angry at how clumsy she had been, and I was affronted by her physical appearance. Mum was never a morning person, and in her slippers and dressing gown, without her make-up and with her hair untidy she suddenly seemed lumpen and slovenly. When she opened the fridge door there was a waft of cheese and cold meat that mingled with her own bed-warm scent. Suddenly, she was no longer the mother I loved unconditionally. For the first time I was aware that she was older than me, a separate physical being and not just an extension of me. And in her clumsiness, in the brutal way she brought her dry, cracked heel down on my little aeroplane she had demonstrated that she was further down the path of physical decay.

It was the first occasion on which I can remember being angry with her, a new emotion that frightened me. I could see that I was partly to blame for the aviation accident, but I simply couldn't understand why she was powerless to prevent me going to school. She didn't seem to want me to go there, and yet she went along with it.

The torture of school didn't last too long, because shortly afterwards I contracted pneumonia, an illness that turned me into a wheezing, bronchitic child forever unwell in what seemed to be the permanently damp Welsh climate. The doctor said the illness would scar my lungs, and sent me to the hospital for a chest X-ray. After that, I remember they put an electric kettle in my room and let it boil continuously so that I would breathe warm, humid air. They gave me antibiotics so strong they stained my adult teeth with white marks while they were still developing in my gums, and twice a day I was supposed to hang over the end of the bed with my feet sticking up into the air and my head over a potty on the floor. It was embarrassing and used to make me feel sick, but the doctor said I had to stay like that for at least ten minutes. The primitive strategy had some merit; I coughed up large gobbets of dark yellow catarrh and sputum that mesmerised me as they swirled on the plastic surface of the potty like rotten egg yolks.

The pneumonia kept me at home for more than two months. I didn't care what happened as long as I could stay at home. It was a situation that my mother aided and abetted, something she continued doing for years afterwards whenever I got 'chesty'. She didn't actually encourage me not to go to school, but she understood why I hated it, and seemed to accept that as long as I was reading books I was probably learning more important stuff than I got from the teachers anyway.

Books were an absolute necessity for Mum. She told me that when she was a teenager her biggest treat was being taken up to Belfast by her father. Each week she saved her one shilling of pocket money so that she would have enough once a month to buy a new book. When they got home, Mum told me that Granny would sneer at her copies of *Wuthering Heights* and *Mansfield Park*. 'Why do you waste your money on those dry old books?' she would ask irritably. Granny thought girls should only spend money on their appearance, and their only goal in life should be to attract a prosperous and respectable husband. In a reaction against her own upbringing, Mum taught me to read before I went to school. That was probably why I found the lessons uninspiring.

Not everything in Wales was bad. In winter we visited crumbling castles where the wind ripped across the ramparts and made your eyes fill with tears. One autumn, when I was five, Dad took us out on a river in a small rowing boat. Mum sat in the stern on a plank seat, holding on to my sister who was just three. Dad always did the rowing, wearing his regular off-duty outfit of twill trousers, a hound's-tooth sports jacket and a narrow regimental tie. On his feet he usually had polished brown Oxford's or suede brogues, and when it was cold enough he wore a tweed cap. All of his officer friends dressed the same way.

I knelt in the bows, with my face inches from the water and one arm dangling over the gunwale. The sound of the river streaming against the wooden hull filled my head as bewitchingly as a Pied Piper song. The air was still, and the surface of the water was a black mirror overhung with gnarled branches. I could see darting water boatmen and diving beetles and occasionally a glimpse of submerged logs, sodden and ebony dark. When Dad rested the oars we would drift under the trees that stretched their arms out from the damp bank forming a canopy that obscured the sky. The air was clammy, heavy with the musty, woody scents of rotting bark and leaf litter returning to the earth. And the only thing I could hear was the water. Reaching my fingertips out to touch its silky surface felt like a guilty pleasure. There was danger in its depths, mystery in its jet sheen and peace in its serene flatness. It felt as if there was no one else alive in the whole of the world, and I never wanted us to turn around and head for land. Time and again, I asked to be taken back to the river.

The other good thing about Wales was Richard, the boy next door. He was an athletic child, who at eight seemed very grown up to me. Stuck in my slow-moving blue metal pedal car, I watched him riding his bike along the path between our houses, and from my bedroom window I would see him climbing the high branches of a tree in his back garden. My hero gave me one of his old books, *Kit Carson's 1960 Cowboy Annual*, and it became one of my favourite possessions. On the cover, Kit Carson had long flowing hair and wore a buckskin jacket with tassels. He galloped across the plains on his white horse without using the reins, twisting around in the saddle to fire his rifle at some Red Indians who were giving chase. The annual was filled with Hurons and Choctaws, rustlers and stage coach robbers, and heroes like Buffalo Bill and Davy Crockett. I never tired of reading the stories over and over, and I still owned it when we went to Africa.

After my prolonged absence from school, two truancy officers from the council came to check up on why I hadn't attended for so long. I could hear the low rumble of those serious adult voices coming up the stairwell from the sitting room below. After they had interviewed my parents the two men were briefly allowed upstairs to see me, presumably to check that I was still alive and looking suitably feeble. Afterwards, Mum and Dad had an argument and then Dad came and sat on my bed and told me that if I didn't go back to school the following week he would go to prison. Dad always presented things that way, any family decisions were always dramatic choices, never easy or subtle. 'Take no notice of your father,' Mum would reassure me when I was older. 'He always exaggerates everything.'

The local doctor told Mum that I would never be free of what he called 'The Englishman's Disease' unless I could be taken away from Britain. It was a phrase she repeated every time I got bronchitis during childhood. Encouraged by Mum and the doctor, Dad was persuaded to ask the Army for a posting to a healthier climate. They offered him a choice between Malaysia and Norway, and there were dinner table discussions about which country would be best. He thought learning to ski would be fun for us all, but for Mum there wasn't much contest: the chance to return to the tropics, where she had lived as a young girl with her parents, was irresistible. The contrast between Wales and Malaysia could not have been more extreme. Living there affected us all very deeply, and kindled the discontent that led us to Africa a decade later.

Spiders, Scorpions and Sunshine

Dad flew to Malaysia, a journey of twenty-four hours with stops in Egypt and India. I was looking forward to going on an aeroplane for the first time, but Mum refused to fly, insisting that the only civilised way for an officer's family to travel was by boat. Before we left, we went back to Ireland to see my grandparents and sort out things to do with a house my parents owned there. They couldn't really afford to buy it, but Mum had persuaded Dad that the house was an investment, and they could let it out when they were abroad. However, at the news that we were going to Malaysia, Granny in Ireland seized this opportunity to suggest that she and Grandpop should rent the house and look after it properly rather than letting some stranger live in it. Mum wasn't entirely happy about the arrangement, but Granny said they were selling their own house and hadn't decided where they would go next.

Getting out to Malaysia was an adventure that began with taking the night ferry from Belfast to Liverpool, and then a train to London to stay a few days with Dad's parents. To me, they were Granny Griffiths (because that was her maiden name, and it conveyed her Welshness), and even more prosaically, Grandfather-in-London. They lived in a smart mansion block with polished brass banisters in Maida Vale. It was very upmarket – Shirley Bassey lived on the same street. The London grandparents had very organised lives, and their flat was the neatest, cleanest place I had ever seen. Granny in Ireland's kitchen was chaotically strewn with cooking utensils and baking ingredients, and there was a coal scuttle sitting permanently by the back door with a sprinkling of black dust along the sill. But everything in London was forensically clean. Inside the food cupboards things were lined up in orderly rows, and anything homemade had a handwritten label (neatly dated) on the bottle or jar. And whereas my Irish grandparents' house was unheated except for the sitting room coal fire, in London they had central heating. The carpets were thick golden-brown pile, and there were portraits of Dad and his sister painted by Augustus John hanging on the wall. We didn't know the London grandparents well, our main contact with them was through Christmas and birthdays. They never sent presents, but always cards containing ten-shilling postal orders. Then Mum made us write thank you letters, because otherwise she said they would say she was bringing us up badly. 'They've never approved of me, because I'm Irish,' Mum would confide. '*And* they never gave us a wedding present. That was a deliberate snub, because they wanted your father to marry one of those heartless society women from London.'

Grandfather, whom the grown-ups called 'W.G.', smelled faintly of cologne and was always immaculately turned out.

For an Englishman he had a very dark complexion, and used to slick his hair back with oil to keep it under control. Because his own father was in the cavalry, he had spent the first twelve years of his life in India. Great-grandfather Harry Ecott, was a legendary figure in the family, a riding champion, a boxer and something of a maverick. His own father, my great-great-grandfather was a hotelier and reasonably well off, but he didn't approve of Harry wanting to join the army. So Harry ran away from home when he was fifteen and rose through the ranks until he was given a field commission during the First World War. Part of the legend was that he had somehow ended up involved with the Cossacks during the Russian Revolution. Dad had a silver dagger with a Russian Imperial crest on the sheath that he said had been given to Harry by the Tsar. Dad spent a lot of time with Harry when he was a boy, and valued his opinion on army matters more than anything his own father said. Dad was especially proud that Harry had become an officer in the cavalry, the snootiest branch of the British Army. In those days cavalry officers had to buy and pay for the upkeep of their own horses. 'Harry's father wouldn't give him a penny as long as he was in the Army,' Dad explained. 'So in India Harry would go down to the bazaar on a Saturday night and take on all-comers in bare-fist boxing matches. He'd take bets on his own fights, and that's how he made the money to keep a string of horses.'

Dad took me to meet Harry in his house on the seafront at Brighton when I was about five. He was eighty-six by then, and still kept his moustache waxed like an Edwardian gentleman. Great-grandfather wasn't a tall man, but even then I remember an aura of toughness. Years later, I would read through his Army records again and again, learning that he'd been an Army swimming instructor and had served in South Africa, Mesopotamia, Persia, Russian Baku and India, returning to England in 1922 aboard the *SS Derbyshire* from Bombay.

At lunch that day I made myself cry because I tipped over a pepper pot and the finely ground powder went up my nose. Harry took me away from the table and into his library where he let me play with a full-sized roulette wheel. He also had a tiger-skin rug with the head attached, and I lay on the floor plucking up the courage to touch the teeth. The tiger had a false tongue made of plaster that was painted too vividly pink.

W.G. couldn't compete with Harry's army exploits and wouldn't even have gone into the Army if he hadn't been called up in 1940. He spent the War as a tank commander in North Africa and worked afterwards in the oil industry in the Middle East. Dad, for whom soldiering was everything, didn't respect W.G., probably because he was more interested in making money than being a soldier. After finishing boarding school, Dad had taken a short-service commission for two years before going up to Oxford. W.G. was well off, and gave Dad a generous allowance while he was at Oriel: certainly enough to allow him to run a fast sports car and pay for large quantities of beer at his rugby club. But during the vacations, Dad always chose to stay with Grandfather Harry, who had a big house on the river at Bablock Hythe, north of Oxford.

'I couldn't bear being at home in London,' Dad always told me. 'And I don't think my parents cared whether I was there or not.' He told me that after Oxford, where he was lucky to scrape through his degree in Classics, he had made the mistake of going back to London for the summer. 'W.G. kept arranging interviews for me with banks and brokerage firms in the City! I couldn't imagine anything more deathly, so I joined the Army again.'

W.G. was a born worrier. In his view, going to the tropics with children was a mistake, and the night before we were due to take the ship to Malaya he regaled Mum with an extensive list of mortal dangers. 'Why are you going by boat? Those kids will be forever going near the railings – if they go overboard that's it – curtains.' Every hazard that he described was accompanied by a small disbelieving shake of the head, and a sharp intake of breath as if he was preparing to blow up a balloon.

'Don't let the children persuade you to keep a dog out there,' he warned, 'you'll have to watch out for rabies . . . And always make the children wear sandals, otherwise they'll get hookworm . . . Check inside your shoes every morning before you put them on, something could have crawled inside them during the night . . . Never eat watermelon or any fruit they sell by the roadside – you'll get dysentery.'

The watermelon warning proved particularly upsetting to Mum. For the first two years in Malaysia she wouldn't let us eat it. Then she realised that if the melons were purchased whole and unopened there was no danger at all, and we absolutely loved them. But she always bore a grudge that W.G. had deprived us of this refreshing pleasure for most of the time we were there. 'The old fool!' she would exclaim. 'He filled my head up with so much nonsense, I was a nervous wreck before I got on the boat.'

Because of his own experiences as a boy in India, Grandfather was also worried that our education would suffer through being away from Britain. 'Put them in a good prep school, that's what you should do.' His solution to my parents' irresponsibility was to buy me a subscription to *Look and Learn* magazine, and every few weeks a meticulously wrapped tube with W.G.'s handwriting on the label would arrive by post with two or three issues inside. My mental image of many historical and biblical characters (lots of scarlet cloaks and long curly beards), is still based on the lavish artwork of *Look and Learn.* My favourite bit was the comic-strip of *The Rise and Fall of the Trigan Empire*, a complex saga about the planet Elekton featuring a hero called Trigo, who also favoured a red cloak.

The train ride down to Southampton seemed to take a long time. In preparation, my sister and I were taken to a toy shop that morning and allowed to choose something for the journey. She picked Tiny Tears, a blonde doll that cried when it was fed liquid from a bottle and closed her eyes in a slow spooky way when she was laid down. I chose two knights in armour on horseback with movable visors, and a single female figure who was meant to be a gypsy dancer. She was a raven haired beauty with a scarlet dress that was hitched up above her ankles at the front to show billowing white petticoats. Her detail included a tiny painted necklace on her pale pink neck and large gold ear-rings. I knew at the time that she didn't fit with the knights, but she was so exotic and beautiful that I had to buy her.

At Southampton docks the air was full of the echoing caw of seagulls and the bustle of departure. I looked up at the vast

ship and the damp air filled my nostrils with the mingled
scents of anchor chain grease and diesel oil as we clattered
across the metal gangplank to board.

We were sailing on the P&O liner, *SS Chitral* on a journey
that lasted about a month. Mum dressed up for dinner most
nights and was escorted to the Captain's table by one of
several young ship's officers. The trip was a prolonged holiday on which every day on the journey south and east brought
warmer weather and new adventures. The *Chitral* had a
luxurious cinema where my sister and I went to watch full
length cartoons of Yogi Bear and Bugs Bunny. In the mornings
we were sent to the ship's playroom where there were uniformed nannies to entertain us. Each stop at a new port was
an education. I saw a pissoir for the first time at Le Havre, in
Lisbon my mother wanted to buy a Siamese cat and smuggle it
onboard, and at Gibraltar, one of the ship's passengers was
bitten by a Barbary ape.

Soon after Gib, the safety net was removed from the
ship's pool and if the sea was calm we were allowed into it
in the afternoons. One day a little girl tried to climb out of
the pool and slipped so that her leg went down between the
wall of the pool and the handrail. She fell backwards with
her head underwater and couldn't pull her foot free. Two of
the male passengers had to support her head above water
while crewmen fetched a crowbar to bend the rail. Even so,
every time the ship rolled the girl's head was submerged and
I remember the tension among the assembled adults gathered at the poolside. I, and all the other children were
removed from the water and wrapped in towels during the
rescue.

The pool relieved the slow hot crawl as the boat passed though the Suez Canal, where there was earnest debate among the military wives about whether it was safe for them to go ashore at Port Said. Dad had instructed us not to, but he had also asked Mum to get him a pair of duty-free binoculars, and Port Said was supposed to have the best deals. One of the other passengers offered to buy them for her and, when the ship's tender returned at the end of the day I was excited by the delivery of the binoculars in their smart leather case lined with crimson felt. Sometimes I was allowed to hold them and open and shut the case, although the binoculars themselves were too heavy for me to use for viewing. Once he got them, Dad said that they weren't quite powerful enough and he barely ever used them, but they were still too precious for me to get my hands on. After more days at sea, there was a party on deck to celebrate crossing the Line, when all of the kids on board were pelted with water and had jelly and ice-cream in the presence of King Neptune.

In Ceylon, we went on an excursion to visit the Temple of the Tooth, and I was entranced by my first sight of an Indian elephant. The mahouts demonstrated how the elephants could move logs, but when they walked past I remember the chains on their legs made a mournful clanking sound. Mum bought a dark sapphire in Colombo that Dad had set into an eighteen-carat gold ring when we got to Malaysia.

As we sailed into Penang, I visited the small shop opposite the Purser's office to buy my mother a present. It was the first time I had ever been into a shop on my own, and the object of desire was a spoon with a circular bowl and a short handle decorated with the P&O crest. Throughout the voyage, it had been displayed on a glass shelf in the window, and I couldn't walk past without stopping to stare at its bright shining perfection. The window display lights made the spoon gleam hypnotically. It cost seven shillings, which I knew was quite a lot of money as the most I was ever given in cash was half a crown. I didn't have any money of my own, so I had to ask Mum to give it to me and made her promise not to ask the reason why. She seemed pleased that I had bought her a gift, but I'm not sure she was quite as enthralled with the spoon as I had been. But ever after, that spoon lived in the family tea-caddy, travelling everywhere in the world with us.

Once in Malaysia I was transformed by the warmth of the tropical climate and an outdoor life. I even learned to love the ponderous tropical rain, so heavy that time seemed to stop as every living thing ran for cover. We cowered under cheap umbrellas made of bamboo and brown paper painted green and lacquered with fish glue that stank when it got wet. Malaya was an assault on the nose, with its rich rotting durian fruits, joss sticks in the Indian trader's shops and the clean fresh air after the rain when everything steamed and thousands of frangipani blossoms littered the ground, their pure white flesh bruised and discoloured.

School finished at lunchtime, and then I had freedom. My scarred lungs were healed and the only time I was off school was when I fell and split open my head and knee. Mum was out shopping at the time and, seeing Dad returning from work, I ran across the garden to meet him. As I got to the edge of the garden I tripped up on one of my flip-flops and went headfirst into the monsoon ditch. Dad jumped out of his army jeep and clambered down into the ditch to get me out. Swiftly, he carried me upstairs to the bathroom and covered my bleeding injuries with damp flannels before rushing me back down to the jeep, shouting at the driver to hurry to the local clinic. I was almost eight, and was amazed that he could still climb the stairs two at a time with me in his arms. And, I remember rediscovering the feeling of security that small children experience when being held by a parent. As an adult he annoyed and frustrated me and sometimes let me down, but he always came into his own in a crisis.

In Taiping we lived in Rifle Range Road, close to the jungle. Our furniture was all made of rattan, and we sprayed the verandah for mosquitoes with tins of Flit attached to a contraption that resembled a bicycle pump. Inside, the chit-chats scampered up and down the walls on their magical adhesive feet, gobbling up the insects with their pale little tongues. Everything in nature was a new discovery, and I was outside all of the daylight hours. Giant spiders, soldier ants, scorpions and snakes were always to be found, and my friends and I invaded the jungle armed with sharpened bamboo poles in search of wild pigs.

I kept scorpions in a jar for a time, until Mum told me to throw them away. I played with knives and made spears, caught soldier ants and used my pocket money to buy stuffed snakes, a three foot long monitor lizard and, pride of the collection, a mongoose with a cobra wrapped around its torso in a life and death struggle.

One night, early on in our time in Malaysia, my mother found an enormous black spider on the wall above my bed. She covered it in DDT powder so copiously that the fumes brought her out in a severe allergic rash. The spider seemed unaffected, so she lifted the upright vacuum cleaner onto the wall and switched it on. The spider was duly sucked up, and Mum went back to bed, but couldn't sleep, troubled by the idea that the spider might somehow find a way out of the machine. Her solution was to get up and throw the vacuum from the bedroom window onto the lawn below, much to the surprise of the gardener when he found it the following day.

I belonged to a gang of boys, all of us army brats constantly playing at soldiers. As this was Malaysia, our enemy was always the Japanese and we persuaded our fathers to pay the camp tailor to make us miniature uniforms. It was up to your Dad to decide what rank badge you got and I was a corporal, but my friend Bobby Caton was given sergeant's stripes. That meant he had the power to order me around. Then a family arrived from New Zealand, and caused a stir. Mum and the other wives commented that the new woman had made most of her own clothes, and listened aghast as she explained how difficult it was to buy things in New Zealand. She told them there was a waiting list of at least six months if you wanted a new car, and that lipstick was hard to come by. Her son was admitted to our gang, and his Dad duly purchased him a uniform so that he could join in with our war games. Shockingly, he was made a lieutenant, and it didn't go down well with the other parents. There were mutterings about protocol, and how typical it was for a New Zealander not to understand that you couldn't just hand out British officer status to children. But in our gang the new boy's rank was unconditionally respected. And that's the way it stayed. We somehow assumed that as an officer he knew best, and he once made us eat tablespoonfuls of salt 'to counteract the dehydration caused by jungle warfare'. We just did it, even though it made us retch.

We lived in Taiping, which was then a very small place, and up in the hills there was an old freshwater swimming pool carved out of the rocks and filled by a natural stream. It trickled down from somewhere higher up the mountain, obscured by a canopy of ferns and branches. The water was always cool and I learned to dive for coins, which glittered against the bottom of the deep dark diving pool. The whole arrangement was shaded by overhanging jungle and in the late afternoon we listened to the sound of gibbons making their mournful whoop-whooping cry through the trees.

In Taiping, I was happy at the small two-class school run by the husband and wife team of Mr and Mrs Holly. He was the Head, and taught one class, while she taught the other. They liked setting general knowledge quizzes for homework, and there were several rows between Mrs Holly and parents about which answers were correct. The Hollys had an old edition of Encyclopaedia Britannica and if your answer didn't match what it said, then there was no way she was going to accept any argument. If you didn't have access to the Encyclopaedia, you had no hope of winning the quiz. And as most of the kids came from army families, the complete thirty-volume set of Britannica wasn't the kind of thing any of us carried around the world. I developed a kind of complex about the Encyclopaedia. I trusted my parents, so the idea formed in my head that Britannica must be inaccurate. For years afterward, whenever I saw the Encyclopaedia sitting on a library shelf I gave it a wide berth. Apart from setting quizzes, Mrs Holly also made us do ballroom dancing instead of P.E., and if you didn't have a partner you had to dance with her. I don't remember much of the general knowledge she taught us, but I'll never forget being twirled around the floor so fast I could barely keep my feet on the ground. My face was pressed into Mrs Holly's slightly sweaty floral-print dress with my head nestled under her squishy bosom. It put me off dancing forever.

The years we lived in Malaysia were a gilded time. My parents were young, and able to enjoy our company without the drudgery of housework or the irksome bills and paraphernalia of cold climate living. This was the Sixties, and it was party time, but without the sex, drugs and rock 'n' roll. We didn't know anyone with long hair, and Mum and Dad didn't listen to the Beatles, they stuck to Bert Kaempfert and Frank Sinatra. We only ever heard from relatives in Britain by post, though once there was a telegram telling Dad that his grandfather Harry had died at the age of ninety-three. Meanwhile, there were servants to do the chores, and an endless round of dinner parties and social events for which my parents could dress up, my father in regimental mess-kit with the smart red stripe down the legs of his trousers. The women, my mother included, had matched sets of Mikimoto pearls and bouffant hair styles and lived lives like the glamorous creatures we saw in the short cinema films advertising Peter Stuyvesant cigarettes. People were all sun-tan and white teeth.

In the middle of our stay Dad went away to fight with the Malaysian army against Indonesia in the jungles of Borneo. It was dangerous and he lived in a damp, centipede infested hole in the ground. I had no thought for the brutality of jungle warfare, and his tales of giant snakes and driving his patrol boat through the dense mangroves held only excitement for eight-year-old ears. When he returned he had grown a beard, an unheard-of indulgence for a British officer, permissible only because the constant humidity in the jungle had given him a skin infection which prevented him shaving. I remember the shock of meeting him at the airport, and my amazement that in spite of this transformation my mother was prepared to kiss him.

Dad later told me that he had been forced to fire shells into civilian villages because the Indonesians used the local people as cover. 'But that was their bad luck,' he said, seeing my shocked face. 'They shouldn't have sheltered the enemy.'

While Dad was away we carried on living the tropical dream in Taiping. Mum had her admirers, and there was a handsome young Malay Captain called Bernard who used to take her out to play golf. Sometimes he came for dinner. One evening as he was leaving the house, I saw him kiss her, in what I called the film-star way. 'Don't worry,' she laughed, 'he's just a boy who thinks he's in love with me. And I've written and told your father all about him.'

When I was older Mum would say that one of the many things that frustrated her about Dad was that she could never make him jealous. I think she would have liked that weapon in her arsenal. 'You never, ever suspected I could be interested in another man,' she would complain. Dad knew she was attractive to other men, but he had an unshakeable belief in her fidelity.

'I just knew you couldn't fall in love with anyone else,' was all he would say on the matter.

'I had my chances you know!' she would retort. This was the signal for us to press her for information about her other boyfriends.

We especially liked a story about a Guards officer she had known when my parents were stationed in Germany in the early Sixties. The dashing admirer had become a frequent visitor to the house and he eventually declared his love for Mum. He even asked Mum to run away with him, although in those days it would have meant the end of his army career.

'He was terribly handsome,' Mum would say with a sideways glance at Dad. 'Yes, he was *extremely handsome* with perfect manners and rich too. He was related to the Wrigley chewing gum family and he had a sports car and a house in Switzerland.' Meanwhile, Dad would carry on reading the paper or pretend not to have heard. 'I *was* tempted,' she would say loudly. 'He even said I could bring you children along, and he'd support you.'

'So why didn't you go?' We always asked, enjoying the ritual of repetition as though Mum was telling a folk tale. 'We could have been rich!'

'Well, he wouldn't let me bring the dog. And I couldn't bear the thought of leaving her behind with your father.'

Occasionally Mum referred to another man she had known before she met Dad. 'I should have married Timothy Bewley,' she would say when he irritated her. I later found out that he came from a very wealthy family in Dublin, and that he had gone to Hong Kong after graduating from Trinity College. Mum said he had become a High Court Judge, and when I was fifteen I discovered a copy of *The Serpent* by D.H. Lawrence in our sitting room book case. There was an inscription inside:*To Pamela, the most beautiful girl in Ireland. Tim Bewley, Trinity Ball 1950.* Suddenly the story had become much more real, and it made me uneasy to know that this man had really existed.

In Malaysia, W.G.'s edict about having dogs quickly crumbled. Mum was incapable of ignoring an animal in need. She couldn't resist puppies and kittens, or small children. They all had to be stroked and squeezed and cuddled. She was always like that with us too, embracing us in a bear hug when we got home from school and smothering us in kisses even when we were adults. Our first dog in Malaya was Fluff, a half-starved russet mongrel brought to us by our cooking amah, Amy Ling. She said that someone in her kampong had abandoned it. Then it was Samson, a scruffy, and minute puppy that Mum heard whining pitifully late one night. The next night she heard the sound again, and Dad was despatched with a torch to find the poor creature who had been thrown into a deep monsoon drain. To me, it was miraculous to wake up and find we had acquired a new dog overnight. Samson never grew very much, but he was a brave little dog and completely devoted to Mum. A neighbour asked us to keep the next dog, a terrier called Blackie, because they were going back to England.

One day Mum took us to Taiping market where the Chinese traders kept rattan baskets filled with day-old chicks. My sister and I persuaded Mum to buy us some as pets. We chose five each, some of them bright yellow and some jet-black. My sister quickly lost interest in the birds, but every morning I would rush to the outhouse to check on them and find at least one little corpse that needed a full garden burial service. After a while only one was left alive. He grew and grew, and because his only companions were the dogs, he copied his behaviour from them. In the heat of the day they all happily snuggled down in a pile under a tree to snooze. The chicken never got a name, but it would run to the front door if a stranger called, clucking loudly to compete with the dog's barking. When Dad came home he waged war on the chicken because it used to roost on the metal magazine rack under the TV while he tried to watch the news. And it was impossible to house-train, so he banned it from the house, and it became aggressive. After a time, I was the only one who could go into the garden and pick it up, and even the dogs were scared to challenge that cockerel. Eventually it had the run of the back garden to itself, and the maids had to arm themselves with a broom when they wanted to get to the washing line. When we left Taiping I was worried about what would happen to my chicken, until Amy persuaded her father to replace his own rooster with mine. For a couple of years afterwards she sent us Christmas cards enclosing a photograph of herself with the chicken to prove to me it was still alive.

When Dad was around we did everything as a family, piling into our black Buick with the brown leather seats and fins at the rear of the bodywork that made it seem much more exotic than English cars. Sometimes at weekends we would travel to the coast and take a boat to a small island where I could swim in the warm sea. I found my first porcupine fish there, and placed it in a bucket where it inflated itself like a balloon – a mass of prickly spines with a small round mouth and two eyes at one end. I let it go. On another occasion I was given a fishing rod with which I swiftly caught a large horseshoe crab.

It was a terrifying sight, like an armoured tank with a long tail protruding from its rear. I cried when I realised I had killed it.

We left Malaya only once, to travel to Singapore on a Comet. It was my first plane journey and we were going because Mum was expecting my brother. He was a Rhesus baby, and the only hospital that could cope with the birth was in Singapore. We had to fly there a month before the baby was due, and we stayed in a small hotel on a hill outside the city. Dad was on his own with us some of the time, and had to find ways to entertain Caro and I.

The day Will was born Mum announced at breakfast that she wanted to go for a boat ride.

'I don't think that's a good idea,' said Dad. 'What if the baby comes?'

'Well, you can stay here at the hotel,' said Mum. 'I'll just find a taxi driver to take me to the docks.'

Naturally, we all went along, and Dad reluctantly found an old Chinese fisherman with a primitive sampan who would take us out into the bay. Caro and I were fascinated by the fact that our skipper had only a single gold tooth. He didn't speak English and headed blithely out towards the open sea where the waves grew rough and ominous clouds gathered above us. 'Isn't this lovely,' Mum said as my sister and I cowered under a flimsy bamboo shelter at the other end of the boat.

'We should head back to shore now,' Dad warned. 'I don't like the look of this weather.'

'Yes, Mummy, we want to go back now,' Caro and I pleaded. For once we were united in our wishes, and convinced that we were going to be drowned in a typhoon.

'Don't be so cowardly,' Mum shouted against the wind. 'I've never seen such yellow-bellies!' she laughed madly, throwing her head back and opening her arms wide to the wind. 'These boats are designed for these conditions.'

That night Mum went into labour, and the storm lashed around our little chalet in the grounds of the hotel on the hill. Dad and Mum set off for the hospital, and Caro asked if she could share my bed because she was frightened. We lay in the darkness listening to the branch of a tree that tap-tapped against the window and sent a gnarled shadow across the room in the moonlight. Dad returned in the morning to tell us that Will had arrived, although he was dangerously ill for the first few weeks and received several blood transfusions before we were allowed to fly back to Malaya.

After three and a half years we returned to Europe, retracing our steps on the *SS Chitral* back to England. Dad was with us on the ship this time, and down in the hold there were seventeen large wooden packing cases filled with our belongings. Like almost every British family stationed in Malaysia, my parents had purchased a carved camphorwood chest and filled it with linen purchased at a fraction of the prices in Britain. The smell of the camphor was supposed to be a lifetime protection against moths. We also had Mum's collection of blue Chinese porcelain, ornate glazed ginger jars, hand-coloured Balinese prints on rice paper, a pair of antique bronze horses, Indian brass tables and lamps, spoons and tankards made from Selangor pewter. Somewhere among the grown-up treasures was my collection of stuffed animals, including the cobra wrapped around the mongoose in that perpetual wrestling match.

Rain, Cats and Dogs

A few months before we emigrated to South Africa, I over-heard Mum talking to Dad about me.

'We've got to get Timmy out of Ireland before he gets much older,' she was saying. My ears pricked up, and I crawled halfway up the stairs to listen in on the conversation going on in her bedroom. 'The next thing you know,' Mum was saying, 'he'll be off to university, a young man about town. And then he'll get trapped by an Irish wife.'

It was a theme I'd heard before. Granny had been making similar predictions since I was ten. Granny's three sons had married women she didn't approve of, one because she was 'common as muck', one because she was 'a divorcee and a hussy' and the other because she was 'already dyeing her hair when she got married'. This low opinion of women tended to include her own daughters, and in any difference of opinion she would always leap to the defence of her three sons-in-law. Their perfection was also enhanced because they were army officers, one of them the son of a diplomat. Granny was living proof that it wasn't just Chinese culture that revered the boy child above the female. 'Make the most of him, Pam,' she would say to my mother. 'In just a few more years Timmy will be off and married, and you'll have lost him for good to some awful creature.'

At sixteen, I didn't feel particularly threatened by the prospect of an Irish wife, or any wife in fact. The only women that featured significantly in my life were Mum, Granny and Caro, my annoying sister who was three years younger than me. My brother Will was younger still, and didn't get in the way much. I was the eldest child, and according to my siblings 'the favourite'. I didn't think it was true, although I secretly hoped it might be.

Apart from hating the hours I had to spend at school, my life was good. We lived in a big house in Ballyholme, the smartest bit of Bangor, a seaside town on the Ards Peninsular. Twice a week Mum drove me out to Breezemount Riding School in Conlig, where I always rode the same horse, Gale, a grey mare who stood 16:2 hands high. My first riding lessons were on a bad-tempered piebald pony called Tempest, before I moved on to Storm and Chinook. They named all the horses at Breezemount after winds. You couldn't always tell the temperament of a horse by its name, but I was frightened of Scirocco and of Breeze, the biggest mare at seventeen hands. The only person who could control all of the horses was my instructor, Wilson Moore. He was a gruff horseman who gave the lessons by barking out commands with a cigarette permanently dangling from one side of his mouth. He had enormous rough hands with blackened and pitted fingernails and was quite unsentimental about the animals. Wilson scared me into attempting jumps that I thought were too high, but I did whatever he asked in order to impress him. He also taught me how to place bets on horse races, showing me how to hedge my losses by placing each-way bets instead of putting money on the nose. What happened at the riding school on Thursday afternoons and Saturday mornings was the most exciting part of my life.

Because of the Troubles, our family outings were limited. Mostly, our family activities were confined to Bangor. Mum sometimes suggested going 'down south', into the Republic, but Dad said he couldn't risk it. As a former British Army officer and because he worked in the security industry, the police had told him he was on an IRA hit-list. There had been an attempt to ambush him when he drove to work one day. Some men had set up a roadblock and tried to flag him down, but he drove through it, knocking the barrier aside with his car, James Bond-style. We had security doors on the house that were supposed to stop a bullet, and blast shutters on the downstairs windows. I wasn't allowed to answer the door without looking through a side window first, and we checked under the car every morning before driving to school for bombs, and we had floodlights to illuminate the front of the house if anyone called at night. Dad kept an automatic pistol in his bedroom. Mum probably felt the strain of the security threat more than the rest of us, but Dad took it all in his stride: he was a soldier. Like most fathers he went off to work every morning and we didn't expect to see him until supper time, except his job meant he sometimes carried a gun. If I fought too much with Caro then Mum would threaten to tell Dad when he got home. Once or twice she actually did it, and we waited in trepidation for his return. But all he did was take us into the sitting room and tell us he was disappointed in our behaviour. 'Don't you understand how much strain it puts on your mother when you fight and bicker all day long?' he would say sadly, trying to appeal to our better natures. 'You're driving her to her wit's end! And you're both old enough to know better.'

Going to the cinema was something my parents always loved doing, and when I was thirteen Mum got me a subscription to *Photoplay* magazine. I would use it to quiz her about old films she had seen long before I was born, and Dad usually joined in too. He would correct Mum if he thought she had made a mistake. I would try to catch him out, but he had an incredible memory for film trivia. 'No, Joan Fontaine was Olivia de Havilland's sister,' he would say, or 'it was Gene Tierney who was admitted to an asylum because she had a breakdown.'

TV wasn't held in the same high regard as cinema. 'Don't waste your eyesight on that rubbish,' Mum would say if she caught me watching something trashy. Or, if I said I wanted to watch something that was on late she would issue the mantra: 'I don't care if *King Kong* is on TV tonight, you're not staying up.' I was about fifteen when the original 1933 version of *King Kong* starring Fay Wray and Bruce Cabot finally appeared on TV, but it was scheduled for eleven o'clock at night. I primed Mum with the news that I wanted to watch a late film. And then triumphantly announced: 'And it IS *King Kong*.' She let me watch it.

Very occasionally we all went to the Tonic Cinema, a grand but faded art deco emporium on the Hamilton Road that boasted being Ireland's largest film theatre. It seated over two thousand people, so even watching a bad film there felt like a bit of an occasion. Usually I sat in the stalls, unless Mum was with me and then we always sat up in the Circle. That was the best place to be and I would stare at the red velvet curtains trimmed with gold that hung down in front of the screen and made it seem enormously high. It was there we went to see *Jaws* (Roy Scheider, Robert Shaw, 1975), one of the few films that whole families queued up for. You couldn't book advance tickets then, and I remember standing in the car park that summer evening hoping we'd get to the front of the queue before the manager came out with his 'House Full' sign and plonked it down on the steps. We just made it, but we had to go back for a second attempt to see *The Towering Inferno* (Steve McQueen, Paul Newman, William Holden, 1974).

The Tonic was originally designed with shops flanking the entrance and some residential accommodation on the upper floors. Gradually the other parts of the complex fell into disuse, and the last one to close was a hairdresser's at the front of the building. Mum would send me in to watch Saturday matinees while she was getting her hair done. I learned not to sit in the three rows that were just under the front rim of the Circle, because kids sometimes threw chewing gum from up there. Continuous B-features like *Tarzan and the Valley of Gold* (Mike Henry, 1966) and cartoons played on Saturday afternoons and I was never told what I was going to see. I just watched whatever was up on the screen when I walked in, and stayed until the feature got to the same scene on the next showing. The cinema rarely got used for anything except films, although when the Bay City Rollers came to Northern Ireland in 1975, that was where they played. My sister was one of the screaming teeny-boppers in a tartan scarf waiting in the queue.

Like thousands of other families, our Saturday nights in winter were passed watching episodes of the *Generation Game*, *Morecambe and Wise* and *Mike Yarwood*. If Granny was visiting we also had to watch the *Val Doonican Show*, and I remember Grandpop liked Frankie Howerd in *Up Pompeii* which I wasn't allowed to see because Mum had classified it as unsuitable. We were ensconced in that Seventies TV womb, brimful with comedy series, awash with catch-phrases: *Dad's Army*, *On the Buses*, *My Wife Next Door*, *Are You Being Served?*, and *It Ain't Half Hot Mum*. Mum had her own ideas about what was suitable viewing, and we learned from an early age that she thought *Coronation Street* and *Crossroads* were 'too common'. *Upstairs Downstairs* was probably the highlight of the week when I got past twelve. Once I had my own TV in my room, films were always my first choice.

In the year before I left school I saw 393 films. I wrote down all the titles and the names of the major stars in my diary. I had rules about what counted as a proper film, and didn't include TV movies, or feature length dramas like *Columbo* (Peter Falk) or *McMillan and Wife* (Rock Hudson, Susan Saint James). 1977 got off to a good start with *Willie Wonka and the Chocolate Factory* (Gene Wilder, 1971), and *Patton: Lust for Glory* (George C. Scott, Karl Malden, 1970) all on January 1st. Within a few days I had watched *The Treasure of Lost Canyon* (William Powell, 1952), *Lady in Cement* (Frank Sinatra, Raquel Welch, 1968) *The Ballad of Cable Hogue* (Jason Robards, Stella Stevens, 1970), *The Long Arm* (Jack

Hawkins, 1956) and *Kings of the Sun* (Yul Brynner, Richard Basehart, 1963).

Apart from the television and horses, the most significant thing in my world was Shandy, a boxer dog who had to put up with being trained as a substitute horse. With a rope attached to her collar she had to jump a series of 'fences' constructed in the garden. After Horse of the Year Show was televised, Shandy was in for a busy time for several weeks afterwards. And we had cats too, half a dozen Siamese that Mum kept for breeding. She sold the kittens and occasionally took one or two of the adults to shows run by the Ulster Siamese and All Breeds Cat Club.

Dad and Mum didn't socialise a great deal, partly because of his security connections, and her unwillingness to get sucked into any sort of circle in Bangor. Perhaps it was because the army had always provided them with a ready-made social network, and in Ireland we had cousins nearby of similar ages with whom we could always play. In Bangor, the adult options were limited to the golf club, the yacht club and the small group of regulars who kept the Little Theatre alive. Mum's acquaintances, and her one or two genuine friends came from the Ulster Siamese and All Breeds Cat Club.

Mum's Siamese cats came from Mrs MacDonald. About once each month she advertised her English bull terriers and Siamese and Persian cats in the *County Down Spectator*. The ad was always the same: *Pedigree puppies and kittens for sale. Ten guineas. Please allow phone to ring for at least two minutes.*

The first time we went to Mrs McDonald's house was when Mum said I could have a dog for my tenth birthday. We had only just moved back to Ireland, and we were staying with Granny and Grandpop while Dad looked for a house. Mum said it was up to me to decide what kind of dog I wanted, and I was allowed to go down to the phone box at the bottom of the road and ring the numbers in the *Spectator* myself. Mrs MacDonald's ad intrigued me and I dutifully waited for the requisite two minutes until she answered. The voice at the other end of the line was breathless, and very, very English. 'You can come tomorrow: six o'clock sharp. You have to stop outside the gate and hoot the horn until I hear you.'

That was how we came to know Mrs MacDonald. First, she sold us a white bull terrier that I christened Happy because he seemed to be smiling. It was an ill-fated christening. One summer's day I tied him up with a chain attached to his collar, the only thing he couldn't chew through, or snap with brute strength. I wanted to stop him roaming the neighbourhood in search of a bitch in heat, and I only left him alone for half an hour while I ate my lunch. Happy was a tremendously strong dog, and he could work out how to solve problems. None of the doors in the downstairs part of the house closed properly because if Happy wanted to open a door he would charge at it with his bullet-hard head. To break the chain he had obviously tried running and jumping in the air, and managed to twist it into a knot that lifted his front legs off the ground and tightened around his throat. He was already dead when I came back into the garden after lunch.

Soon after we bought Happy, Mrs MacDonald sold Mum a Siamese cat. Then some more cats. Until we had seven, and Mum was in the business of breeding and showing the animals herself.

Mrs MacDonald lived alone in a massive Victorian house at the end of a long overgrown driveway. The house was obscured by a miniature forest of tall Scots pines, and it had about ten bedrooms. In the garden there were large kennels and dog runs enclosed with sturdy wire mesh where the breeding bitches, about a dozen of them, lived. That was why you had to let the phone ring so long, to give her time to get back to the house if she was out in the yard. On subsequent visits we got to see the house properly. Each bedroom was home to three or four cats, either fluffy Persians, or sleek Siamese. The dogs were all English bull terriers, with good pedigrees.

I liked going to Mrs MacDonald's house, even though most people said she was scary, and mad. And everyone agreed that up close, she didn't smell good. No one ever saw her in anything but baggy green or brown corduroy trousers tied up with a thick man's leather belt. Winter and summer she wore long-sleeved plaid shirts, and her hair was always, always back in a greying bun. I used to hear the other cat-breeders making fun of Mrs MacDonald, and saying things about how crazy she was because all she cared about was her animals.

Inside the house the air was thick with drifting piles of cat fur. Clumps of fine Persian hair puffed from the carpet when you walked on it, and it coated all of the surfaces in all of the rooms. In the kitchen, which was the only room Mrs Mac-

Donald seemed to use herself apart from a bedroom, there was an incontinent bull terrier with wonky back legs that dragged himself around on his forepaws. Mrs MacDonald said he was a faithful friend and she just couldn't bear to have him put down. Sometimes she offered us something to drink and Mum would shoot us a warning glance not to accept anything. If Dad came with us then he would accept a cup of tea and we would watch him trying to drink it without letting his lips touch the china. The entire house was filthy, and Mrs MacDonald had hands that were as coarse and chapped as a navvy. I didn't mind the dirt but the hallway did frighten me. Opposite the grand front door there was a Christmas tree, so old that all of the needles had dropped off leaving a desiccated brown skeleton. There were decorations visible here and there among the branches, although the layers of dust and matted cat hair made it seem as if the tree had been sprayed with one of those cans of fake snow.

One day, while my mother was looking at the cats, I plucked up the courage to ask Mrs MacDonald about the tree. She told me it had been there since 1943. Tears rolled slowly down her ruddy cheeks as she told me that on Christmas Eve of that year she had married an Air Force pilot. On Boxing Day, he was shot down and killed flying over Germany. 'If I take down the tree, I'll really know that he's not coming back,' she said quietly. I didn't know what to say or do. Then Mrs MacDonald rubbed her blackened hands roughly and swiftly across her face and stomped up the stairs to see to the cats.

After that I got annoyed when I heard other breeders laughing at Mrs MacDonald. Once she fell onto the luggage carousel at the airport when she was trying to retrieve a cat box from the belt after taking it to a show in England. Those who saw it happen said the last thing they saw was Mrs MacDonald's bottom in its expanse of corduroy as she was trundled through the rubber curtains that led back to the baggage area out of sight from the other passengers. The incident was the talk of the Ulster Siamese And All Breeds Cat Club for years. But, I think the main reason people talked about Mrs MacDonald was because she was English. And, I suppose I liked her for the same reason. Perhaps if they had known the story about the Christmas tree they might have been more tolerant.

Market People

Mrs Meerblat was one of the Hillbrovniks, the mittel-Europeans of every variety who lived in the apartment blocks around Hillbrow. She was a tiny old woman with a solid girth and sparse hair that was dyed jet black to match her quite dense moustache. Mrs Meerblat lived in a block that seemed to be entirely populated by elderly Jewish widows. She, like a significant number of the old ladies who came into The Whatnot once rolled up her sleeve to reveal a number tattooed on her forearm, showing that she had been processed in a Nazi concentration camp. She had lived in Johannesburg since 1948, but her accent was impenetrable. She rarely bought anything, and Mum would duck into the back room and pull the curtain when she saw her coming.

'Vere iss de lady? De lady in de gveen dwess?'

I tried my hardest to make her leave so that Mum could emerge from her hiding place. She probably suspected the truth, because whatever I said she simply repeated her question. 'De lady? She's dare?'

'I'm afraid she's out. She may not come back today at all.'

'But I mussst see dee lady. She's dare, or she's not dare?'

'She's not here.'

'Okay den. I vill vait.'

This was torture. Mrs Meerblat would make a painfully slow circuit of the entire shop picking up every single item on display and peering at the price sticker as if she was a serious customer. In seven years of haunting the shop, she only ever bought one cracked willow-pattern china plate from a box of odds and ends.

'I vont to see de gveen lady. De propriedor. I haf zumzing to giff her.'

Mrs Meerblat lived in an apartment block which had a communal restaurant on the ground floor where residents, all of them very aged, could take breakfast and dinner if they wished. Breakfast was included in the rent, but for dinner you paid extra. When Mrs Meerblat said she had something to give to Mum, we would brace ourselves. 'Leave it on the counter,' we would bark rudely, trying not to make eye contact. But inevitably, she would rummage in her handbag and produce one or two lumps of tissue paper, folded pass-the-parcel-style around something she had filched from the breakfast buffet. 'Itz a pwesent fud djor mudder,' Mrs Meerblat would say gravely. 'Dell her, I gum back lader.'

When Mum emerged from her cubby-hole my brother and I would taunt her. 'What can it be? A present. Open it! Open it!'

Inside would be a stale roll, sometimes a lump of gooey cheddar or even on one occasion a half-dozen portions of butter wrapped in their little silver-foil envelopes. They oozed melted butter all over the counter. Mum would threaten to eject Mrs Meerblat from the shop if she ever came again, but we knew she didn't have the heart.

'I know she's lonely,' Mum would rant, 'but how dare she think I'm so poor that I need leftovers from her breakfast table!'

It really upset Mum that old Mrs Meerblat called her the 'green lady'. It was because her wardrobe consisted of two basic outfits, both of them green. It happened to be her favourite colour, but when I saved up enough money to buy her a new outfit she insisted on a blue skirt and blouse.

Zenobia De La Porte was another regular. Tall and elegant, she started coming to the shop about once a week as a customer. She wasn't the sort to stay and to join the gin and beer fuelled parties on a Friday night, but when she did come, she usually bought something so Mum didn't mind chatting to her for a while. Gradually, we noticed that she seemed to be paying Mum more attention than normal, giving her compliments. 'You're very young looking to have such grown-up children,' she would say. Zenobia had long, dark hair wound into a tightly coiled plait that she pulled forwards over one shoulder. One day she came into the shop and we barely recognised her. Her hair was dyed blonde and cut and curled.

'I've always wanted hair like yours, Pam, don't you think we could be taken for sisters?'

Mum didn't know what to say. Zenobia was six inches taller than her, a big boned woman with a prominent jaw. We had got used to Market People and the customers making outlandish claims over the years, and Zenobia's desire to become just like our mother didn't seem especially strange.

Like many of the people who came into the shop, Zenobia seemed to enjoy experimenting with her own life-story. 'My son is one of the top surgeons in the world,' she would claim. 'He's very wealthy and he sends me tickets, First Class, to visit him in London.' At other times she talked about her son 'the architect in Hong Kong', but another of the dealers who knew Zenobia said she had no children.

After the copycat hairstyling incident we didn't see Zenobia in the shop for a few weeks, but the next time she appeared it was to make another revelation. 'I've changed my name,' she announced. 'Everyone has to call me Pam. But, I don't want people mixing us up, so I'm moving to Cape Town to open my own antique shop.'

There was always some drama at the Village Market. Shopkeepers fought with each other, and their customers. There were love affairs and robberies, bankruptcies and raids by the municipal authorities or the police.

The shops in the arcade were extremely varied. Apart from the Velvet Heart sex shop, there was also Sophie's Choice, run by an eponymous Greek lady. Sophie specialised in risqué lingerie and did a good trade with the many call-girls who used the local hotels and bars for their trade. Then there was a hairdresser for white people called In Style. It was next door to an African salon named Ebony. The African salon was run by Robbie, the son of an English vicar. Next door was a tiny bookshop selling religious pamphlets, financed by Robbie's father's congregation back home. Robbie was never to be found in the pamphlet shop, spending most of his time running Ebony with his two African girlfriends. They were tall curvaceous women who dressed like twins, often in bright yellow hotpants held up with braces. 'It would kill Dad if he knew I was living in sin with a black girl,' Robbie confessed with a manic laugh. 'But two black girlfriends, wow, man, that would really freak him out!'

Next door to Vintage Vinyl was Scots John, an ex-British Army sergeant who sold militaria, medals, uniforms and guns that had been made legally inoperable. Naturally, the guns could be quickly made functional, for a fee. Scots John's shop attracted ex-soldiers and mercenaries who were passing through Johannesburg to various small wars in other parts of Africa. A surprising number of Americans seemed to be involved, and they brought him captured insignia, Russian-made cartridge cases and disarmed grenades that he could sell to collectors. One of his regulars was a man from Alabama who befriended my brother. Mum didn't encourage him into The Whatnot because his favourite topic was what he had achieved as a member of the Ku Klux Klan, the reason he had to leave the USA.

One night when my brother was about ten, Scots John asked him if he would go with him to collect some stock from a nearby apartment block. He needed help carrying some pistols that he didn't want to be seen with in daylight. Will was happy to help, but when they reached the street, Scots John decided that he wanted to take a covert route. In between the forest of apartment blocks of Hillbrow there were narrow service alleys leading into back courtyards where the dustbins could be stored. 'Let's treat thus as a mishun,' Scots John said conspiratorially. 'You'se need to get in a wee bit o' trainin' laddie. You'se wint ta be like yure Daddy, don't ye? Ye wint ta be in the SAS, noo?'

Scots John ducked into an alleyway and flattened himself against the wall. 'C'mon laddie, we've to go all the way like thus. We'll nort let inywun see us taneet. Ye must preten' you'se ur in the Brec-un Beec'ins. Ye ken? The Brec-un Beec'ins. Tharts whayre the SAS de all thair trainin'!'

Half-crouching and occasionally kneeling they crept along the alleyway behind the well-lit length of Pretoria Street. When they reached the end of a block, Scots John decided they should run quickly across the road dodging the traffic as if they were being pursued by the enemy. As they reached the next alleyway, Scots John tripped and went headlong into the dirty dark space. My brother carried on a little further before he realised that John wasn't following. Retracing his footsteps, he found John prone on the ground. 'Come on John,' he said enthusiastically. 'We're on a mission aren't we? In the Brecon Beacons – just like the SAS?'

A low groan was all he heard at first, followed by a string of expletives. 'Fock the fockin' Brec'un fockin' beak'uns. An' fock the fockin' S. A. fockin' S. Ah'm away hame to ma bed.'

Most of the Market People seemed to have a story, and whatever it was they shared it with Mum. Gimpy Aubrey was typical. He was a slim pale boy of around nineteen, good looking with glossy black hair that curled into ringlets at the temples. He dragged one leg slightly, and had a club-foot and his general manner was effete. Something had gone wrong during his birth, and although he spoke beautifully, his words came out slowly and there was a lot about the world that he didn't seem to understand. Aubretia, Aubrey's mother, claimed she earned her living as a fortune-teller. Aubretia wore black kaftans with motifs embroidered in gold thread and heavy ethnic jewellery, studded with amber and quartz. In reality, Aubretia was a prostitute, who made some extra money by selling drugs to her clients. She had brought Aubrey up on her own, and from an early age he knew that he had to stay in his room and not come out when she was 'telling fortunes'. As he got older, Aubretia allowed him to walk around Hillbrow, and visiting Mum at the shop was one of the things he did to pass the time.

Aubrey sat in the shop and was happy to talk to the other customers, but left alone with any of us he asked incessant questions about England. We discovered that Aubretia had brought him up believing that he was the illegitimate heir to a title and a large estate. She claimed that he had been born after an affair with a Duke, and Aubrey dreamt of going to England one day and claiming his inheritance.

'Actually,' he sighed, 'I'd just like to meet my English relatives and get to know them. Don't you think they'd like to meet the South African branch of the family?'

Aubretia was fond of Aubrey, but she didn't seem to mind that he was being targeted by Natie, a middle-aged neighbour who paid him for sex. Natie had an enormous belly, and always wore ultra-white shirts open to the midriff that showed off his deep tan, as well as a jungle of grey chest hair and gold necklaces. He wore his sunglasses perched on top of his head and always carried a bunch of car keys and a packet of cigarettes in one hand. If Mum spotted Natie coming towards the shop, she would bundle Aubrey behind the curtain into the back room to hide. Aubrey was very naïve, and didn't really seem to know if he was gay or straight.

'I don't have to do very much for Natie,' Aubrey told us candidly. 'My bum hurts a bit afterwards, but I'm getting used to it, and he gives me money which comes in useful.'

Markus the sex shop owner felt sorry for Aubrey and was keen to convince him that he wasn't necessarily homosexual. 'We've got to show Aubrey that there's another option when it comes to sex,' Markus confided in Mum. He then paid a prostitute to ask Aubrey out on a date. She was instructed to have sex with Aubrey, but not to reveal that she was a professional.

'So how did it go, this date?' Mum enquired when she next saw Aubrey.

'It was okay,' he replied. 'But I think I'll stick to being gay.'

'Why is that?'

'I quite enjoyed the sex part, but' – and he pulled a face – 'it was very hard work what with my weak leg and all.'

Soon afterwards, Mum asked Aubretia whether she minded that Aubrey was being buggered by Natie, the portly neighbour.

'I suppose it's not ideal,' Aubretia conceded, taking a drag on a cigarette, 'but what other options does a boy like that have?'

In the Shadow of Irish Mountains

When they weren't away with the Army, Mum's family lived
in Newcastle, a small seaside town at the foot of Slieve
Donard. Now, after years of travelling, the mountains and
the nearby sands of Dundrum Bay feel as much like home to
me as anywhere. Mum and Dad were married in St John's
Church at the end of the bay, and I was christened there.
Returning, I can still marvel at how much greener the landscape is than England. When I told people in Africa that I was
from Northern Ireland they expressed sympathy, and I knew
that their minds filled with images from the Troubles. Like
many people from the Province, I have a split identity: part-
Irish and part-English, part Northern-Irish and part-British,
and part-wanting-nothing-to-do-with-the-place at all. When I
visit, I sometimes let my English accent act as a disguise,
allowing myself to be welcomed as a holidaymaker. That way
I can't be judged: is he Catholic or Protestant? Nationalist or
Brit? It's easier to keep my insider knowledge, and connections, to myself. North and South of the border, I can enjoy an
Irish welcome without being spotted as a native.

Newcastle holds the most vivid memories. At the edge of the town, the Mountains of Mourne are as ancient and Gaelic a landscape as any in the whole of Ireland, a mysterious world of empty space and spirits which looks out imperiously over the neatly ordered Protestant farmlands of the north. From Belfast, which is thirty miles away, the Mournes rise high above the low rolling hills of County Down. At school I was told that these hills are called drumlins, and their regularity and smoothness earns them the geographers' nickname, 'eggs in a basket country'. It is a landscape both smooth and sharp, with verdant greens and bare browns fashioned by ancient glaciers which scoured the low hills clean, and left the granite peaks alone. The Kingdom of Mourne contains twelve mountains in excess of two thousand feet, and yet the entire range is less than seven miles wide, creating some of the most dramatic countryside in all Ireland. No roads span the interior of the range, leaving its Celtic heart untrammelled.

These mountains inhabit my earliest memories, and I learned to walk beneath the great blue shadow of Slieve Donard. Unfailingly, a return to the slopes recalls the presence of absent family members, living and dead. They are companion spirits as I climb into the clean fresh air. At one edge of Newcastle's long sandy beach, the Slieve Donard Hotel is a great red Ruabon brick castle, dressed with Dumfries sandstone and topped with a roof of green slate. The building stares out at the breakers rolling onto the strand and draws golfers from around the world to play on the famous Royal County Down course beside the sea. Mum learned to play the game there, and on her secret nine-handicap she enjoyed beating male players who thought they faced no challenge from her slim frame.

From the beach in front of the hotel, the mountains fill the sky, now blue, now purple, then green as the sun shifts its angle and the clouds and the heather, the shale and the granite play tricks with the spectrum. The names of the peaks and hills form a litany of glottal stops and consonants in my head: Donard, Commedagh, Binnian, Slievenamady and Slievenagloch, Tievedockaragh and Drinnahilly. When the rain obliterates the tip of Donard, and her sister peak Slieve Commedagh, they seem dark and grim, a truly forbidding kingdom where, as a boy, I could easily imagine malevolent spirits. But when the days are lighter, and the clouds are not filled with rain there are sights in the mountains that gladden my heart. Up there is the Glen River, a clear mountain stream which tumbles down the cleft between Donard and Commedagh for two miles. At the head of the valley between the peaks there is a dry-stone wall, part of the twenty-two mile barrier erected in the 1920s to keep livestock out of the water catchment for the Silent Valley Reservoir. When a mist strikes unexpectedly, or a rain squall hits hard, the wall is a walker's friend, a shelter and a guide.

Up above the birch and Scots pine forest there is a valley lit with the golden-topped heather which carpets the peaty subsoil. Ahead, the Mourne Wall links the switchback of the peaks like a crazy stone-age roller coaster track. Walk up to it and peer over the wall and you will see the Brandy Pad, the old smugglers' path which leads from the coast across the interior of the mountains. Ahead and to the west, the path finds the Hare's Gap, a natural flat break between Slieve Bearnagh and

Slievenagloch. Bearnagh's jagged top is the most forbidding of the Mourne peaks – a dizzy, craggy tor. They call Bearnagh the 'unfinished' mountain, it's ragged granite silhouette forming a natural amphitheatre where hikers peer down at the valleys below. Up here the air is fresh and empties your lungs and head of city dust and untidy thoughts. The view extends past Slieve Binnian (mountain of little horns) and Slieve Muck (the pigs) then on to the entrance to Carlingford Lough which separates the North of Ireland from the South. A hundred years ago the lowlands around the Mournes were potato country, and the crop was fertilised with seaweed from these shores. Hauling it over and around the mountains was tough work, but it made the difference between life and death in these parts when the yield was low.

The last time I climbed Commedagh there was a peregrine falcon being mobbed by five black ravens. Stooping high above the heather, the falcon hoped to raid the ravens' wind-blown nests, but after several minutes of tumbling and wheeling it was driven off by the big black birds. Up here, over 2000 feet above the waters of Dundrum Bay, the ravens make their home, sustained by mice and blaeberries, but feeding mostly on the carcasses of mountain sheep rotting in the heather. From below, the mountains look best when the wind strikes them clear of cloud and rain and in the late afternoon there are slivers of granite on the flanks of Slieve Donard that shine like precious metal in the softening light.

Beneath the shoulder of Slievenamaddy and at the base of Shan Slieve there is the Donard Wood. The slopes are soggy with soft peat and cold mountain water that seeps into your shoes. From the age of about three, it was Grandpop, my mother's father, who took me walking there. When I was a little older, he liked to hide among the dark trees, tormenting me by leaving me alone in the forest until I started to cry. He would bribe me with a thru'penny bit not to tell my mother what he had done and, although he regularly repeated the cruelty, I never learned to be unafraid. It didn't stop me wanting to go into the forest with him, but it gave me a lingering fear of dark untended nature that lasted well into my teens. There were imagined hidden things among the clustered pine trunks, tall towering ferns and rotting stumps, and underfoot a bed of countless pine needles softened the sounds of footfall and birdsong. Grandpop had grown up in the country and knew the names of the plants and birds. Sometimes, as a treat, he would stop on the way home by a little cottage at the edge of the demesne where 'Paddy' Taggart lived. There was always a wisp of smoke coming from the chimney and the heartwarming smell of the smouldering peat filled the air in the lane outside. Paddy had a horse and cart, and he would let me sit up on the driving seat and hold the reins as we clip-clopped back along the road to where my grandparents lived.

Like many 'Northern Irish' families, our political allegiances could shift depending on the circumstances. Granny's family came from Dublin while Grandpop was a staunch Protestant from Lurgan. On the other side, Dad was completely English, but he fell in love with Ireland when he was stationed there in the 1950s. Although he was in the British Army he thought that there was nothing illogical or wrong about a United Ireland. But it didn't mean he wouldn't fight the IRA.

Dad met Mum in England. She was in the Territorial Army, and had gone to Cornwall in 1953 to do her annual two-week camp. He told us that he had been looking out of his office window one morning when he saw her marching across the parade ground. He said she looked like Doris Day. 'I'm going to marry that girl,' he announced to the other officer in the room.

Mum didn't like him at first. 'He was very arrogant,' she would say with a smile. 'He expected me to jump into bed with him, like all of his other girlfriends.' She wasn't like them – not in any way – and he followed her home to Northern Ireland for an old-fashioned courtship, braving the eagle-eyed scrutiny of Grandpop. Six months later they walked out from the little church at the foot of the mountains in Newcastle, County Down, through an archway of raised officer's swords held aloft by a guard of honour. Their relationship was tested almost immediately, because Dad volunteered to fight in Cyprus within six months of the wedding. For the next two years they lived apart, seeing each other twice a year when he came home on leave. But that's what being an army wife meant, and it was a life my mother accepted. It was a pattern that allowed them to live in separate countries and yet remain emotionally centred on one another. Theirs proved to be an unshakeable love.

In 1969, Dad was sent back to Northern Ireland when the Troubles broke out. And that was where we stayed until we immigrated to South Africa in January 1977. In all that time we only had one holiday, when we took the ferry over to the west coast of Scotland and visited Glasgow, Stirling and Troon. Mum and Dad had lived in Troon when they were first married, and she often mentioned the house where the wind came whistling under the front door and lifted up the carpet.

That trip to Scotland was the only time we left Bangor until we moved to Johannesburg, although Dad sometimes went to London on business. Not many people seemed to go on foreign holidays then, and the places you could fly to from Belfast were quite limited. Sometimes Mum would say she wished we could sell our house and buy a boat to sail around the world. 'Plenty of people do it!' she would tell Dad when he pointed out the practical problems involved. The Army was supposed to have been Mum's way of getting out of Ireland. 'I married a British soldier only to become marooned here,' she complained bitterly. As I got older I began to understand how seriously she meant it.

Mum's father and her three brothers were all in the British Army, and her two sisters married army officers too. Both my sister and my brother were born in military hospitals, one in Germany and one in Singapore, and lots of our cousins were born somewhere 'abroad'. My parents' friends were almost exclusively brother officers and their wives. As a child, I came to regard civilians as slightly inferior creatures, and I was more than a little suspicious of them. I couldn't really imagine how they managed without any connection to the Services.

Living in Northern Ireland during the Troubles didn't seem strange to me. We watched the local news every night and saw what was happening, but Bangor was relatively unaffected by what happened in Belfast and other hot-spots closer to the border. The IRA was just another name among the list of enemies that cropped up in stories about most of our male family members. By the time I was seven, my head was already filled with tales about the Mau Mau in Kenya, the communist insurgents in Malaysia and AOKA in Cyprus.

We saw my grandparents several times each week, and Mum would often call in on them to see if they needed any shopping, or a lift somewhere since they didn't have a car of their own. I was close to them both, and loved sitting with Grandpop and asking him about his youth. He told me stories of a tough childhood, growing up on a farm with his five brothers. I liked hearing about the time he dropped a cat down an old woman's chimney to give her a fright, and I was shocked to hear that when he was eight his father decided that he was too old for Christmas presents. Waking up on Christmas morning he went to open his stocking hanging beside the hearth, only to discover that it contained nothing but a lump of coal. Most of all I wanted to hear about the First World War. Granny always left the room, unimpressed with my interest in things military.

'Bah! Haven't we heard enough about the blinking war?' she would exclaim. 'I don't know why you can't forget all about it.'

As Grandpop got older he lost the use of his right arm, the one that had been wounded twice on the Somme. Granny told me that he had a weakness in that side of his body due to a slight stroke he'd had when he was about sixty. 'It's better if he thinks it's because of his war wound,' she confided in me.

In the summer Grandpop's main activity was gardening, but in the winter he stayed indoors reading Zane Grey novels, or simply sat by the coal fire puffing away on Embassy No. 1s. He blamed his terrible coughing fits on being gassed in the trenches rather than the steady sixty cigarettes a day he'd consumed since the age of fourteen. Often, he would simply stare silently into the flames in the hearth for hours on end. When I asked him what he was thinking about, his answer was always the same: the war. And though he had been active in 1939–45, I knew he meant 1914–18, when he and his brothers served in the Royal Irish Fusiliers. Best of all, I liked hearing about his experiences in the trenches, and how over the course of one week in the depths of winter everyone in his platoon except for Grandpop and two other men had been killed. One night they piled up the bodies of the other soldiers, covering them with all of the blankets so that they formed a platform they could sleep upon. He said it was the only way they could keep themselves dry in all the snow and mud. I also liked hearing about how Grandpop and two of his brothers had gone over the top on 1 July 1916 at the Somme. As they raced towards the enemy, sixteen year old Ernest, the youngest of his five brothers was hit and fell down. Grandpop and his other brother Ivan knew they couldn't stop to help Ernest, but at the end of the day they were given permission to leave their trench and go to look for him. They never found his body, though his grave is in the war cemetery in Beaumont-Hammel. The gravestone gives his age as twenty-two, but that was because he had lied about his age to join up with his brothers.

On just a few occasions, I persuaded Grandpop to tell me the story of how he was wounded. The first time he was shot, it was in the shoulder and after an operation in France he was sent back to Ireland to recuperate. He always laughed when he told me that when he was well enough to walk about, he had been stopped in the street by a woman who handed him a white feather. It was a symbol of cowardice, an insult intended for men who hadn't joined up to fight. I knew the custom from watching Ralph Richardson and C. Aubrey Smith in *The Four Feathers* (1939).

'What did you do?' I would ask, hoping that he had pulled back his coat to show off his bandaged shoulder. 'I just took the feather,' he answered. 'Stupid people like that aren't worth bothering with.'

The second injury came during a night reconnaissance with his best friend, Bill. The German troops spotted them crawling across no-man's land and opened fire, hitting Grandpop in the arm. He crawled back to the trenches where the doctors wanted to amputate his hand. He refused, although they said he would die of blood poisoning. His friend Bill was shot full in the face. The Germans picked him up and bandaged him as best they could, then pointed him back towards his own lines. Bill was blinded, and had lost his nose and most of his jaw too, but he didn't die. For several years after the War, Grandpop visited him in a nursing home in Brighton. 'Bill liked to smoke, but he had no proper way to keep a cigarette in his mouth. I used to inhale on a cigarette and blow the smoke straight out towards where his nose was meant to be.'

It upset Grandpop to talk about Bill, but he couldn't just forget about him. Granny's reaction was different. She would react with a full body shudder and a grimace at the mere mention of his name. 'I could never bear to visit that man. All those dreadful injuries.'

Granny exhibited the same twitch when she mentioned her daughter-in-law Barbara. Granny never called her anything but '*that* Barbara'. Barbara had been rather beautiful, but became disfigured after fainting and falling onto a coal fire. Consequently she wore a wig, and the left side of her face was badly scarred. As teenagers, my cousin and I would try to engineer a conversation in which Granny was forced to mention Barbara by name, and we awarded points to the one who could trigger the accompanying shudder.

Like all of the soldiers in the family, Grandpop was virulently anti-war. I asked him if he disliked the Germans. 'No, they were good soldiers, very brave men,' he would say. 'But I hated the Turks at Gallipoli, they used to come out onto no-man's land and torture any of the wounded they found still alive.'

Everyone we knew served in the military. If you didn't join the Army then you had to be in some way deficient. And it was the way to see the world. Souvenirs dotted around my relatives' houses included spears and tiger skins, blow-pipes with poisoned arrows and murderously sharp kukris. There were carved tables inlaid with ivory from India and animal hide shields from Africa, a mounted deer's head trophy with massive spiral horns and even an elegant pair of ladies stilettos made from zebra skin. For my fifteenth birthday, Great Aunt Prudence sent me a lion's skull that her husband had shot in Bechuanaland in the 1930s. Tucked away in drawers were medals from China and Mesopotamia and the Boer War. Like many families, we had a hoard of First World War ephemera including those brass chocolate boxes given as gifts to the troops in the trenches, and two framed 'mentions in des-patches' for my great-grandfather. They were signed by Winston Churchill when he was First Lord of the Admiralty, and I would stare at his inky scrawl and marvel that the great man had held those very bits of paper in his hand.

Stories about India featured in much of family history, with both sets of grandparents having been stationed there for almost a decade. Great-grandfather Harry had served in the 14th King's Hussars and both of my grandfathers – one English, one Irish – were in the British Army, one in the Royal Tank Regiment, and one in the Royal Irish Fusiliers. Great-grandfather had been at the relief of Ladysmith, and Grandpop had been unlucky enough to be at both Gallipoli and the Somme.

Grandfather-in-London had fought in North Africa, and Mum's elder brother, Herbert, had been wounded at Anzio. A few months before we went to Africa, Grandpop died and Uncle Herbert came over from England for the funeral. He stayed with us, sharing my bedroom on the night of the wake. Watching him put on his pyjamas I was thrilled to catch a flash of the deeply recessed scar on his back. It was triangular, as if someone had taken an iron and pressed it into the flesh. I didn't dare to ask to look at it closely, but that glimpse confirmed the seriousness of the injury.

In the family albums I saw photographs of grandfather riding a camel at the pyramids, of great-grandfather in his jodhpurs supervising disembarking troops and mules at Baku, and my mother sitting beside the Taj Mahal as a little girl. The legacy was all-encompassing, and it embarrassed me that amongst all this exoticism and derring-do I had been born in Ireland. Even worse, I discovered I had been born in a distinctly provincial local hospital, though my mother always reassured me I had at least been delivered in the private wing.

Mum hated Ireland. And her mother felt the same. She too filled my head with stories of living in India, and the regimental dances she loved to attend. Travelling with army husbands had spoilt their appetite for provincial life, and closed their eyes to the beauty of the green hills. In common, I suspect, with so many British women of their time they longed for the simplicity of a foreign posting – especially when living abroad meant having servants. Mum was a hopeless case, born in Egypt en route to spending the first nine years of her life in India, she never stopped dreaming of a return to the tropics. When we stepped ashore in Columbo en route to Malaya she grasped me by the arm. 'Oh, can you smell it?' she gasped. 'This is how the air should be. I am at home!'

I inherited that discontent, believing that we were destined for greater things and bigger places. Walking home from school on darkening winter afternoons I craved the light of the tropics, and wished that something, anything would happen to get us away from Northern Ireland.

Confessions of a Bored Housewife

In Bangor, County Down, I went to the boys' grammar school where most of the teachers were sadistic and dished out punishments that would be illegal these days. It was an old fashioned regime, you got the cane for serious stuff and, in 1970, when I was in First Form, we witnessed a few public canings during morning assembly. Every day we said prayers and sang the school song: *Comgall noster, Columbanus,// Sanctus noster Gall, Britannos// Effecere Christianos,//Floreat Bangoria, Deo laus et Gloria.*

It was a male world perfumed with pubescent sweat and rugby socks, and where acne and homework were more pressing interests than girls. There were only two women in the whole school, Miss Addy the Art teacher, and Mrs Sangster, the school secretary. Miss Addy was almost seventy when she taught me, and about the only teacher that we respected. She was a kind old lady, who could make us listen while she taught us the difference between the Ionic and the Doric without terrorising us into submission. One morning, she came into class and stood very still in front of the blackboard. With tears running down her cheeks she told us, her bemused and largely ignorant audience, that Picasso had died. In contrast, Mrs Sangster didn't have much contact with the boys, and you only got to see her if you were on your way to the Head. She was a petite woman with immaculately coiffured ash-blonde hair and exceptionally good legs. She click-clacked around the corridors in high heels and a tight pencil skirt and all conversation stopped when she went by. Her manicured but mature sexuality made us all uneasy. All of the other teachers were men, and with few exceptions they used physical threats and punishments to keep discipline. We just put up with it, because almost everyone suffered equally and our parents weren't interested in hearing about what went on.

For six years my main enemy was 'Stringer', the history teacher, who wore cheap navy blue suits that stank of cigarette smoke. He often picked his nose while he was marking our essays, and would throw the bogey-ridden books back at our heads hoping we wouldn't see them coming. Stringer asked you a question and then pulled you out of your chair by the short hairs above your ears while you answered. The younger boys squealed while they tried to remember the answer. We sat at wooden desks and if your feet poked out into the aisle he would take a little skipping jump and land on your toes. As we got older it was a point of honour not to show the pain. The only way to fight back was to belittle the masters without appearing to plan it. One day, Stringer asked us if we could explain how fashions changed over the centuries. Taking stock of his outfit, I said that once upon a time it had been considered very low class to wear brown shoes with a blue suit, but that not many people noticed such things anymore. From then on, I became his favourite victim. He tried to exclude me from his A-Level class and put me in the lower grade group, until I pointed out that I had a better O-Level grade than two of the boys he had selected for the top group. I like to think our feud acquired legendary status within the school, and even when I was applying for University he wrote me a very poor report. The Head called me in and asked me to explain why Stringer's report was so much at odds with those of the other teachers. I gleefully told him the story of the blue suit, and was able to show that in the course of seven years the man had barely ever given me a good grade for an essay.

We called our maths teacher Hook, because he had a deformed right arm that didn't bend. School lore had it that his elbow had been knocked off while he was driving with his arm dangling out of the window in some unnamed tropical country. It meant he had to contort his whole body to write on the blackboard, and when he tried to hit you he had to jump up and down to get enough leverage for a decent blow. His black gown flapped wildly like a giant bat-wing sending out clouds of chalk dust as he tried to get his arm high enough to give you a decent whack, and even if you were the one on the receiving end you had to try not to laugh.

The masters had to ride a fine line, if they were too nice the boys ran riot and they got no respect. Our French teacher was like that, a kindly man who treated us as if we were young gentlemen. But his problem was that his initials were J.E.S., so we always called him Jessie. Mr Brown was 'Pogle', which seemed to have a strange sexual connotation, but nothing you could define precisely when adults asked. Physically, he was a flabby, pallid man with a comb-over hairstyle and large square-rimmed spectacles. We all knew Pogle was obsessed with sex. One of his duties was teaching Religious Instruction, but mostly he just wanted us to talk about masturbation and give him lots of detail about who was doing it, and how often. He banned me from his classes because he said I was too argumentative, and asked too many insolent questions about religious doctrine. Most of us sensed there was something unhealthy about the way he lingered in the showers after games, and there were rumours about which boys he had actually molested. I can remember him in the changing rooms at the swimming pool, a large belly spilling over his tight black Speedos, and his very white feet at the end of stumpy legs with fat thighs. The boys he targeted attracted scorn, and no one ever thought to sympathise, or report what we knew. Twenty years after I left Bangor he was finally arrested, and sentenced to seven years for sexually abusing boys.

Home life was always better than school, but Mum and Dad tried to make me understand that I needed to apply myself seriously to my work. Convincing me to take school seriously was an uphill battle. 'You're just too comfortable at home,' Mum would say. 'I should be cruel to you so that you would enjoy school more.' There was some truth in the idea, but Mum didn't know how to be cruel. When I failed all of my mock O-Levels, the best she could do was to confine me to my bedroom at weekends for two months before I sat the real exams. The TV was confiscated, and I was told that I had to stay at my desk revising. It worked, and I amazed myself by getting good enough grades to stay at school.

We were well off. We had two cars and a big house, and were the first people I knew to get a chest freezer. 'You've got it easy,' Granny would say if Mum complained about housework. 'I brought up six children without an electric washing machine.'

Mum was an avid reader, and every week without fail she took us to the Carnegie Library to get new books. On Thursday mornings she often went to Ross's auctions on Central Avenue to buy furniture, or just to see what might be up for sale. Sometimes she bought things she could renovate and sell through adverts in the Spectator newspaper, or smaller items like jewellery and porcelain that she could sell to antique shops in other towns. In the holidays we went with her, rummaging through the box-lots to check if there was something valuable inside that the dealers might have missed. She loved to find a bargain, and loved the challenge of securing a piece that she knew would bring a profit.

To help with the housework we had a char lady who came twice a week to do the ironing. Mrs Mac was in her seventies, someone Mum had employed when I was a baby and who now needed some extra money. 'Och, I remember you'se when ye wuz a wee babby!' she would say to me almost every week. 'You'se wuz a dear wee thing. Gord luv ye.'

Mum always offered Mrs Mac some fruit to take home when she left the house. She usually took two apples, one for herself and one for her husband, Tommy. Once, when we didn't have any apples Mum offered her bananas instead. 'Ay couldn't touch thut! Aend ay woodint' know what tay do wi'it!' she exclaimed. 'Ay niver even saw a beenana till efter the war.'

Mrs Mac had to be home by five o'clock to get her husband Tommy his tea. That was the main meal of the day, and it mustn't be late. According to Mrs Mac, Tommy had never eaten a meal, or even drunk a cup of tea outside his own home. 'Tommy says that's wha' kills peeple!' she explained. 'Ye never know whit gairms thair mait be in ether peeple's hises.'

Bangor seemed to have everything we needed. Mum's main activity was going into town to do the main grocery shopping at Wellworths supermarket. Confusingly, it was almost next door to the local branch of Woolworths. The High Street was still quite traditional: a couple of pubs, a bakery, a wool shop and a general hardware store. As the High Street joined the esplanade there was an Irish Linen shop stocked with tea-towels decorated with shamrocks, ornamental shillelaghs carved from blackthorn and pieces of Belleek china. Once you got onto Quay Street on the seafront, there was a crumbling crenellated building with a sign proclaiming Barry's Amusements. Once upon a time it had boasted a haunted house, and there were the faded silhouettes of ghoulish figures painted on the façade. The haunted house was already closed when we moved to Bangor, or so Mum always told us, but Barry's still ran a miniature roller coaster on the esplanade opposite. It was barely ten feet off the ground, but its creaking and groaning rails produced a terrifying ride as it hurtled you towards the sea.

We rarely shopped at the bottom of the hill. Halfway down, Cecil Greenwood ran what we called the joke shop, a seedy newsagent's where you could buy comics, *Commando* magazine and novelty bags containing things like itching powder, whoopee cushions and plastic flies to put in your parents' tea.

I wasn't allowed to visit the shop on my own, even when I was older, because behind a curtain there was a section selling adult material. I found Cecil himself a bit creepy, always wearing a cloth cap and a long overcoat while he stood behind the counter. A few doors higher up the hill, Mum sometimes went into McVeigh's, a little shop where chaos reigned. Two elderly women, one fat and one thin, sold all kinds of lingerie. They sat in the middle of the shop surrounded by mounds of unlabelled boxes, and cabinets filled with narrow drawers with glass fronts. Inside the boxes and drawers there was a seemingly limitless range of lingerie. The dimensions of the shop, and the lack of labelling meant it was impossible for the customers to do any browsing. Mum and the other customers would mutter their orders in hushed tones to one of the shopkeepers, who would then begin to move boxes around the tiny space, adding to the disorder. Miraculously, and often without rising from their chairs, they would then produce the requisite garment.

Woolworths and Wellworths were the biggest shops in town, and in 1974 they were both obliterated by fire bombs along with much of Main Street. We were out walking the dogs on the beach that Saturday afternoon when we heard the explosions, and then watched the black smoke filling the sky above the town centre. The Co-Op went too, and a couple of other small businesses. It was a shock to genteel Bangor, but I found it more exciting than frightening, and later we all walked down to the top of Main Street and stood behind the police barricade to watch the fire brigade trying to clear up the mess. After that we started going over to Bangor West to use the VG Supermarket and the new shopping centre at Springhill.

Once, I signed up to go on an early morning excursion with the Nature Club from school. One of the masters had agreed to take us out badger-watching, and we were told to assemble outside the train station at four thirty a.m. Mum agreed to drive me down there, and insisted on keeping me in the car with the heater on until the master arrived. The other boys in the Nature Club were all older than me, and I was humiliated to be seen with my mother let alone kept in the car 'out of the chilly morning air'. I pleaded with Mum to go home, afraid that the adolescents would see me as the little boy in the charge of his mother. But she wouldn't leave. Suddenly, things became even more embarrassing. 'Oh my God, Timothy!' she exclaimed. 'Quick! Get out of the car – there's a bomb on the back seat.'

I looked around, and sure enough, on the rear seat of the Mini-Clubman was something that did indeed look like a bomb. There were ominous coloured wires and trip switches and an electronic timer. We stared in horror at the device.

'It can't be a bomb,' I argued without conviction. I had no thought for the lethal possibilities of an explosion. All I could think about was the mortifying embarrassment of telling the sixth formers nearby that we had a bomb in the car.

'You get out,' Mum said tensely. 'I'll drive the car away.'

A few minutes later she returned, having left the Mini at a safe distance and called my father at home from a telephone box in the station to tell him the news. 'Oh, I'm sorry,' he said groggily when he answered. 'It's okay. It's been defused and I forgot to take it out of the car last night and leave it at the office.'

Dad had taken Mum's car to work the previous day, because his own car was being serviced. He didn't know that she needed the Mini in the early hours, and hadn't bothered to reveal the presence of the bomb. 'We're going home,' Mum said, still shaking from the shock. 'You can forget the badgers.'

At the height of the Troubles we rarely went into Belfast as a family. But when we did, it was thrilling. It was a proper city. Behind the grimness of the barbed wire, body searches and steel barricades, I could imagine a different untroubled world through the stories I had collected from Mum and her parents. I could see that Belfast was more than just a place where bombs made gaps in the streets, or where people were murdered in alleyways for going to the wrong church. It was a proud mercantile city where solid granite office blocks housed insurance companies and department stores, buildings that grew from the profits of the great Ulster Linen makers, tobacco importers and the shipyards that built the Titanic. Right in the very centre stood the Edwardian City Hall, Belfast's grandest architectural statement. Its Portland Stone façade dominates the middle of Donegal Square, and the central domed roof is sheathed in copper, now elegantly green with verdigris.

Opposite City Hall, Mum and Dad had their bank account at the Northern Bank, an imposing building with a shining marble foyer where Dad would be summoned to explain his overdraft to the manager once a year. We could tell when the allotted day was approaching because his mood would be more than usually irascible. We knew from an early age that Dad never liked facing up to his finances, and Mum liked to open his bank statements while he was out at work. If she didn't intercept the post before he came downstairs he would either ignore the letters from the bank, or worse, open them and start raging about how much money she had spent from their joint account. Mum only let him see the statements if she thought he was in the right frame of mind. It was the same with my school reports. 'We'll keep this quiet,' she would confide to me when I brought the dire paperwork home at the end of each term. 'I'll show it to your father when you're asleep, and when he's in a good mood.'

Facing City Hall, at the head of Royal Avenue, stood Robinson and Cleaver's – the largest, smartest department store in town and the most exciting place I could imagine. From an early age, I would wait and hope for Mum to announce that we were going on an excursion to Cleaver's. Even older than the City Hall, it was decorated with dozens of heads depicting patrons of the firm, including Queen Victoria, and an Indian Maharajah. Inside, the shop was a cornucopia of household goods complete with elaborately made-up women behind the cosmetics counters on the ground floor. A vast sweeping marble staircase adorned with crimson carpet held in place with polished brass stair-rods led up to the other floors, including of course ladies' lingerie, gentleman's formal wear and, best of all, a toy department. Mum only went to Cleaver's once or twice a year, usually when she wanted something special to wear. While she was closeted in the changing rooms discussing purchases with assistants who called her 'madam', I would sit on the thick carpet of the sales floor or stand watching the mysterious goings on at the cash desk. When it was time to pay, the cashier would stuff a copy of the sales slip (along with my mother's cheque or sometimes just cash) into little glass canisters with brass ends protected by a felt covered cap. By lifting a flap on a compartment attached to the wall they could insert these canisters into a pneumatic transport system. I was fascinated by the soft vacuum hiss that pulled the flap closed, and the way the solid canisters disappeared up a tubular chute. A few moments later, the canisters would plop into the same transportation chamber and be retrieved. Inside, as if by magic would be the receipt. I longed to be allowed to have a go, but never dared ask.

Apart from its fading mercantile glory, and its ongoing dismemberment at the hands of the IRA, to me Belfast symbolised something else. It was where family members went to get the boat to England. England itself meant very little to me, but from there you could get boats to other more exotic places: India and Egypt, Nigeria and Hong Kong, Cyprus and Suez. These were the destinations where family lore was created, and it gave me a sense of being something other. As I grew up, those stories collected in my head like a film show of images and people and places that helped me understand the present. They made sense of who my parents were, allowing me a backward glimpse in time to when they had their own lives: before they were just Mum and Dad.

When my mother's generation was young, the overnight ferry from Belfast to Liverpool was the only affordable way to get to England. The adventure of travel became inextricably linked to the rituals of the dockside. At the ferry terminal the rattle of idling engines at the taxi rank signalled the start of a journey, or the joyous arrival of someone who had been away.

On board there were stewards in starched white jackets and, for those who could afford it, a saloon where they served perfect scrambled eggs. The toast racks and the cruets were solid silver plate. Arriving at Liverpool the boat train would be ready to take you the rest of the way to London. And, as an adult, travelling down the length of the Lough away from the lights of Belfast and Carrickfergus with a chill breeze whipping in from the Irish Sea brought a sense of parting and sadness even when you had a good reason for leaving.

Stuck at home, Mum dreamed of getting away from Ireland again. She wasn't a fan of housework, and cooking was never part of her plan. She found the daily grind of feeding us and looking after the house unutterably tedious. On Sundays tensions ran high as Mum battled with the logistics of a family meal. She often cooked a leg of lamb and Yorkshire pudding with roast potatoes, a major undertaking that made the kitchen windows steam up and filled the house with the smell of gravy made with Bisto. The food she cooked was edible, but the ritual of creating the traditional meal, complete with homemade mint sauce always put Mum in a bad mood. It was even worse if my grandparents joined us, because Granny would appear with an apple pie she had made especially for Dad. 'I feel so sorry for you, Stuart,' she would say. 'You do *love* your pastry, but I can't always be here to cook it.'

During the week, boiled frozen peas and egg and chips was our regular fare. Luckily, I liked tinned rice pudding. In summer it was cold ham with lettuce, spring onions and boiled new potatoes. For dessert we ate prodigious amounts of strawberries with cream. Mum said she dreamt of being

94

able to give us packets of astronaut food that would meet our nutritional needs without requiring preparation. Her wish virtually came true, because by the time I was at secondary school she could buy me Bird's Eye boil-in-the-bag curry that I could cook for myself. Boil-in-the-bag kippers were another favourite, and fortunately, I was happy to cook and eat both concoctions. However, Mum made sure the fruit bowl was never empty and we weren't allowed biscuits or sweet things between meals. Even so, I think we could have developed scurvy if she hadn't made us made us eat a daily Haliborange tablet from the age of five.

'I'm a bad mother,' she said to me once. 'You deserve a proper Irish mother: someone who'd enjoy baking you cakes and scones, pies and potato bread.'

Slowly, over the years, Mum got fat. She dieted. She became depressed, and started sleeping during the day. She got fatter. It was such a gradual decline that we children didn't notice. She was just Mum, the same person who always kissed us when we got home from school every day and cuddled up to us on the sofa when we watched TV. We knew she thought she was too fat, because she started cutting herself out of family photographs with a pair of nail scissors. She destroyed any that weren't flattering, and as she put on weight that meant almost all of them. Very few survive. 'Age is a terrible curse,' she always told us. 'I wish I'd been ugly as a young woman, then I wouldn't care what I looked like now.'

One summer Mum went into hospital. Her doctor arranged it, because he couldn't understand why she was putting on weight. He didn't believe that she was sticking to the diet he'd prescribed, so he had her admitted to the metabolic unit at the

Royal Victoria Hospital in Belfast. She was kept on a strict diet of one thousand calories a day, but after six weeks she had only lost four pounds. I visited her there once, in a stark simple ward where all of the other patients were painfully thin. When Mum returned home she brought one of the other patients with her, a thirteen-year-old girl who came from a family of twelve children. Her name was Mary, and she had anorexia. Her family were farmers down on the border, and she was a sensitive little bird whom Mum said needed to see a different view of the world. Mary was a pale withdrawn creature who barely spoke to me, and only smiled at Mum. After a week, the family, including seven of Mary's horde of siblings came to collect her. They filled the sitting room, the parents drinking tea and the children consuming lemon-cream biscuits. They stared at us awkwardly, as if we were from another planet. Mum cried bitterly when Mary left, and told her she should come back whenever she wanted. 'She'll never get better, those parents don't have time to look after her,' Mum said. Sometimes Mary would telephone and Mum would stay on the line for an hour, but she was never allowed to come back.

One day my sister fell over at school and broke her collar bone. She needed a general anaesthetic to have it fixed, but they couldn't administer the drugs without Mum's consent. The hospital rang and rang the house for hours, but she was sound asleep and didn't answer the phone. She was taking barbiturates at the time to blot out the day. When she told me about the pills, I thought she was turning into a character from *Valley of the Dolls* (Sharon Tate, 1967).

When I was fourteen, I came home from school and found Mum in a very buoyant mood as we had our afternoon tea. It was our regular after-school ritual at four o'clock: tea and a piece of toast. 'Guess what?' she announced triumphantly as I sat down. 'It was on the Jimmy Young Show on the radio today, that they've discovered an illness called "Housewife's Syndrome". Listen, I've written down the symptoms,' she brandished a sheet of note-paper above the tea-tray. ' "Lethargy, depression, inability to function". Apparently, they've known about it in America for years, but I've definitely got it!'

The fact that they knew about it in America was the absolute seal of approval. In Ireland, North or South, there was an unshakeable faith in anything new or modern that came from the USA. If such discoveries aroused suspicion in England, all the better, it was evidence once again that the Irish were one step ahead of their neighbours. Mum was an avid collector of all health related information. The *Pears Medical Encyclopaedia* was always at hand and I often saw her sitting up in bed reading it for general interest. 'I'll look it up in my Pears', she would say, if any of us had an ailment. It wasn't that she didn't trust doctors, not a bit of it, but she did like to be able to put forward a challenge to their diagnoses. She wasn't a hypochondriac either, but she did have great faith in pills, and happily swallowed anything that was prescribed.

Housewife's Syndrome sounded sinister to me. Mum cooked our dinner and organised our birthday parties, and she was the one with the answer to all of our problems. To me, she was the perfect mother, unfailingly kind and loving and, above all, brave. She stood up to Dad when he was angry, and laughed at me gently when I was afraid of going to the dentist. The suggestion that she could be in any way psychologically weak didn't fit. But Mum seemed very relieved that there were other people out there in the same state of mind. And I was struck that she was telling me the news before she told Dad.

Heat and Dust

The night before we left Ireland the snow came. Towards midnight I was woken by the sound of a foghorn sounding across Ballyholme Bay. It was the Liverpool ferry, heading offshore from the mouth of Belfast Lough. That night, the noise of the ship was soft and muffled by the white storm. In seven years in that house I had never seen snow. The salt air from the sea just a few hundred yards down the hill kept it away – or that's what I was told. I crept to the window and saw the garden disguised in its covering of whiteness. There was something about the stillness of the night and the newness of the snow that was both eerie and comforting. Then I remembered the journey ahead. We were leaving for Africa that day, though we would not be taking the boat. I was escaping from school. From the grey January skies and from the suburban life that was slowly killing my mother.

In the morning we drove to the airport, snaking our way slowly along slippery country roads, stopping now and again to pass through the army roadblocks which dotted the route. Then, at the approach to the airport there was the final police

checkpoint, a steel and concrete bunker with gun-slits and
bullet proof glass in the tiny windows. Burly men in dark
green Royal Ulster Constabulary uniforms stamped their feet
in their hard-toed black boots against the weather. They blew
into cupped hands to warm them and left their guns hanging
over their shoulders. Further up the road there were British
soldiers and an armoured vehicle.

'Are ye goin' far the day?' the policeman asked.

'They're going to Africa,' said the farmer's widow, a friend
who had offered to give us a lift. She said it with a mixture of
awe and disbelief, clearly doubting the wisdom of the move.
Why would anyone leave Ireland for Africa: so far away and
so foreign?

'They've enough luggage anyway,' the policeman nodded at
the mound of suitcases in the back of the estate-car. I sensed
some unspoken agreement in his solid Irish tone, reminding
me of my own English, and therefore foreign, accent. He had
no interest in searching us or the vehicle. We were just
baggage, ignored in the exchange between him and the driver.
No longer real people.

Just as we had on our way to Malaya, we passed through
London again, where Dad had arranged for us to stay a night
at an hotel close to Heathrow, before the long flight to
Johannesburg. My aunt recommended a place she liked,
mainly because it was a completely circular building. The
experience taught me that hotels should not be chosen according to their shape: back then it was a dump, but staying the
night allowed us time on the day of our flight to make the
ritual stop at my grandparents in Maida Vale. 'I hope you
know what you're doing,' W.G. would state at intervals

during the day to Dad, even though he had no direct experience of South Africa.

It was only when we had said goodbye to W.G. and Granny Griffiths and travelled by taxi to the airport that it dawned on me that leaving Britain might involve any degree of risk. This was a not a foreign posting with the support network of the Army behind us: we were civilians now. At Heathrow, Uncle Herbert and his wife appeared to say goodbye. We sat in a smoky airport bar while they drank too much gin and tonic and chatted. Herbert had been stationed in Swaziland in the sixties and had once driven to Johannesburg. While he and Dad reminisced about their army adventures, I overheard my aunt telling Mum that she had friends who had recently returned to Yorkshire after living thirty years in Johannesburg.

'The wife's not very well,' my aunt said conspiratorially, 'so they want to be here, at home, you know . . . if anything bad is going to happen.' This remark was accompanied with a nod in my direction, implying that whatever the illness was, it wasn't something suitable for teenage ears. Her words made me nervous. I wondered what kind of place we were going to, somewhere that after thirty years might still not feel like home.

British Airways did not deliver us in style. The Boeing 747 was crammed full, and in addition to a scheduled stop in Nairobi we were forced to land at Entebbe in Uganda to make some kind of technical repair. The doors were open during the four-hour stop, letting in the humid tropical air that brought the smell of the African night. We weren't allowed off the plane, although I didn't mind because I had recently watched the high-jacking drama *Raid on Entebbe* (Peter Falk, 1977). Overall, the delays extended our flight from twelve hours to more than nineteen, and we arrived at Jan Smuts Airport in a state of exhaustion. The only redeeming feature of the journey for me was that I saw my first in-flight movie: *Shout at the Devil* (Lee Marvin, Barbara Parkins, 1976).

In Johannesburg people told my mother she had beautiful Irish skin, and that she should keep her children indoors as much as possible. They told us the sun was especially dangerous because we were six thousand feet above sea level and the air was so thin. Coming from an Irish January we had wanted sunshine, but not like this. The sun was so bright it went beyond yellow – just a searing all day whiteout. During those first few months the pitiless sky was permanently blue, and I longed for a cloud to bring the promise of rain. It made me think of John Mills and Sylvia Syms struggling to escape from the Germans across the desert in *Ice Cold in Alex* (1958).

For the first three days, the heat made me so ill I had to stay in my bed at the Sunnyside Park Hotel. We had a week there until our rented house was ready for us to move into. Dad had always stayed at the Sunnyside when he visited Johannesburg, and on one occasion had met Britt Ekland (*The Man with the Golden Gun*, 1974) in the bar. On another visit he saw Terry Thomas (*Monte Carlo or Bust*, 1969) walking around the grounds and leaning heavily on a walking stick. Dad said hello to him and I was thrilled to be told that the actor had flashed his famous gap-toothed grin and responded with a plummy, 'Good afternoon old chap.' We saw no film stars, and during the day there were hardly any other guests around. At night I woke up breathless with the sense that the air had been sucked from the city. In the day I returned to the room to nap, drifting in and out of sleep, feverish and afraid. Everything here was strange.

Our household belongings were coming by sea, and wouldn't arrive for about eight weeks. My dog, Shandy, was coming by air, as well as the seven Siamese cats but they were all scheduled to arrive a few weeks after us. The most interesting thing we had to do was going to the shops on Saturday mornings to buy the stuff we needed for our rented house. The shops closed at one o'clock on a Saturday afternoon and didn't reopen until Monday. We hired a TV, but there wasn't much to watch, just two hours of English programmes each night and the only half-decent programme was the American soap-opera, *Dallas*. We hadn't bothered watching it in Ireland, but in our new world it became the highlight of the week. We weren't the only ones who refused to miss it. Johannesburg restaurants started closing on Tuesday nights because hardly anyone went out when *Dallas* was on. The government had only allowed TV into South Africa about a year before we arrived, and only after a lot of debate about whether it would make the black South Africans discontented by showing them what the rest of the multi-racial world was like. They told us not to let our maid, Rebecca, watch it. We did. She had rarely seen any TV, and she clapped her hands together with excitement and did a little curtsy when Mum said she could watch the news in Afrikaans, but otherwise it didn't seem to make her behave dangerously. Apartheid meant that most British TV programmes weren't available to South Africans, and we learned to appreciate the cowboy series *Bonanza* on a Friday evening as another cultural gem in the output.

Dad had rented us a house in a new suburb on the northern outskirts of Johannesburg, where the roads were still made of dirt and everyone drove around followed by their own little cloud of dust. You had to drive slowly or you could skid just as badly as on ice and it made going to the shops feel like a safari. There was open countryside at the end of the road and in the mornings we often found snakes in the swimming pool that I would fish out with a net. That was the only fun thing about having the pool. The filter didn't work properly and the water was already turning green with algae when we arrived at the house. The pool shop sold us new parts for the filter, and then lots of expensive chemicals, but it didn't help. Dad said he couldn't afford to buy a new filter and soon the water was almost black. Toads started breeding in it and I sat by the edge of the pool trying to catch them and wishing that we'd never left Ireland. We'd had a pool there too and it had been my job to keep it clean, a chore I had never tired of.

Standing by the glistening water I used to swirl the net in a rhythmic pattern and watch the miniature eddies and ripples that drew the leaves and insects into the mesh. The sound of the water was hypnotic and calming. The hollow metal handle shivered against my palms and sang out *tung-ting* when I tapped the long-handled net against the wall to empty it. Winter and summer I scooped out the leaves, and when it got really cold I used the handle to break up the ice so it didn't crack the sides.

One night when the ice was thick enough I tried to walk across the surface and fell through the middle. One of our Siamese cats did that too. After school one winter's day I was scooping out the leaves in the fading light when I found Tina's body under the ice. She was just a clump of dark matter at the edge of the frozen water that I couldn't recognise at first. Irregular shards of ice stuck up proud around the body, spoiling the smoothness of the evenly frozen pool. In the gloom of that wintry afternoon I fished her out, only recognising her face as I drew the net close. She was hard as a stuffed toy, her silvery blue coat flattened and dull. Her legs felt brittle like they would snap if I dropped her. Tina's offical name was Dooneen Platina, and she was a highly pedigreed blue-point, the very first Siamese Mum had bought from Mrs MacDonald. Unlike the other breeding queens, Tina was allowed to live in the house rather than the cattery, and she preferred to use the upstairs lavatory instead of the litter tray. She would squat on the seat and defecate very neatly into the bowl, though she couldn't flush. I found deep scratch marks on the pool ladder where she had tried to scramble from the water, but her claws couldn't get a grip on the varnished wood. I didn't tell Mum that bit.

The African pool was warm. For a couple of weeks, until the algae got really bad I could just about bring myself to swim in it, but only in broad daylight. At night there was a big round lamp at one end that was meant to illuminate the whole pool but it just shed a dull glow in the thick murk; like an alien eye.

Johannesburg was further from the sea than I'd ever been. The new house felt like a prison. We didn't know anyone and never saw any other people on the empty dusty roads nearby. That was something we learned: white people didn't walk. Most people had vicious dogs to protect them from African intruders. They roamed the big yellow gardens in packs and ran at the fences barking madly as we passed. I was lonely, and bored.

My younger brother and sister were enrolled at private schools, the best available. They both wore blazers and straw boaters and went through arched gates into school quadrangles that looked like they had been plucked straight from *Goodbye Mr. Chips* (Robert Donat, 1939). As it happened they both hated their new schools and begged to be allowed to leave. There were horrible scenes in the morning with both of them in tears when they were dropped at the gates. It was ironic, because in Ireland it was me that tried to 'mitch off'. Both of my siblings had always loved school, and in Ireland they never chose to stay at home on a flimsy excuse. My sister had even been given a certificate in recognition of only missing one day of school in five years: the time she dislocated her shoulder in a playground accident. But in Johannesburg, I got my wish to stay at home.

I was meant to be going to school, but a short interview with the head of the private school where Dad said I could be enrolled revealed that their curriculum didn't match what I'd been studying in Ireland. We had barely made it out of the school car-park when Mum and Dad started arguing furiously about the assurances he'd given us that 'there would be no problem fitting in with the South African schools'. Under questioning from Mum he admitted that he had simply asked other parents he'd met in Johannesburg if it was possible to do A-levels. It was, but only those set by the Cambridge Examination Board, and not the specific syllabus that I was more than half-way through. It was another sign that something wasn't quite right about our move. And more evidence that Dad was not infallible.

At first, not going to school didn't seem like a problem for me: it was what I'd dreamed about for years. Mum and Dad discussed sending me back to Bangor to my old school, but I refused. They agreed that I would have to stay at home every day, and revise the books I'd been studying in Ireland until the time came to sit the exams. It was possible for me to have the Northern Ireland A-level papers sent to the British Embassy in Pretoria. The embassy would also invigilate the exams for me, and make sure I sat them on the same day as my classmates back in Bangor, although that was all six months away.

Dad was always obsessive about my education. Before we left Ireland, he said that he had found me a school where I could continue my A-levels. I knew it was important to him that I got the right qualifications to go to university, and Mum told me that it was because of my schooling that Dad left the Army. Although he was frustrated by my lack of interest in schoolwork, he blamed his army career for not providing me with a more settled childhood. As I got older the only realistic option would have been for me to be sent to boarding school.

Even though she hated the thought of sending me away to school, Mum never thought of asking Dad to leave the Army, because she knew that he would find civilian life difficult. The Army weren't enthusiastic about Dad's resignation either. Officers could apply for what they called the 'golden bowler hat', a kind of redundancy package that gave you a cash settlement for leaving the Army earlier than retirement age. They wouldn't give it to him, but he was determined to leave so that I could stay at school in Northern Ireland, where he knew the educational standards were high. I didn't think about it much at the time, but now I realise that leaving the

Army was a huge sacrifice for him. In 1973, he took a civilian job that paid well, but soon became boring, another factor in the decision to emigrate.

As a teenager, I began to argue with Dad over many things, most of them to do with school. He forced me to keep taking French even though I loathed it with a passion, and he had to help me with the grammar. Having studied Latin from the age of five and taken Classics at Oxford he simply couldn't comprehend why I had such a hard time with tenses and cases. I had wanted to study biology or art, but Dad said they wouldn't help me get a career, or allow me to study anything useful at university. His view of my future was quite traditional, and he was the one who decided which A-levels I should sit. Our homework sessions at the dining room table usually ended in blazing rows and if I provoked him long and hard enough he would slap me across the face, the last time when I was well past my sixteenth birthday. When things got heated Mum would intervene, and I would tell her how much I hated him.

'You have no idea how much he loves you,' she would always say, to soothe me. More than once, when I knew that Dad had hurt her own feelings, I asked her why she put up with his outbursts. Although he wasn't physically violent towards her, she sometimes threatened him with divorce, telling him that he was subjecting her to 'mental cruelty'. In the main, this consisted of trying to separate her from her own siblings, whom he found irritating in varying degrees. His own dispassionate family background made him incapable of understanding that for Mum, close contact with her three brothers and two sisters was important. 'I had a lot of friends before I married your father,' Mum would say when we were alone. 'But he drove them all away.'

Dad's moods were a source of misery. Mum said that within six months of marrying him, she had started having what she called 'ulcer attacks'. Her stomach would start churning over, and eventually she was diagnosed with a peptic ulcer. 'Old Dr McClean said that it was the shock of being married. My whole circle of friends just faded away,' she said. 'I was constantly being invited to parties or to play golf and tennis, but your father doesn't want to see anyone when he gets home from work. Sometimes I think he'd only be happy stuck in a little stone croft on an Irish mountain.'

Mum had her theories about Dad's antisocial temperament. One of her favourites was based on his severe colour blindness. We knew from an early age that Dad had a problem because he sometimes asked us what colour shirt or trousers we were wearing. Once he bought a new car and told me proudly that I would easily spot it because it was bright red. In fact it was dull brown, the colour, I told him, 'of a dry dog turd.' I also knew that he'd originally wanted to join the Navy rather than the Army, but he was rejected because he couldn't tell if a ship's navigation light was red or green. 'Everything's always been grey for him,' said Mum. 'That's why he doesn't notice that things in Ireland are the same dull shades most of the time, so it doesn't get him down. As long as there are a few hills and trees he's happy – but he can't really appreciate sunshine and the colours you get in the summer.'

Even so, she always made excuses for his behaviour. 'I can never forget what a lonely childhood your father had,' she would say. 'When I think of that dear little boy being sent away to those *awful* schools, it makes me cry.'

Apart from his time at Oxford, Dad had known nothing else but the military since his own school days. I knew he had been to boarding school at the age of four, and he once told me that his earliest memories from that time were of having to make the headmaster a cup of tea each morning at seven a.m. and take it up to his bedroom. In consequence, his relationship with his own parents was always distant. I was fascinated by the idea that my grandparents had sent him away at such an early age. It was the absolute opposite of everything my own parents wanted for me, and I couldn't imagine the pain of being separated from them.

As I got older I began to understand that the Army was very much Dad's home. It was the place where he knew all the rules. Even as a civilian, he had continued to work closely with the security services in Northern Ireland, taking a job where he was responsible for safeguarding the electricity supply for the province. Commuting to an office in Belfast each day had been a difficult adjustment for him, though he only told me years later how much he had hated the daily routine. It made sense that he wanted to try something new, in Africa.

As time went on, I came to understand that a lot of things about the move to Africa were ill-considered. But Mum and Dad didn't choose South Africa just because of the sunshine. They went because Dad was offered a partnership by an Irish businessman called Patterson, who wanted him to start up a security consultancy. Their paths had crossed when Patterson had supplied the government with some high-tech security cameras, and after working together on several large scale projects he suggested that Dad could do better for himself by working in the private sector. Patterson thought that Dad's army background, and previous work he had done for the Northern Ireland Government, made him the ideal person to advise South African businesses on how to minimise the impact of any possible terrorism campaign devised by the ANC. He was sure they could make lots of money, and said he would provide the capital for Dad to set up as a consultant in Johannesburg. In business terms, any civil unrest and the increasing international isolation of South Africa because of apartheid were good things, they made people think about how to protect themselves and their assets. Dad's role would be to offer strategic advice and expertise on how to protect the big stuff: power stations, docks and airports so that the economy wouldn't suffer if they became targets.

In 1976, Dad and Patterson flew to Johannesburg and came back with glowing reports about how ripe the place was for their type of business. The whole family was excited by the prospect. We all liked Patterson and his attractive wife Kitty who had been an air hostess in her youth. Kitty's jet-set credentials were further enhanced when she told me that her passengers had included Robert Stack (*The Last Voyage*, 1960, with Dorothy Malone – whom I thought Mum resembled) and Sterling Hayden (*Ten Days to Tulara*, 1958). Still pretty, and always immaculately turned out, Kitty would sweep into our house with a heady waft of perfume. I was captivated by the scent, and made Mum ask her what it was: *Moon Drops* by Revlon. I liked it so much I made Mum buy some for herself.

Compared to the old maids in the Cat Club, the Pattersons seemed impossibly glamorous and exciting. He even had his own seven-seater aeroplane with his own pilot, and was talking about setting up an airline. He would arrive at our house in his red Rolls Royce Silver Shadow, or if we were lucky his canary yellow TR7 sports car with pop-up frog headlights. The Pattersons didn't have any children and lived in a big house on the outskirts of Belfast with what seemed to me like the height of sophistication – an illuminated rockery. Patterson knew that Dad was an expert in his field, but what he hadn't counted on was that Dad knew everything about security, and nothing about how to run a business. Meanwhile, Dad treated Patterson like he was a brother army officer and didn't understand that their relationship was based purely on profit and loss. Patterson provided the money to start up the African venture but, as Mum pointed out later, he wasn't the one who had to uproot his family to start a new life in another country.

When we first arrived in Johannesburg Dad was preoccupied with getting the business started, and flew around South Africa making pitches for big security contracts. We were stuck out at the house with Mum, where I was supposed to be studying on my own. On Saturdays, when Dad didn't need the car to go to work, he would take us sightseeing. We lived in one of the newer suburbs, affluent enough, but not populated by old money. Closer to town we passed through the older, classier districts like Parktown, Essexwold and Saxonwold. They had immaculate lawns tended by black gardeners who needed a government permit, the infamous pass-book, to live on the property. The owners sat on the *stoep* drinking sundowners while inside, the maid in her polyester uniform from the OK Bazaars cooked dinner. The biggest and best houses looked like they had been lifted straight from Surrey in the 1930s. Dad said we'd buy one of them when his business took off.

Visiting the city centre was a novelty for us. Sometimes we went shopping but often we just drove around and looked at the skyscrapers. To us, Johannesburg had all the glamour of Manhattan. Away from the affluent suburbs it wasn't an elegant city, but it oozed raw power. As you drove south the city became more industrial, the houses smaller and the landscape littered with mine-dumps, the great flat-topped pyramids of yellow sand created by the workings from the gold mines. In winter the wind blew the dust around the city centre and some people thought the dumps were ugly. But as the sun went down they caught the low golden light and seemed to hold on to it, lustrous evidence that this was a place where people could get rich through hard work.

Driving in from the north the first big building we saw as we approached the city was the Strydom Tower, a bleak toilet-roll tube of concrete with a bristling crown of telephone antennae. It was Johannesburg's Post Office Tower and there was a revolving restaurant at the top which wasn't open long before the government decided it should be shut for security reasons. Further downtown, in the financial district we gawped at the Standard Bank headquarters, which Dad told us was the only building in Africa that had been constructed as a central core from which the floors were suspended on cantilevered arms. It looked like something a child would make from wooden building blocks, but we were impressed that this was the kind of city where such things existed.

'This place is unique in the world,' Dad would say as proudly as if he'd been born and bred in Johannesburg. 'It's one of the only major world cities that isn't built beside a river. And do you know they've knocked the whole place down and rebuilt it three times in a century? People don't stand in your way here, not like in Britain where there's always a reason why you can't do something!'

Everything was brash and bold and Dad had fallen in love with the chutzpah of Johannesburg. 'I've got a good feeling about this country,' he would declare. 'I just *know* South Africa is going to be lucky for us.'

His business premises, named Securicentres, were at the bottom of Main Street not far from the Stock Exchange in a district known as Marshalltown. His office was just above street level, and the entrance was on the corner of the building. I thought it was extremely smart, with its black granite entrance, glass double doors and steel security gates with brass handles like in an old bank. Dad had a surveillance camera mounted at the entrance with a TV monitor on the receptionist's desk. To get to the office we drove through a forest of tall office buildings sitting on bedrock that had been plundered for gold. Late at night, or on a Sunday afternoon when the streets were deserted of traffic, you would occasionally feel the tremors when rockfalls occurred deep underground in the old tunnels.

Right at the heart of the city grid, about six blocks from Dad's offices, was the Carlton Centre. The Centre occupied a whole block and was dominated by a fifty-storey office tower fronting onto the busy thoroughfare of Commissioner Street. At over seven hundred feet high, the office tower was not just the tallest building in Johannesburg, or even in Africa, but in the whole of the Southern hemisphere. Sometimes Dad paid for us to ride to the top of the tower in the express lift that was so fast it made your stomach flip. At the top there was an observation deck with floor-to-ceiling windows on all four sides. Mum refused to go near the biggest windows but I dared myself to stand flush against them, pressing my nose against the glass and inducing vertigo if I looked down to the street over six-hundred feet below where all the cars looked like toys. In the distance you could see the aeroplanes landing and taking off at Jan Smuts Airport, and stretching to the horizon was the great flat plateau of the Witwatersrand.

Above ground the grey granite complex contained not just the office tower, but also Garlicks department store, an ice-rink and the curious inverted Y-shape of the Carlton Hotel. The widened base of the hotel at ground level housed the lobby, but as it rose the hotel tapered inwards so that the upper floors became gradually narrower allowing the guest rooms to be located in a vertical tower. From the observation deck of the office block we looked down onto the hotel which was a mere thirty storeys high, and had a circular swimming pool on top, covered by an electrically operated sliding glass roof. The round blue pool was surrounded by trees and large shrubs and one of the flower beds was an aviary containing small songbirds to add to the jungle-in-the-city ambience. The Carlton had six-hundred bedrooms, and was listed in the phone book as Africa's Greatest Hotel. Anyone important or famous who came to South Africa was bound to stay there. At ground-level in the middle of all these tall buildings was a glass cupola that let light into an underground shopping mall containing two hundred shops. Escalators led straight down from the pavement to the shops and the whole complex had a space-age feel. In fact, the glass cupola immediately reminded me of the rotating disc that sent people to their doom when they reached their thirtieth birthday in *Logan's Run* (Jenny Agutter, Michael York, 1976). The Carlton Centre was a city within the city, and our Saturday outings almost always ended there.

When we'd finished window-shopping, the best part of an excursion into Johannesburg was to go into the Carlton Hotel itself. Revolving doors led from the bustling shopping centre into the vast ground-floor lobby, a calm and civilised haven of deep-pile carpets, huge, soft cream and brown settees and smoked glass coffee tables. Dad and Mum would order gin and tonics that came with a Carlton swizzle stick in the upside down Y-shape of the hotel. I would ask for a chocolate milkshake, something they didn't have in Bangor, or anywhere in Northern Ireland to my knowledge. At The Carlton, my drink always came with a straw in a paper sleeve that the barman would twist into a twirling tail that hung down over the side of the glass.

In one corner of the lobby there was the small and intimate Clock Bar, a dark space modelled on an English gentlemen's club and decorated with numerous brass time-pieces on the walls. Against the same wall and separated from the bar by the entrance to the lifts that took guests up to their rooms or to the glittering pool deck on the roof, there were two small but exclusive jewellery shops. They sold gold and platinum rings, diamond bracelets that cost more than our house and watches by Piaget and Cartier encrusted with emeralds and rubies. We would stare at the spotlit window displays choosing our favourite items, and I would ask Mum to pick out one ring or a watch, which I would buy her when we got rich.

At the opposite end of the lobby was the Koffie-Huis, where the waitresses wore blue and white checked gingham and little Dutch bonnets. Blue Delft plates decorated with windmills and Dutch country scenes hung on the walls beside gleaming copper warming pans, and you could get waffles and pancakes served with syrup and cream at any time of day. The managers in the Carlton restaurants seemed to have been picked for their good looks and would glide through the public areas dressed in smart blue blazers with dazzling white shirts and neatly knotted ties, sharply creased grey slacks and highly polished shoes. All along one wall of the vast lobby there was the marble-topped reception desk with clocks on the back wall telling you the time in London, New York and Tokyo.

While Mum and Dad had their drinks, I would take the lift up to the pool deck and look at the guests sunbathing thirty floors above the street. They lay on sun-loungers with plump yellow cushions beneath that sliding glass roof, sipping their iced drinks and listening to the songbirds that chirruped in the aviaries around the pool. I would ride up and down in the lift time and time again. If any of the genuine guests got into the lift with me I waited to see which button they pressed, and then selected a different floor for myself. You didn't have to actually touch those magical buttons, they were heat sensitive so that they lit up the instant before your finger hit them. The tinkling chime that sounded when the doors opened was as sweet as the notes from a cocktail bar piano.

When it was time to leave, we took a different lift from the lobby to the underground car park. It was gloomy down there, an echoing arcade filled with petrol fumes and the shrill squeal of tyres on the smooth cement floor. On the drive home, I dreamed that we would one day arrive at the Carlton by taxi. A doorman in a grey tailcoat, top hat and white gloves would open the car door, and we would walk along the red carpet through the main entrance. And then we would be given our own solid brass key and ride in the lifts to our room.

Bakkies and Bailiffs

On Sundays, when the shops were closed and the heat made us all irritable, Mum made Dad take us out for longer drives in the countryside, which we had now learned to call the *veldt*. A few minutes from the house there was an old single-track road that went, eventually, to Olifantsfontein. The days when the elephants came there to drink were long gone, but the road dipped down towards a thin dry river bed lined with ancient willows. Somehow, they survived from one rainy season to the next, but that year the leaves looked as though they had been dipped in the dust. Along the road itself there were tall spindly gum trees with blue foliage and pale flaky bark. Once we left the shade of the old road, we were surrounded again by that flat brown earth being baked hard by the relentless sun.

I longed to get out of the car and walk, but the heat and the dust and strangeness of the land made it seem impossible. And Dad told us it wasn't safe for white people to wander around the countryside. Those country drives made me afraid, and I wondered what we would do if we ever broke down. For the first time in my life I preferred being in the city, where we were at least allowed to walk. South Africa seemed like an endless space where people spoke a different language, even when they spoke English. We had to use their words if we wanted to be understood: traffic lights were *robots*, small vans were *bakkies*. No one knew what a roundabout was, you had to call it a *traffic circle*, and electric light bulbs were *globes*. Mum was the first to adapt, but we sniggered when we heard her using the new vocabulary.

About a month after we arrived in Johannesburg, bad news came from Ireland. Dad told us that the sale of our house in Bangor had fallen through. He was relying on the money to pay off the mortgage, as well as his overdraft. The bank was less accommodating now that he had left the UK, and under pressure to pay off his debts he told the estate agents that he needed a quick sale. Late at night, I would hear Mum and Dad talking about money as they sat up in bed. Soon afterwards, they told me that our house had been sold, but for just enough to pay the bank what was owed. We later found out that the buyer was a friend of the estate agent, and six months later the house was back on the market at a greatly inflated price. But for a time, Dad seemed less worried. Then, in June, just as the highveldt winter finally brought relief from the strength sapping heat, there was a bigger problem. Back in Ireland, Patterson had decided that his other business interests needed all his available cash-flow. He arrived in Johannesburg to discuss ways of minimising the overheads on the business with Dad. He checked into the Landrost Hotel in the city centre, and after several days it became obvious that he wasn't going to come out to our house for a visit. I was disappointed.

'Patterson isn't here with Kitty,' Mum was forced to explain. 'But he's travelling with another woman, and he doesn't want us to meet her because he knows we're all so fond of Kitty.'

It was my first direct encounter with someone having an affair, and it made me uneasy. More dramatically, Dad told us that Patterson was intent on starting up his own airline and suddenly, it seemed, South Africa wasn't a priority.

Over the course of several days, Dad went for meetings at the hotel, and then came home and shut himself in the bedroom with Mum to discuss the latest developments. We were excluded from the conversations, because they didn't think we should know how serious things were. Eventually, Dad and Patterson had a bitter argument. I wasn't there, but I suspect Dad probably swore at him and said things that a business partner wouldn't be able to forgive. Patterson had agreed to pay Dad a salary for the first year of operations in South Africa, but instead he pulled out. Overnight, the bank account was virtually empty and we were on our own.

We weren't quite destitute: Dad's business was just starting to bear fruit, and several large companies had already asked him to conduct security surveys of their operations. For a time, there would be a limited income from these contracts, but it was clear that we couldn't afford to stay in the house we were renting.

Mum decided that she had to take charge of the family finances. She knew that she had to find us somewhere else to live, and quickly. Dad then revealed that he had signed a year's lease for our house, and that there might be legal difficulties if we didn't stay for the whole period. Mum sent him to the landlord to explain the situation, hoping that he might have some sympathy with a family in financial difficulties. Rather than default on the lease, Dad offered to pay a reduced rent as a gesture of goodwill, and returned claiming that the man had agreed. Three days later the landlord had changed his mind, and sent a legal summons demanding full payment of the year's rent. We didn't have the money, so Mum began a daily ritual of buying the *Johannesburg Star* newspaper as soon as it hit the streets at lunchtime, and scouring the lettings section. Hurriedly, we started viewing properties that were big enough for us, and our pets, and yet were affordable. After two weeks, and with the rent on our existing house due, she found somewhere that was available immediately. Unlike many of the other properties she'd seen, it seemed like a bargain. Naturally, there was a catch: the owner was offering it at a reduced rent on condition that the tenant signed an agreement to purchase the property after six months. Desperate to find a home for us to live in, Dad signed the lease. 'Who knows what will happen in six months' time,' he said. 'The business should be healthy enough by then for us to arrange a mortgage.'

Two days before we were due to move to the new house, and exactly six months after arriving in Johannesburg, we were evicted. It was a Thursday afternoon, and we returned from doing some shopping at the supermarket to find our maid, Rebecca, outside the house in tears. Two African men in overalls were standing beside a lorry parked in our driveway, while a short white man with a clipboard waited at our front door. He was the bailiff, and he presented Dad with a sheet of paper informing us that he was to take possession of the house and everything in it, except for personal belongings such as clothes. Under South African law he was empowered to take all of the furniture including our beds – but not the mattresses or the bedding. The bailiff had a cheerful face, and seemed slightly embarrassed by his job. Dad stood on the front drive smoking while the bailiff went efficiently about his task. Dad didn't speak to anyone while it was happening, and the whole thing took place very calmly. We watched as the men rolled up the rugs that Mum had bought for the sitting room and all of the bedrooms. She followed them around the house as they worked. 'Surely that's not worth taking?' she would quibble over one or two objects in each room. The Africans never spoke to us, they simply manhandled the furniture along the corridors and onto the van under the direction of the bailiff. The house had stone floors, and the noise of the removals began to bounce off the walls once the rugs were taken out. Then they took the dining table and chairs, the curtains, the TV and the bookcases. In the kitchen they took the freezer, the fridge and the washing machine, though they left the cooker because it belonged to the house. We were allowed to take the food from the freezer. Afterwards, my mattress lay on the floor of my bedroom strewn with the contents of my bedside table: a Parker fountain pen, my diary where I recorded the films I had watched, my alarm clock and a copy of *Moll Flanders*, one of my A-level texts.

None of the neighbours saw what was happening. The big gardens surrounded by high walls and security fencing made our humiliation private. We knew one family, who lived a couple of streets away, and Mum went over to their house and asked if they had room in their freezer for our food. She had to explain what was going on, and they said we could stay the night. Mum then used their telephone to ring our new land-lord, and asked him if we could move in the next day. Meanwhile, the bailiff was sympathetic, and he said we could leave our remaining belongings in the garage until we could get a removals van the next day. Inside the garage, we also had several wooden packing crates containing personal posses-sions brought from Ireland. Kindly, he said he would pretend he hadn't seen them.

We moved to the new house in Ferndale the next day, sleeping on the floor on our mattresses and counting ourselves lucky that we had a roof over our heads. That was when Dad started hating South Africa. Overnight, it was transformed from the land of opportunity into 'this bloody country'. I remember Mum pointing out that our problems had been caused by his Irish partner, and not by South Africa, but the trauma of being evicted had been too much. He said we should go back to Ireland, and started making enquiries about finding a job there.

A new kind of life started then. In the short term, we needed to replace the domestic items seized by the bailiff. That's when we began going to second-hand shops, and the best one was a place called The Swap Shop on Jan Smuts Avenue. We had driven past it many times, and I had seen the furniture displayed on the pavement beside the busy main road, and the windows stuffed with other people's discarded belongings. Mum found a lounge suite there, a simple 1960s design that she decided was 'rather Danish' because of its clean lines, exposed wood and plain fabric. We scrubbed it with soapy water and bleach and left it out in the garden in the sun to dry before she declared it was clean enough to use. I was glad that we didn't have any friends in Johannesburg who would see the Swap Shop furniture. Subsequent trips produced a dining table and chairs, a fridge and an old Decca record player that allowed us to listen to the music we had brought from Ireland.

Deprived of television for the first time in years, we started playing board games unearthed from the packing crates. Night after night we endured marathon sessions of Monopoly that often lasted until one or two in the morning. Because he was still working, Dad usually went to bed early, but the rest of us sat up until the games were finished. When we tired of Monopoly our other favourites were Mah-jong, played on a set Mum had bought in Malaya and almost never played with in Ireland, and Masterpiece – the Art Auction Game.

In our new circumstances, we couldn't afford to go to the cinema but occasionally we would go to the drive-in, another South African novelty which we knew only from American films. The whole family could get into the drive-in for just two Rand, about the price of a single adult ticket at the cinema. Sometimes we had to smuggle my little brother in under a blanket, but he usually went to sleep during the film anyway. A slightly more expensive option, but still cheaper than the cinema, was to hire a home movie. In the days before video players, South Africans were accustomed to hiring feature films on thirty-five millimetre reels and playing them at home with the aid of a projector hired from the same shop. We would drive along Louis Botha Avenue to Orange Grove, a suburb with a predominantly Italian population where there was a shop called *Pik-A-Movie*. The first film we hired was

Gone With the Wind (Clark Gable, Vivien Leigh, Olivia de Havilland and Leslie Howard, 1939). It came as seven reels of film and lasted more than three and a half hours. None of us had seen it before, and Mum invited Rebecca and her boyfriend, Johannes, in to watch with us. Rebecca asked us which country the story was taking place in, and found it difficult to understand that the events depicted were historical, perhaps unsurprisingly because the plantation scenes weren't so far removed from the way many black South Africans lived at the time.

Very soon after the move, I got my exam results. Although I had scored an 'A' grade in English, I had failed French, and without it I couldn't get into university. The news didn't help Dad's mood. He decreed that I was to be sent back to school in Ireland. The plan was for me to lodge with my mother's sister until the rest of the family could return. But it soon became clear that Mum and Dad disagreed about the wisdom of leaving Johannesburg. 'The reasons we came to Africa haven't changed,' I remember Mum saying. 'We left Ireland to get away from so many things – and now you want to scuttle back. We haven't the money to buy a home of our own, and I'm not going to live in some filthy rented house at my time of life!'

Mum and Dad couldn't talk about anything except money. Every day seemed to bring another financial worry. The car was leased, and would be repossessed unless the payments were made on time. Meanwhile, Dad's offices were in an expensive part of town and he couldn't afford next month's rent. One Sunday afternoon we drove down and retrieved everything inside the office, stationery, telephones, filing cabinets and the electric typewriter. For years afterwards, we used the headed notepaper as scrap. The red and black logo of Securicentres seemed as fake as Monopoly money.

Getting back to Ireland wasn't as easy as it sounded. Dad couldn't afford to buy me the plane ticket, let alone tickets for us all. It was decided that Caro and I should go back first, so that we could resume our schooling. That was when Mum started taking things to antique shops and selling them. One by one, our wooden packing cases were opened up as she looked for things that might be worth some cash. 'You see,' I remember her saying triumphantly, 'if I hadn't been to all those auctions, we wouldn't have these things to sell now.' Objects she had acquired in Ireland purely for their decorative value were now important assets. She had a collection of antique copper warming pans, jugs, griddles and kitchen ladles. The warming pan and the griddle allowed us to keep the car for another month. Then, driving into town one day, we saw a large billboard advertisement for British Airways. Underneath a picture of the Tower of London complete with beefeater, the slogan said; *Fly Now. Pay Later.* In the family it became known as the *Fly Now, Sue you Later* scheme, because Dad failed to keep up the instalments and was eventually taken to court by the airline. But that was all in the future. For now, I had a ticket to go home.

That last month in Johannesburg was a strange time. We were all befuddled by our reversal of fortune. There was a constant atmosphere of tension, and a sense of threat. At the weekends, Mum still insisted that we went on excursions, and one Saturday we drove out to some riding stables where there were Lipizzaner stallions. The white horses were famous for having been rescued from the Spanish Riding School in Vienna during World War II, and Mum wanted me to see them. But when we arrived at the stables she realised we couldn't afford the entrance fee. 'Never mind,' she said. 'We'll do it another time.'

Nothing about the future seemed in any way certain. One day in Garlicks department store we saw an African man running down the 'up' escalator. He had been shoplifting, and as he reached the bottom of the escalator he tripped and fell, giving the guards time to catch him. There was a scuffle as he was arrested, but the white shoppers carried on as if nothing had happened while he was led away with his arms pinned behind his back. I wished he had escaped, and wondered if I might ever have to steal something to survive. For the first time in my life, I began to feel deeply anxious.

My diary bears witness to the change in me. I kept up my habit of listing the films I watched, and the sequence of things happening to my parents, but it also became a conduit for my fears. The daily entries became fetishistic and compulsive, and always had to end with the same talismanic formula. *I hope tomorrow is a better day.* Gradually, the way I wrote the words also changed. I became convinced that certain portions of the page were 'luckier' than others, and I began avoiding certain parts of the paper because they were either positive or negative. Sometimes it would be the left-hand side of the page, sometimes the bottom or the top that mustn't be written upon. After the eviction, a full-page entry would be squeezed into a column at the right hand margin just two words wide, so that none of the entry appeared on the 'negative' side of the page.

I developed other compulsive behaviour. When walking, especially on a busy city street, I would have the sensation that there was a black rope stretched across the pavement at ankle height. The rope was never more than a few inches in front of me, but if I walked quickly enough I could catch up with it and step over it. Crossing the road couldn't protect me, because the rope was of infinite length. More frustratingly, the imaginary rope was an animate thing, and could anticipate my actions. I had to pretend to be ignoring it for a while, then try to outwit it with a sudden move. Like some fiendish playground skipping game, I could sometimes get one foot over the rope, but rarely both. Then, in my imagination, it would hobble me, snagging against the other shinbone and threatening to trip me up. I would have to change step, like a horse, in an attempt to free the other foot. Other symptoms surfaced. When I was leaving a room in our house at night, I had to switch off the light in a special way. My fingers all had to touch the switch at the same time, and stay in contact with it as I flipped it upwards. And then I had to step out of the room with my right foot first.

The only time we all seemed to be able to relax a little was during the evenings. As far as we knew, none of the people to whom Dad owed money had our new address. Night-time was the safe zone when the telephone didn't ring and the debt collectors wouldn't turn up at the door. There was security in Monopoly and Masterpiece, and always, above all, in reels of movie film.

Family Secrets

Flying back to London, I retraced the journey we had made as a family nine months earlier. It was the first time I had travelled further than my Granny's house without my parents. Until then I had only ever spent two nights away from home, when I had been in hospital for a dental operation the year before we left Ireland. The night before the flight, we hired *Gone With the Wind* for a final time. It was my sister's choice, but Mum said she wanted to see it too. We all watched it together, and once again I had to see it all the way through, because I was the only one who knew how to thread the rolls of film onto the projector. We finished screening it after midnight. Rather than go to bed, Mum and my sister said they wanted to see it again. That's what I remember of our last night together as a family.

Even though I was seventeen, back in Ireland I had to learn to do almost everything for myself for the first time. I had to open a bank account and manage what little cash Caro and I had between us to buy clothes. In some ways I enjoyed the freedom of managing my own daily life, and it felt grown-up to have a chequebook with my own name on it. Dad sent us money to pay my aunt for our food and keep, though it wasn't much. We got ourselves to and from school, did our own washing and ironing and generally grew up. But I missed home life terribly, and Christmas was miserable. Ireland was home, but not without Mum. At school, unexpectedly, people treated me with more respect, even the teachers, because they knew my parents weren't around. I felt like an orphan.

I was unable to communicate with my parents except by letter and, very occasionally, a brief telephone call. My aunt had a telephone, but it didn't make outgoing calls because she had failed to pay the bill too many times. Auntie Viv had undergone a parallel reversal of fortune. Like us, until recently she had lived in Ballyholme in a big house in a smart road. And like Mum, she had married an English artillery officer, although their relationship was always tempestuous. The marriage finally collapsed when she took a lover, a teenage boy who was less than half her age. She was now living in a tiny two-bedroom cottage without central heating. It was the best scandal to hit the family in years. Just like Mum, Viv hated to be told what she could or could not do, though her preferred route for rebellion was often sexual. 'Of the three girls, Viv was the "wild one",' Granny would admit to me.

'I could never control her,' Granny mused at the height of the toy-boy crisis. 'When she was sixteen she started wearing jumpers that were too tight; that was the fashion, though I know she had an eye for the boys. And she was very highly strung, so I didn't like to tell her off for fear of what she might do.'

'Pah!' Mum said, when I told her what Granny had said about my aunt. 'She wasn't highly strung – just neurotic. She just wanted to be the centre of attention. I remember a group of us going to the Palace Cinema to see *From Here to Eternity* (Burt Lancaster, Frank Sinatra, Deborah Kerr, 1953) and the only seats we could get all together were in the Circle. There we all were standing at the box-office, when Viv suddenly announced that she couldn't sit up there because she suffered from vertigo. There was a huge argument and we all went home again, having waited weeks for the film to come to Newcastle. She ruined the whole evening. That was typical!'

Life with Auntie Viv was an education, and I watched her negotiating the pitfalls of a new relationship with her children in tow. It was a shock to see my aunt with her young boyfriend, sometimes ignoring her responsibilities as a parent. But like Mum, I could see she relished the freedom of her new life, even though it brought financial hardship. For the first time, I began to understand that mothers had their own desires, things that had nothing to do with their children.

Mum wrote almost every day, and I did too. I was back at my old school, repeating the final year, an isolating experience since all of my contemporaries had already gone on to university or out to work. Meanwhile, the letters from Africa claimed that Dad was 'sorting things out', and just before Christmas came the news that he had been offered a job in Belfast. He was due to start work in February, and I started counting the days on my calendar until we would all be together again. As the weeks went by, the reassurances from Africa remained the same. Mum also told me in her letters that she was successfully losing weight for the first time in years. In six weeks, she had already lost nine kilograms on a strict diet and had begun a course of treatment with a doctor who had guaranteed its success. She explained that the course involved regular injections of something extracted from sheep. Dad was going to be administering the injections and she said he'd been practising using the hypodermic on oranges, but I never found out exactly what the medicine contained.

In February, Dad returned to Ireland alone to take up his new job in Belfast. He told me that Mum had moved into a flat, and would stay there until she had finished her slimming treatment. Meanwhile, in her letters, she explained that she had found herself a job, working as a secretary at the British Consulate. She always sounded optimistic that things would change for the better, and reassured me that she didn't want us to carry on living apart. Soon afterwards, a letter came with a picture inside. It was her monthly bus pass embellished with a laminated photograph. Mum wanted me to see how much thinner she was. She asked me to show it to Granny to demonstrate the success of her treatment regime, but I didn't. When I looked at the photograph, it made me cry, because for the first time, in my eyes, she looked old.

Dad made it sound like everything was a positive development. Although he had a job, he kept trying to find ways of making extra money. His schemes usually involved acting as a broker for military equipment, and he kept in touch with a network of ex-military men in London whom he said, 'had the right sort of contacts'. For years, he pursued a succession of deals, and I soon learned not to get excited when he discussed the latest money-making scheme, because none of them ever came to anything.

Sometimes he made a hasty return trip to South Africa or to the Middle East with a sample of some kind of equipment. He didn't tell me where he was going, but sometimes a postcard would arrive from Sharjah or Sana'a or Zurich. There were infra-red night sights for rifles, and encryption machines for sending coded radio messages. He set up meetings with Colonels and Generals in the South African Defence Forces, and returned with high hopes that they would place an order which would make him a fortune in commissions.

'You never know,' Mum would say when we were in the grip of a particularly severe financial crisis. 'One of these days one of your father's schemes might come off, and we won't have to worry about money any more.' But at other times she would laugh at him and say he that he was a cross between Walter Mitty and Rambo.

Dad never referred to the events that had happened in Africa, and always talked as if Mum and my brother and sister would return in the near future. His new job in Belfast was similar to the one he'd done before, but not as well paid. He had enough money to rent a house and support me, but very little extra to send to Johannesburg. He bought a secondhand car from Gethin's, the local garage where we regularly used to fill up our two cars when we lived in our old house. Mum had bought a brand new Mini-Clubman Estate from Gethin's a couple of years before we left Bangor. It was dark red with a wooden trim along the sides, and the stretched boot was perfect for carrying the dogs and cats to shows or to the vet. In memory of those years of good custom, Mr Gethin allowed him to buy a car on credit, and was relatively tolerant if Dad couldn't make the monthly instalments. Usually he filled up the car with petrol at least once a week but I knew that if Dad ever went to another garage it was because he was hiding from Gethin. Sometimes he sent me to fill up, and instructed me to tell Gethin that he was away on business.

So that I could have as little disruption as possible to my studies, Dad rented a house close to my old school, potentially large enough for Mum and my siblings to live in too. We fell into a routine, where Dad did all of the shopping, the cooking and washing, and went out to work. We did the weekly shopping in Wellworths and I walked into school in the mornings just as I had done for the six years before we went to Africa. For a brief time I had been magically transported away from everything I had hated about Bangor, and school, just as I'd so desperately wished for. But now I was back again, and it was as if our African adventure had all been a dream: except that half of the family was missing.

If Dad was depressed by the cycle of domestic duties, he never said so. Boarding school and the Army had left him well equipped to look after himself. I visited Granny several days each week after school, walking across town to see her and taking a detour to avoid passing by our old house. It was the only one that had a large plane tree growing beside the front gate, and I could see it clearly from the end of the street. If I had to pass the end of the road I would sneak a glance at the tree, a comforting shape that had always been visible from my bedroom window when we lived there. I didn't want to get close enough to see the house itself, or to know what the new owners were doing to it.

Granny sometimes asked when Mum was coming home, and I repeated what I had been told, that she would be back when she had finished her weight-loss programme. I tried not to think about the future, and still assumed that somehow Dad and Mum would make things alright again. I was close to Granny, who was by then a widow, and she was always glad of my company. When we were alone she liked to tell me stories about her life in India, and I would quiz her about family history.

———————

Saturday morning was story time in our house. Mum couldn't, or wouldn't, speak to anyone before she'd had a cup of tea, but after that she would sit up in bed and tell us stories. Propped up on pillows, she would sip it slowly, keeping her eyes closed tight to ward off conversation until the cup was empty. Our first question, once the tea had given her a kick-start was always: 'Did you have any dreams last night?'

I learned to be scared of Mum's dreams. She had them every single night of her life. They were always in colour, and they were often outlandish, and sometimes they were premonitions. If Mum was edgy, or irritable, it usually meant she'd had one of her bad dreams. We all learned the codes when we were very young. Any dream with kittens in it was a seriously bad omen. In spite of our family military connections, soldiers in uniform were a sign of bad news, but nothing was as sinister as newborn babies. If Mum had a dream about babies then the whole family was on red alert: unnecessary trips by road had to be cancelled, or plans to visit a relative postponed. Dad would even cancel a business meeting if Mum had a really negative dream.

'I had a dream about "Pig" Morton last night.' This was a phrase I learned to dread. It could cast a pall over the entire family for several days as we waited for something to happen. Morton had been her boss when she worked as a secretary at an insurance brokers in Belfast before she got married. According to Mum, he was a weak, lascivious character who could never be trusted with money. He was also lazy, and let her do a lot of the work while he went off to play golf. She admitted that he wasn't really a genuinely evil character, but if he appeared in a dream it was a sign that we needed to be ready for bad news. As I got older I tried to distance myself from the dreams, and would refuse to even hear about them. The trouble was that when Mum had a horrible dream something bad usually came along. It might just be a threatening letter from the bank manager, or even just contact with someone Mum didn't want to see. Two or three days of bad dreams meant that a minor car accident or losing something valuable was a real possibility. Even Dad, who liked to claim he didn't believe in anything that smacked of what he called 'mumbo-jumbo' (and that included anything to do with God), didn't take any major decisions without checking with Mum. And if she had a bad dream, he would get nervous. 'Don't anyone answer the phone this morning,' Mum would some-times say. 'I don't want any bad news.' I was happy to accept this ruling, believing somehow that negative events could be fore-stalled by refusing to let news of them into the house. I tried ignoring the dreams for a long time, but it didn't really work. Too many of them came true.

If Mum didn't have a dream worth telling, there were always stories. Like most children, I was fascinated by my parents' youth, and things that happened to them before I existed. If the stories had a hint of glamour, or an encounter with danger, so much the better. There was the time Mum had been asked to go for a drive in the countryside with a man who stopped at a secluded spot and then produced a pair of handcuffs. He asked her to try them on 'just for fun', and we listened in amazement every time she told us the story. She allowed the man to put the handcuffs on her wrists. 'Now, I can do whatever I want and you can't stop me!' he said. 'No you can't,' Mum replied, dropping her hands and allowing the cuffs to slip off her slim wrists.

There were some stories that we never tired of hearing. A favourite tale concerned Mum walking down a quiet country road on a balmy summer's evening. 'I saw a police motorbike coming towards me, followed by an enormous black car with a flag on the bonnet,' she would recount misty-eyed. 'I stopped and stared and as the car passed it slowed right down and the most gorgeous man in uniform leaned out, and very gallantly gave me a salute.'

The handsome officer was Prince Philip and Mum would never hear a negative word about him for the rest of her life. Dad had a seemingly inexhaustible supply of army stories, but to compete with Prince Philip, Dad could muster only a small selection of celebrities. Serving in Cyprus he had once had to share his tent with the comedian Reg Varney (star of *On the Buses*) who had come to entertain the troops. He had also met Frankie Howerd in similar circumstances. His most famous encounter had occurred in Hyde Park, while he was out walking two English bull-terriers that belonged to his father. Suddenly, a glamorous woman came cantering up to him on a pure white stallion.

'Zose are ze most beeootiful dogs in ze world!' she purred. 'Zey vill match my horse perfectly. Please. Tell me vot zey are called.'

It was Zsa Zsa Gabor, and she offered to buy the dogs. My grandfather wasn't interested in selling, but the next day the same thing happened, and Dad decided that he would let Zsa Zsa continue negotiations over a drink. 'And, so, what happened?' we would always clamour.

'We went to Quaglinos night club for a drink that evening.' And that's all Dad would say.

I especially liked the stories Mum told about her own family, because her five siblings were a rich source of scandal and amusement. I stored up the anecdotes like a jigsaw in my head, matching and cross-matching the details of names and places so that I could understand my uncles and aunts, and my parents, better. As a teenager, I began to notice how some stories induced discomfort, or in some cases a categorical denial from the participants that they had ever happened. And then there were stories that Mum trusted me alone with, and I felt privileged. Gradually, I learned how selective memory could be, and that some people are adept at erasing whole chapters from their own lives, if it suits them.

It was thrilling to know things about my elders. I collected the family stories, especially the ones that came with a whiff of scandal – an unplanned pregnancy, marital problems and general gossip. Most of the information was inconsequential, but I knew when one of my aunts had been having an affair, and that another found ways to buy herself extra clothes by fiddling her housekeeping allowance. If I found out something that I thought was quite secret then I would hoard it, squirrelling it away in my memory until I could verify or amplify the facts. And, that knowledge brought with it power.

Granny featured in many of Mum's stories. I felt it was part of her charm that she was a prodigious snob, even though her life in Newcastle, County Down, was as small-town as you could get. However, Grandpop's army record, and his position as a Colonel in the Home Guard during the War, and later as a local policeman, gave Granny a certain standing in the local community. She also had a deep belief in keeping up appearances, and much effort was put into maintaining her small-town respectability in the whirl of Newcastle society. Grandpop was a member of the Royal County Down Golf Club, and she was a regular at the Bridge Club that met in the Slieve Donard Hotel.

Granny had high hopes that her daughters would marry well, and expended great effort in raising their expectations. At one time she tried to get a local aristocrat interested in marrying one of the trio. The Northern Irish gentry has always been thin on the ground, but in Newcastle there was a local landowner named Lord St John. 'He was at least forty,' Mum said, 'when Granny had the idea that he might like to marry me, or Viv, or even Constance who was only about fourteen at the time.'

After months of cultivating Lord St John, Granny managed to get him to agree to come to her own modest house one Sunday afternoon for tea. The three girls were instructed to put on their smartest dresses and to be on their best behaviour. Grandpop was not appraised of the plan, because Granny had hoped that he would be at the Golf Club that afternoon. Notwithstanding his military career, Grandpop was a farmer's son and entirely without airs and graces, most unlikely to impress Lord St John with his breeding.

As they sat at the table taking tea and scones served off the best crockery, Grandpop, who was outside gardening, shambled past the window. To Granny's horror, he was wearing an old hat with holes in the brim, a collarless shirt full of holes and trousers held up with a piece of brown string. 'Who's that?' enquired Lord St John.

'Oh, that's just the gardener,' Granny rejoined calmly, shooting a steely glare at the three girls. Shortly afterwards, the gardener came into the house and joined the rest of the family for tea. Greedily taking a swig from the dainty bone-china, he spat it back into the cup with a grimace:

'Aaagh! Mona, what's this muck?' To impress Lord St John, Granny had served Earl Grey, rather than the customary strong Irish blend. Granny tried to maintain her composure, but then Grandpop lifted his plate and inspected it carefully before commenting, 'I've never seen this crockery before, where did it come from?'

Grandpop's two unguarded remarks became catch-phrases in the family, but Granny harboured a grudge that he had let her down in front of Lord St John. But for him, she might have married one of the girls into the landed gentry. At the bridge club, Granny would make friends with elderly women, hoping that they might remember her in their wills. She referred to this habit as 'cultivating', but so far as anyone knew, it never paid off.

When it came to social climbing, her three sons were something of a hindrance, because they each provided Granny with daughters-in-law of whom she disapproved. Herbert, the eldest, fell for the charms of an Englishwoman whom Granny never liked, principally because she believed she lied about her age. When he was just eighteen, Lewis, her second son, met a Catholic girl from a poor family and got her pregnant. An irate mother appeared on Granny's doorstep, demanding that Lewis marry her daughter immediately. Grandpop refused to cooperate at first, and told his son he would give him the money to escape to England and hide from the harridan. But Granny was afraid of a scandal, and persuaded Lewis to marry the girl 'to protect your father's reputation'. He did as his mother wanted, and endured a desperately unhappy relationship for many years. Mum's youngest brother, Doug, was Granny's favourite. Mum called him Golden Boy when she wanted to sneer at the way Granny doted on him. Unlike the elder pair, Doug was an academic child who managed to get a place at Queen's University in Belfast. After graduating, and like his siblings and his father before him, Doug went into the Army, and was sent to Nigeria. There he met and fell in love with another man's wife, a woman who already had two children. For Granny, the liaison was never satisfactory, and the adulterous wife was forever referred to in private as 'that brazen hussy'.

Granny's redeeming charm was that she had an irrepressible sense of humour. Mum told me that during the war she had once gone to the cinema in Belfast and as they filed into their seats, Granny sat down onto a man's lap. In the darkness she hadn't noticed that the seat was already occupied, but instead of getting up, she went into a state of helpless, hysterical laughter, with tears rolling down her cheeks. The more the man struggled the more helpless Granny became. I witnessed the same performance once as a child when Mum was giving Granny a lift somewhere. The passenger door hadn't been properly closed, and as we pulled away from the kerb, Granny fell out of the car. Horrified, Mum screeched to a halt and we all jumped out, to find Granny lying on her back at the kerb, relatively unharmed but still unable to stand up because she was having a laughing fit.

She was a tiny woman, exactly five feet tall. She never gained weight and she had good legs. 'That's because I always loved dancing,' she would tell me. 'Oh how I miss it. In India we went ballroom dancing every week without fail.'

Granny's full name was Mona Mary Aynho Ellen Phillips. Grandpop called her Mona, but everyone else in the family called her Aynho. No one in the family could ever explain why, though there was a theory that her eldest son, Herbert, started using Aynho when he was about eight and his siblings followed suit. Granny was frustratingly vague about her own parents, and I was intrigued by the fact that her father had changed his name from Phipps to Phillips. Granny claimed that this was because he had fallen out with his father – allegedly one of the wealthy Sainsbury family – and had decided to separate himself from the clan. According to Granny, her grandfather 'Phipps' had been killed falling from a horse in a hunting accident: a suitably aristocratic death. His son, her father, had been adopted by the Sainsburys who were cousins of her grandfather. Granny had two sisters, Josie and Ella. I never met Josie, who died in the 1950s, something Granny didn't like to discuss. There were doubts over Josie's demise: either she had accidentally overdosed on sleeping pills, or she had committed suicide, or possibly been murdered by her husband. Granny preferred the murder option, and would only say: 'Her husband was the one who always gave her the medicine.' I could never get her to tell me any more than that, but it seemed like the suggestion of murder was more acceptable that the stigma of suicide.

Ella, Granny's elder sister, was more interesting to me, and I looked forward to her coming over from England on a visit. She always stayed in the Royal Hotel, the smartest Bangor had to offer. She had a prodigious tolerance for alcohol, and when Grandpop died she consumed seventeen gin and tonics over the course of an afternoon and evening wake. It was my job to mix the drinks for the assembled relatives, and after a few hours Ella decided that the gap between refreshments was too long. She took up station beside the Welsh dresser which we were using as a bar, and started mixing her own drinks. Her feet were planted squarely apart, steadying her as if she were on deck. I was fascinated by the fact that she was never seen without her very curly black wig. She didn't deny wearing it, and in combination with large amounts of scarlet lipstick and false eyelashes she was a doppelganger for Blanche Hudson in *Whatever Happened to Baby Jane* (Bette Davis and Joan Crawford, 1962). I found her frightening and fascinating in equal measure, and I cooperated when she asked me to call her Prudence. She didn't like being called Ella, but Granny refused to go along with her new name. Given that Granny happily switched between 'Mona' and 'Aynho', this didn't seem entirely reasonable.

Granny told me that Ella had been married three times. In fact, Ella was only married once, but as a Catholic had been unable to divorce. It was easier to talk about her three 'husbands' than acknowledge that she had lived with two other men after her first marriage. Granny didn't mind dispensing gossip, but anything that threatened propriety had to be hushed up. Ella's husband Eddie had shot himself in South Africa after the War, reputedly because he had been swindled by a partner over a diamond mine. According to Granny, Eddie was wealthy, handsome and dashing. Great Aunt Ella liked to tell me about her glamorous youth, and I loved hearing about Eddie, who had been a bomber pilot during the War. Ella said the noisy engines of the Lancasters had affected his hearing, and his worsening deafness had contributed to his depression while he was in Africa. She didn't seem to mind talking about the way he had blown his brains out with a hunting rifle in Africa. That was the kind of dramatic family story I liked best, but according to Granny, Ella's version of what happened to Eddie wasn't entirely complete. He had shot himself, it was true, and perhaps he had been losing his hearing. But what really depressed him was a letter that he had just received from Ella telling him that she would not be coming out to Africa to join him. She preferred to stay in London 'living the high life', as Granny put it with a shake of the head, and having an affair with Eddie's best friend. It was Prudence, or Ella, who sent me the lion's skull which I eventually took back to Africa. Mum put it up for sale in the shop, but the air conditioning dried out the skull and the magnificent incisors started to split and fall out of the jaws.

Prudence regarded the world with a certain cynicism, while Granny maintained a degree of naïve optimism. In fact, Granny was the youngest person I've ever known, and mostly laughed at herself. I remember sitting with her one afternoon when an elderly neighbour whom she'd been 'cultivating' in the hope of an inheritance, approached the front door. 'Oh blow!' said Granny in a stage-whisper, 'it's that old Miss Smythe – she's such a bore, we'll never get rid of her. Don't answer the door, and don't speak in case she hears us!'

I sat immobile in my chair, hoping that the net curtain at the front window made it impossible for Miss Smythe to tell that we were at home. Meanwhile, Granny decided to crawl across the sitting room carpet, raising herself on her elbows on a chair beneath the window to peer out and see if it was safe to resume making a noise. At the same time, Miss Smythe was pressing her nose up against the glass from the other side, and could see Granny quite clearly. 'Hello . . . Aynho?' she shouted through the window. 'Are you alright?'

'Keep quiet!' Granny mouthed at me, ignoring the plain truth that she had been spotted.

'She can see you!' I hissed. 'We'll have to answer the door.'

As I stood up, Granny realised that she had embarrassed herself. But when I came back into the room with Miss Smythe, it was to find Granny giggling on her hands and knees, and totally unable to get to her feet. I had to haul her upright and let her subside onto the sofa, still speechless, and helpless with laughter while I busied myself with offering the unwelcome visitor some tea. 'Is your grandmother quite well?' the spinster enquired. Granny was clasping her arms across her stomach by now and there were tears rolling down her cheeks.

'Oh, I think so,' I stammered lamely. 'I had just told her a funny story about something that happened at school.'

'It must have been very amusing indeed,' said Miss Smythe tartly. 'Perhaps I'll come back another time.'

Surprisingly, Granny was the great keeper of secrets. It continually amazed me that she often didn't let her own children know what any of their siblings were doing. Perhaps her greatest secret was concealing her own religion. Grandpop wasn't particularly religious, but he came from a staunch Protestant family. He met Granny when he was stationed in Kent after the First World War, and they married when she was just sixteen and he was twenty-two. Although his approach to everything in life was scrupulously honest, he decided that it would be best if his family didn't know that Granny's family were originally from Dublin. And that they were Roman Catholics. Taking a Catholic wife back to Northern Ireland in the 1920s wasn't going to be easy for him. Mixed marriages, as they liked to call inter-faith unions in Northern Ireland, almost always brought complications.

Because Grandpop was in the British Army, Mum lived in India until she was ten. She might have stayed longer, but she was struck down with an illness that affected her left eye. She and her older siblings returned to Ireland with Granny, a little while before Grandpop. In Ireland the doctors were mystified by Mum's illness, and, after a series of operations they said there was no choice but to remove her eye. Most people, including me until I was about sixteen, never even suspected that Mum had a false eye, and it didn't stop her driving, or playing games like golf or badminton. It was only as I got older that I realised that if I crept into Mum's bedroom when she was on the telephone, she wouldn't notice me until I spoke. The telephone was on the right hand side of the bed, the side with her good eye. But I never dared to ask her about it. Then I remembered that as a small boy I had discovered a little box at the back of Mum's shoe cupboard. Inside there was a set of six glass eyes, all beautifully painted and extremely realistic. I was allowed to get them out and look at them, but I was too young to understand their purpose.

After the operation, Granny decided that she would send Mum to the local Catholic girls' school. Communicating with Grandpop in India by letter, she explained that the convent school was the best option available, and that Mum would only go there until a place became available at the nearby state, Protestant school. But, in order to get her into the school, Granny arranged for Mum to be Confirmed as a Roman Catholic. At the convent, the Mother Superior made a daily addendum to the morning prayer service for Mum, and one other child. 'And now, let's say a special prayer for Pam and Phyllis,' she would say, 'because their fathers are Protestants.'

Mum was instructed that she must never tell her father that she had been Catholicised, and she never did. As a child, I assumed that this had been simply a ruse, a ploy by Granny to get my mother a better education. It was only years later, when I was at university, that I discovered there was more to it. At weekends, I would sometimes spend the night at Granny's house. Grandpop was dead by then, and she was living alone in a small bungalow in the seaside village of Groomsport. We would stay up late drinking tea and eating her homemade shortbread while we watched old films. She was always encouraging about my studies, reassuring me that I would pass my exams no matter how difficult I was finding the course. Lying in bed late one night on one such visit, I heard a voice coming from Granny's bedroom. Thinking she might be calling out because she was unwell, I crept towards the door. For several moments I couldn't make sense of the low incantations I could hear. *Hail Mary, full of grace, the Lord is with me . . .* I stole away from the door, hoping fervently that she wouldn't hear me.

Later, in Africa, Mum told me the whole story of my grandparents' secret. Knowing that she was Catholic didn't affect my relationship with Granny in any way, but I was amazed that she had been able to submerge her faith for so long. A few years later, when Granny died, it became clear to me that my aunts and uncles were in complete ignorance of their own mother's Catholicism. Arrangements for the funeral were being made, and I was in the house with one of my aunts when the Protestant vicar arrived to discuss the funeral service. Shortly after he left, the doorbell rang and it was the local Catholic priest. Like the vicar, he thought Granny was one of his own flock and was expecting to conduct her funeral. To avoid giving the rest of her assembled relatives yet another shock, she was eventually buried as a Protestant. I sat through the service in discomfort. I didn't feel that the vicar knew her particularly well, and I was struck by the hypocrisy of the divided faiths. Granny was gone, and now her spirit was being invoked in a ceremony which seemed hollow. While my assembled aunts and uncles sobbed in their pews, I marvelled at the fact that she had kept the secret of her dual faith so successfully for the sixty-two years she had lived in Ireland. That would have made her laugh. Helplessly.

Mum's relationship with Granny was ambivalent. 'Your Grandmother is *incredibly* stupid, but very, very devious,' she would say. And yet, she was unfailing in her support for her when she got old.

When Dad lost his money in Africa, Mum told me that she felt partially responsible for the situation. 'I've never brought him any luck when it comes to money,' she said. She then revealed that one of the reasons we had been so heavily in debt in Ireland before we emigrated was because of Granny. It didn't make much sense to me until she reminded me that Granny and Grandpop had been living in our house while we were in Malaya. For Mum and Dad, the house in Newcastle had been intended as an investment, an attempt to get a secure footing on the property ladder while Dad had access to subsidised housing in the army. Granny and Grandpop had initially paid rent on the house, but this stopped after about a year. Dad and Mum only became aware of a problem when they received a letter from the bank asking for the arrears on the mortgage. Dad then wrote repeatedly to Grandpop to ask what was happening, but received no reply. 'Granny was intercepting the letters,' Mum explained. 'Because she knew Grandpop would rather starve than owe us money.'

When Mum finally made contact with Granny, she claimed that she was behind with the rent because of the expenses of my aunt's wedding. Granny was enjoying a minor success in her social climbing with the marriage of her youngest daughter. Like her two sisters, Constance was to marry an army officer, but Granny's new son-in-law brought with him the added prestige of being the son of a diplomat, who had even been knighted. Naturally, she wanted to give her youngest daughter a suitably grand send-off, especially as the groom's family were well-to-do, and she didn't want them to think she couldn't compete. It sounded like a plausible excuse, but Mum later found out that Granny really needed money because my uncle Lewis was in prison. It took years for the whole story to come out. It seems that Lewis got into financial difficulties over maintenance payments for his wife and seven children. Granny needed the money for the subsequent court case, or possibly to support his family while he was inside. The only way Granny could come up with the money was to live rent-free in my parents' house. Granny's skill at keeping things quiet meant that Grandpop never knew that his son was in prison in England. And he never found out that Mum and Dad weren't getting any rent for the house he was living in.

Mum wasn't bitter about what her mother had done, though she was angry that her siblings didn't know. Dad had to sell the house in Newcastle, and Granny and Grandpop had to find alternative rented accommodation. Some of the family criticised my parents for, as they saw it, forcing Granny and Grandpop to move out. In their eyes, my parents were simply making a profit by selling the house, little knowing that they had to do so in order to repay the bank, which had continued paying the mortgage while we were abroad. It was a financial blow from which my parents never fully recovered, and another factor in their decision to emigrate.

Plenty of things would have stayed secret if we hadn't gone to Africa.

Riding on Trolley-Buses

After re-sitting my A-levels, Dad said that Caro and I could go back to Johannesburg for the summer. All being well, I had a place at Queen's University in Belfast to study English starting that autumn. The idea of going back to Africa was scary, but I felt I had to visit Mum.

'Perhaps you can persuade your mother to come back with you,' Dad said quietly as I kissed him goodbye at the airport. He looked around furtively when I kissed him in public, always offering a formal handshake as if he hoped one day I would make do with that instead. Later, as an adult, if I told him I was going somewhere in Africa to report on an election, or travel into a remote area he never expressed any fears for my safety until I was on the point of saying goodbye. 'Mind how you go,' was the most he could manage. That was how he did things, never broaching an emotional or deeply personal topic when there might be enough time to discuss it properly. We'd spent almost every evening alone together for several months, and yet we had never talked about why she hadn't returned. The only time I saw him get really excited and happy was when there was an international rugby match on TV on *Saturday Grandstand*. He also got engrossed watching Bodie and Doyle in *The Professionals* on a Friday night.

That was the difference between Mum and Dad. At best he was sheepish, and at worst blundering, unwilling to acknowledge his own feelings, and nervous that anyone else might. As he got older, he became angry if anyone questioned how he might manage some task on his own. 'I've been looking after myself since I was four years old,' he would snap. 'No one's ever helped me – so you don't need to start now!'

Dad didn't expect to be asked how he felt about anything, and it never occurred to him that anyone else might want to talk about their feelings. Mum was the opposite: sensitive, but persistent. And no topic was out of bounds, however deeply personal the subject matter, she would cut to the chase and make you confront whatever was making you unhappy. Even so, like most mothers, she sometimes jumped to irritating conclusions, combining her own broad-minded approachability with an annoying set of small-town prejudices. Once, possibly after watching *The Turning Point* (Mikhail Baryshnikov, Shirley Maclaine, 1977), I told her that I had developed an interest in ballet, and wished I could have been trained as a dancer. The conversation happened to coincide with a period when I was unhappy at university and felt unsure about whether I had chosen the right subject for my degree.

'You're gay, aren't you?' she said calmly as we drank tea in her bedroom. 'I just knew it.'

'No, I just think ballet dancers are amazing athletes, and I wish I could do something like that.'

It was too late, the conversation was already out of control.

'Timothy.' She only used my full name when she wanted my full attention. Then she took my hand in hers and squeezed it hard. 'Something is making you unhappy. Believe me, I've had so many shocks in my life, one more won't matter. Just admit it, you know it won't affect how I feel about you. You're gay.'

'No,' I protested, snatching my hand away. 'I'm not. You can like ballet without being gay.'

'Hmm,' she said, narrowing her eyes disbelievingly. 'But you said you wanted to be a ballet dancer.'

'No, I said I wished I could do what they do – there's a difference.'

She never forgot a conversation, even when it was seemingly trivial, and my chance remark ignited a spark of suspicion that hovered in her imagination for years. Until I got married, or fathered a child, Mum was not going to let go of the idea that I was homosexual. Her suspicions only abated when I started introducing her to my girlfriends.

Almost a year after I left, I returned to a Johannesburg in the grip of the cold highveldt winter. During the day the sun shone down on the city streets like a spotlight behind glass, the heat filtered out through the smog that hung over the skyscrapers in a nicotine yellow cloud. White office workers hurried along the pavements in mismatched winter clothes, poorly insulated in their cheap sweaters made of viscose and nylon. The really cold weather usually only lasts about two months, but even so, sometimes we saw rich women in floor-length mink coats and stoles with matching hats as if they had just walked off a street in Gstaad during the skiing season.

The Africans wore knitted woollen hats and shawls made from ragged blankets. Usually, by lunchtime, if they could find a sunny spot and there was no wind sweeping down the razor straight city blocks, the office workers could sit outside in shirtsleeves. But by late afternoon, the permanently cloudless sky whipped the heat away again like a quilt snatched by a lover in the night.

For ten months, the only direct news I had from Johannesburg had come in Mum's letters, at least two or three each week, to which I faithfully replied. She usually sent aerograms, single sheets of franked blue paper that you had to fold in three and glue down with adhesive flaps. The aerograms were covered in printed instructions about how to fold them, which flaps to cut first and where you should write the sender's address. *Sluitings word nie toegelaat nie. Enclosures not permitted.*

Mum's letters were always upbeat, and she never wrote without telling me how much she loved me. She said her treatment with her diet doctor was almost finished, the reason she originally cited for not coming back to Ireland with Dad. She would encourage me to work hard at school and ask me if possible, not to argue with Dad. 'Try not to grit your teeth when he talks to you,' she wrote. 'He loves you very much and he's doing his best to look after you so that you can go to university.'

My own letters were filled with inconsequential news about school, and messages from Granny. I never asked Mum directly if she was coming home, because I think I already knew that she wasn't. She never revealed what a financial struggle her daily life in Johannesburg had become. She told me about the people she worked with at the Consulate, that she took the bus to work and that my brother was now at a state-school within walking distance of the flat. Sometimes she wrote that she was 'saving up' so that she could afford to bring the pets back from Africa too. The seven cats we had taken from Ireland originally were down to five. Mao-Tse the tomcat had been run over, and Mae Ling the tabby-point queen had simply disappeared. But Shandy the boxer had now been joined by a stray called Hennie.

Mum found Hennie running through the traffic at the bottom of Claim Street in the middle of the city, and he had adopted her completely. He was a little grey and white scrap of a dog, with a bushy moustache, dark button eyes and snaggly teeth that sometimes trapped his upper lip in a quizzical smile. Hennie was some kind of terrier, with a little bit of poodle mixed in, but we never knew how old he was or where he came from. His breath always smelt bad. Mum called him 'Hennie' because it was a sound he seemed to recognise. She didn't like it when people asked if he was named after the stereotype Afrikaaner, Hennie Van Der Merwe, a stupid yokel who was the butt of many South African jokes. There was nothing stupid about Hennie. He anticipated Mum's every command, and seemed to be able to sense what she wanted him to do. Years later when he was killed, Mum told me she loved him more than she loved Dad.

Mum brought Hennie to meet me at the airport. He was in a brown leather bag, hidden by a chiffon scarf draped over his head. Dogs weren't allowed into the arrivals area, but Hennie knew when he had stay hidden. Mum would just say, 'In the bag, Hennie,' and in he would hop, staying quiet and still until he was tipped out. The bag was quite smart-looking, and it had a flat base so it stood upright like a bin. Hennie even went to restaurants and to the cinema that way, and no one ever spotted him.

I saw Mum straight away when the sliding doors opened into the arrivals hall. Her smile was the same, but not much else. For a start, she was wearing trousers, something I'd never ever seen. And she was much thinner – the same size, she said, as when she got married in 1955.

'I can't believe you're home,' she kept saying on the bus ride back into the city. She held my hand between both of her own, squeezing it rhythmically and pulling me close against her. 'You're so brown and healthy,' she said. 'Look at me, living in Africa and as white as a ghost!'

I was glad to see her, but everything was filtered through that surreal, spaced out feeling you get after an all-night flight. This wasn't home, and I didn't like her calling it that. She didn't even seem like the mother I had left behind almost a year earlier. So much had changed.

This time there was no car journey to the leafy northern suburbs. The bus headed straight back to the heart of the city and then we took a five-minute taxi ride from the terminus to her one-bedroom flat. Mitchell Court was one of the last buildings in Kotze Street before you got to the Old Fort. They took the prisoners from there to Pretoria when it was time for them to be hanged. From Mum's sitting room window, we could see the barbed wire on top of the perimeter wall and the rooftops of the gaol.

Dad sent Mum money when he could, but didn't have much to spare. Mum's secretarial job paid just enough for the rent and to feed herself and my brother. In the winter she couldn't afford to heat the flat with its electric fires. Once, she told me at the end of the month she couldn't afford pet food either, and she stayed in bed to keep warm while the cats paced around and around the flat yowling like wild beasts. She wouldn't get rid of any of the pets, they were part of the family. And the Siamese cats sometimes produced kittens that she could sell.

We lived on the first floor, at number 109. The building had ten storeys with ten flats on each floor. The whole thing was built out of dark red bricks which made it seem to disappear into the night sky. Because of the prison, the road between us and the Fort didn't get too busy, and it was relatively quiet compared to the rest of Hillbrow. Two blocks east and things got busier where Twist Street cut north-south across Pretoria and there was Highpoint centre with the big OK Bazaars store and a Fontana bakery. Nearer to our block, we only had the Vasco Da Gama late-night shop just around the corner on Klein Street.

The apartment entrances were all on a common balcony that led around the inside edge of the three-sided block in the shape of a squared-off U. From the balcony you looked down into a bare cement courtyard, and beyond it the rear wall of the run-down Quirinale Hotel. Even in summer, it was cool and gloomy down in the courtyard, but in the winter it was bitter because the sun only reached the ground for about an hour every day. No one ever went down there except for the maids, because that was where the big dustbins were kept. Sometimes they would sit down there on upturned milk-crates during their lunch break and exchange gossip about their madams. The maids ate *bunny-chow*, half loaves of bread with the centre scooped out and filled with meat and gravy. The loaves came in a thin plastic bag with a blue and white-striped pattern so you could hold them without getting covered in the hot gravy. The only other reason to go down to the courtyard was if they had rubbish that wouldn't fit in the metal chute that allowed you to dump stuff straight off the ends of the balcony. The chute smelled bad because people emptied their kitchen bins into it, and all kinds of other things went down too: empty glass bottles and toothpaste tubes, used nappies and leftover food, milk cartons and old vegetables. Everything hurtled down into the darkness with a tremendous clattering and thumping and banging, so you weren't supposed to use the chute after eight o'clock at night. One day somebody threw a dead cat down the chute and Mrs Trubbock, the building supervisor, tried for days to find out who owned it. She got one of the maids to retrieve the cat's body and left it out in the courtyard on a piece of newspaper. She knew no one would admit owning it, but she wanted to punish them with the sight of their dead pet. Everyone who lived at Mitchell Court was scared of Dollie Trubbock.

Trubbock was a stout woman with steel grey hair. Chain-smoking had blackened the teeth in her lower jaw and the ones at the front had tips that were so ground down you could see the insides, like chopped tree-trunks. Her skin was heavily wrinkled and she had large liver-spots on her cheeks and around the eyes. Her eyes were like little brown beads, permanently screwed up tight against the veil of cigarette smoke that enveloped her.

Mitchell Court had two creaking lifts with great metal doors that were always highly polished. Some of the old ladies who lived in the block had to wait for someone to come along to open the doors for them they were so heavy. Dollie Trubbock had an African maid called Ellen who had to keep the public areas clean. I never saw her without a duster in her hand, and when she wasn't polishing the lift doors she was buffing the lobby floor with a giant tin of red Johnson's Wax. 'You never know,' Dollie would say portentously, 'when the owner of the building might stop by.' No one who lived in the building had ever seen the owner, and we doubted that he ever bothered to visit. Dollie never called Ellen by her name. If she saw one of her favoured tenants struggling with a heavy load of shopping she would say, 'Leave your bags in the lobby. I'll get my *munt* to carry that them up for you.' And if Dollie was angry she would scurry along the balcony shouting, 'WHERE'S THE MUNT?'

After a time we stopped taking the lift up to our flat because Dollie kept her apartment door open so that she could hear who was coming and going. If the lift stopped on her floor, she would come to the door to check who was in it, and if you were in her good books she invited you in for a cup of tea. Once you were inside she could talk for hours, mostly gossip about other tenants in the block. She got offended if you tried to leave too soon, probably because she was short of company. 'The trouble with being the supervisor for the building is that I can never leave!' she would whine. 'My job is like being a doctor, you know, I have to be on call twenty-four hours a day in case of an emergency, and in case the owner makes a surprise visit. He relies on me to keep up standards, you know.'

Back in Ireland, Dad had told me he had found Mum a great place to live, with a lovely woman in charge, who would look after Mum. Dad had found the apartment from a newspaper ad, which was cheaper than going through an agent. Dollie had turned on the charm to get Mum and Dad to rent the flat. 'When is the Major coming back again?' she would enquire with a simpering smile. 'Such a handsome man, your father. We need men like that in the building.'

It was part of the supervisor's job to make sure none of the flats stayed empty and she would promise new tenants whatever they wanted to hear to get them to sign a lease. Dollie was a pathological liar. I met her the day Mum collected me from the airport and I could tell she was deranged. 'Your Mom has told me all about you,' she oozed. 'And how clever you are. Don't worry about going back to Ireland for University – I know all the Professors here, and I can get you in to Wits. No problem.'

The University of the Witwatersrand, which everyone called 'Wits' (though with her strong accent she made it sound like *Vutz*) was not far from Hillbrow in the neighbouring district of Braamfontein. Dollie and her family weren't South Africans, they were Rhodesians who had fled south because of the guerrilla war. Noticing that I wore glasses, she asked me why I didn't get contact lenses, and then said she was a qualified optometrist and could fit them for me and give me a good discount. At other times she said she had worked as a veterinary surgeon in Rhodesia, and then a few days later would say she had been a nurse. The claims she made were so outlandish that no one bothered to challenge them.

Dollie was married to Geoff, and they had two obese children, Norma and Brendan. She didn't want her son doing military service. 'My boy isn't going to be killed by the bloody *munts*,' she would say. Part of the deal with being supervisor of Mitchell Court was that they didn't pay rent.

The only time we took the lift was to get up to the tenth floor. From there you could take the stairs up one more flight and get onto the roof. Albert, the night watchman had a shack on the roof and he slept there during the day. Mum kept our wooden packing cases up there and she sent me up occasionally to check if anything had been stolen. The roof areas of all the apartment blocks in Hillbrow were forbidden, forgotten places where the raw working parts of the buildings were hidden. Up there you could see the clutter of TV aerials on all the other buildings, like a metal forest sticking into the sky. On our building there was a big metal water tank and a few brick outhouses which had originally been built as servants' quarters. Dollie Trubbock didn't allow anyone to keep a maid on the premises so people used the shacks to store things they didn't want in their apartments. Mum didn't like going up there. I would walk to the edge of the roof and look down onto the street and wonder what it would be like to jump.

———————

Mum went back to work the day after I arrived in Johannesburg and I was on my own. She explained how to catch the bus into the city so I could meet her during lunch hour. Suddenly, in this city where she had made a new life, I was being treated as an independent adult.

Getting the bus was a good thing. Sunbeam electric trolley-buses ran between the terminus at the bottom of Troye Street towards Hillbrow and the northern suburbs. They looked just like London double-deckers except they were dull maroon instead of red, and they were powered by overhead electrical cables that made a *click-clunk* sound as the connector crossed over a join in the wire. At night you could see sparks flaring from the power line as they went over a bump in the road, *fizz-thwunk*. For us, the easiest route from the city centre was to take the Number 18 to Hillbrow, or the Number 19 to Yeoville though it meant getting off at the end of Pretoria Street and walking back. Sometimes I took the 79A Parktown North (via Zoo Lake) because they carried a better class of passenger. For about twenty minutes I could pretend I was one of them, going all the way to the smartest part of town. The Parktown buses were never so busy either, because not many people out there needed to take the bus anyway. I liked sitting upstairs in the front seats. When pedestrians crossed in front of the bus the flat front made it seem as though they were going under the wheels for certain.

On cold winter mornings the buses were deliciously warm, and in summer storms there was nothing to beat the muggy feeling of being inside when the hailstones came down like machine-gun fire on the metal roof. Then the windows fogged up and the schoolgirls from Jeppe High drew their initials inside love-hearts with arrows and wrote obscene messages on the glass with their fingertips. The traffic slowed to a crawl but the showers passed swiftly, and afterwards the hot tarmac gave off little clouds of steam and the wheels made a juicy *squish-thrumm* through the puddles.

From the top deck, I looked down at the busy pavements and the purposeful walkers who I imagined all led more normal lives than we did. On Pritchard Street, shoppers crowded into John Orr's department store and the giant OK Bazaars. Down on Von Brandis Street I would see the advocates scurrying up the steps to the Supreme Court in their gowns and white wigs and pin-striped trousers. Riding on the bus made me feel safe. Those short journeys were a time of sanctuary and calm, all for the price of forty cents.

Staying with Mum meant getting a job. Going to university and leaving her behind didn't seem like a realistic option anymore, and I wrote to Dad and told him I wanted to defer my place at Queen's. Then, I answered an advertisement in the *Star* and started selling household items door-to-door in the evenings. In those days you could still walk up to people's houses at night and not get shot at. The business was run by an Englishman called Terry, and his very beautiful wife Shelley. She was South African and officially classified as Coloured, but to live in Hillbrow they pretended she was from Mauritius, which was where they went for their wedding to get around the laws preventing mixed-race marriages. Terry hired students to sell things like dusters and aprons, gardening gloves and sponges to housewives in the white suburbs. We were all trained to tell the customers that we needed the money for our studies, and that a proportion of the sales went to an animal welfare charity. We had photocopied letters from the Johannesburg municipal authorities verifying Terry's charitable status and most people would buy something.

Three nights a week Terry took a team of six or seven of us out in his minivan and dropped us outside a block of flats or at the end of a road and left us to sell. At the end of the night we got paid our commission in cash. After a few weeks, I realised that the job wasn't going to earn me enough money to make a real difference to our lives but at least I gained some selling experience. In Ireland I had never had so much as a paper round. Then I answered another ad, this time for a job with a company called Systems for Education.

The idea was to sell home-education kits for parents, and cash in on South Africa's relative isolation from the rest of the world. There were almost no educational programmes on TV for young children, and in the provincial towns it was hard to find books. The product was a subscription to a service that delivered everything parents needed to give their pre-schoolers a 'hunger for knowledge'. Once you paid up, you got everything you could need to stimulate your toddler to take an interest in the alphabet, spelling, reading and maths. It was all carefully structured and designed by teachers to allow the parents to tutor their kids up until the age of seven. The product was perfectly good, but the selling was high pressure. Once again, I joined a team that canvassed a neighbourhood in the afternoon, trying to set up appointments with housewives to return that evening to make a presentation to them and their husbands when they got back from work.

In order to sell effectively I had to get both parents to sit through a forty-five minute presentation using a flip-chart and examples of the teaching materials that they would receive from the company as their child grew. The husbands were usually tired and grumpy after a day at work, and not impressed that their wives had committed their evening to a door-to-door salesman. The key to success was getting 'positive feedback and engagement' from both husband and wife during the tightly scripted demonstration. If either one of the couple didn't speak up and say 'yes' at any stage of the presentation, I was taught to stop and go back over the point and ask them again if they thought the system would be a 'good way of teaching your child how to read?' If they mumbled or didn't seem to be paying attention, then we were taught to stop altogether. 'I'm sorry Mrs Smith, your husband doesn't seem to agree that this system will give your child an advantage when it comes to starting school.'

Usually, this would embarrass the husband into affirming his commitment to giving his child the best possible start in life. If I made it through the entire presentation and got positive feedback at every stage of the process then there was no logical way that the parents could argue that they weren't sure the product was right for them. The only possible reason they could give for not purchasing the system was lack of funds. Even then, I was taught to go through the family budget, and ask if they thought the cost of two packets of cigarettes per day for the next seven years was too much to pay for their child's future. It wasn't exactly blackmail, but it had a similar effect.

Turning up on people's doorsteps and trying to convince them to sign up to an expensive monthly subscription wasn't easy, but most people were friendly. Sometimes they took pity on me and offered me cups of tea, or a cold drink as refreshments. 'You poor dear,' an elderly woman said to me one day. 'You're not used to this climate – let me get you a drink.' She produced a deliciously sweet pink liquid which left a gritty sensation on my teeth. 'That's guava juice,' she announced. 'You've never had it before have you? Well, let me tell you it has more vitamins in it than any other fruit. Make sure you keep drinking it as long as you live here.'

The real snag with the job was the dogs. Most of the houses were surrounded by chain-link fencing, and on the gate would be a small pressed metal sign saying *Beware of the Dog*. Usually, it was bilingual: *Pasop vir die Hond*. And the dogs were always large breeds, especially Rhodesian ridge-backs, dobermanns and rottweilers. Often, they lived perma-nently in the gardens and weren't what I would call household pets. There were stories in the newspapers about African maids and gardeners going to visit neighbouring servants and being torn to pieces by vicious dogs. I quickly learned that dogs belonging to white people were usually only aggressive towards black visitors. They might run towards me and bark madly, but they stopped short of an actual bite. Even so, the sight of three or four dobermanns running towards me across the lawn was unnerving. After a few such incidents, I learned that it was best to rattle the gate as loudly as possible before walking up the front path. Any dogs roaming the property usually pricked up their ears at the sound of the gate and came out to investigate. If I ruled out the houses with the warning signs on the gates I wouldn't have made any sales at all. One night I called at a house and rang the bell. There was no reply, and as I turned to leave I found the way barred by a large male boxer dog. It didn't bark, and it hadn't made any sound as it sneaked up on me. But when I tried to move away from the door it bared its teeth and uttered a long, low, deep growl. It was clear that if I took more than one or two steps from the door it would attack. I had to stand motionless on the front step for an hour before the owners returned.

Another day I approached a house in the working-class suburb of Alberton, south of Johannesburg. The house was set well back from the gate and I walked up a brick driveway leading up one side of the house, hoping to find the front door. Rattling the gate had not produced a sign of any dogs. A metal door led into a yard behind the house, but it was locked and I realised I could not get to the front door. As I retreated down the path a woman's head appeared at a high window on the side of the house. She seemed to be standing on a chair to reach the narrow skylight window and from behind burglar bars she whispered; 'Where's the dog?'

'Good afternoon, Madam,' I began my spiel. 'I'm in the neighbourhood today talking to parents with young children, I wonder if I could—'

'KEEP QUIET!' she hissed. 'Where's the dog?'

'I haven't seen a dog, can we talk at the front door?'

'No!' The woman seemed terrified. 'I can't come out. The dog will kill me! You have to leave.'

It was clear that this was no ordinary dog, but the path and front garden were empty. The front of the house had a sliding glass window facing the lawn, and I told the woman that I would meet her there. 'Then you can take me to the gate,' I suggested.

'Why did you come into my garden,' she continued, still whispering. 'There's a sign on the gate warning you about the dog.'

'Everyone has one of those signs,' I answered. 'I rattled the gate, and there was no dog.'

'Quickly, get round to the front of the house!' Her head disappeared and the window slammed shut.

As she opened the sliding door I attempted to continue my sales routine. 'Shut up! You don't understand. MY DOG WILL KILL YOU!'

The woman was pale and nervous. Suddenly, all I wanted to do was leave. But the front gate seemed a long way away. Just as she was explaining that her husband was the only person who could control the dog, I saw it. It was coming around the side of the house at speed, its mouth agape in a state of high excitement. An enormous red tongue lolled from its mouth, spraying drool as it ran. It was the biggest, heaviest dog I had ever seen, something like a mastiff crossed with a great dane. It didn't bark or growl but it had red-rimmed eyes and it was coming in for the kill. I just had time to swing my briefcase with all my strength and catch the dog in the eye as it lunged for my leg. Looking down I saw that it had turned its head to one side – like a shark – to take my whole thigh into its jaws. Without thinking, I pushed the woman out of the way, not noticing that there was a sofa behind her. She toppled backwards, legs in the air as I fell through the open door and slammed it behind me. There were four holes in my trousers and I could feel blood trickling down my leg. I ran through the house looking for a bathroom where I could inspect the damage. Luckily, my blow had made the dog hesitate momentarily as it clamped its upper and lower canines around my thigh. If it had bitten down hard, the back of my leg would have been taken off. Seconds later, I heard the woman screaming.

'We'll sue you! The dog's all excited – he's jumped over the gate. If he finds a child he'll kill it!'

As I mopped up the wound I tried to reason with the woman, who was now hysterical. 'I'm phoning my husband! He'll have you arrested for trespassing. Give me your name!'

'Tom Jones,' I babbled, and ran down the path, all the time looking out for the hound from hell. It was nowhere to be seen. I limped as far as I could and lay down in the shade of a hedge for the rest of the afternoon and evening. Later, I saw the woman with a man whom I took to be her husband driving around the streets looking for the dog. For about a year I carried four dark marks on either side of my thigh as a souvenir.

One day the sales leader told me I had to go on a road trip with two of the Afrikaans speaking team. Kobus and Willie were not the brightest members of the sales force, and a large part of the five-day trip was spent arguing about how to find our way from one town to the next. Kobus had a battered Ford Escort with filthy leather seats. The back seat, which I occupied, was littered with sweet wrappers, a spare car battery, odd pieces of wire and dog-eared copies of *Scope* magazine with its signature photos of busty young women. Kobus drove fast, and I was in a permanent state of fear that we were going to die in a head-on collision with one of the articulated lorries that thundered towards Johannesburg carrying produce from the farmlands. For hour after hour we drove along the straight featureless roads of the Transvaal, passing through dull, heat-stricken *dorps* with names like Bakerville and Koster. The tarmac shimmered under its heat halo and dirt tracks led off to unseen farmhouses tucked behind clumps of thorn trees. Once a secretary bird with its elegant stilt-like legs and knobbly knees walked onto the tarmac ahead of the car. Kobus swerved to make sure he hit it and, as I looked back, I saw the bird struggling to rise, flapping one intact wing wildly from a jumble of feathers and gore. He and Willie laughed thuggishly when I said we should stop and make sure it was dead.

They conversed in Afrikaans almost all of the time, and it was clear they didn't like having me along. To save money we grilled sausages and lamb chops beside the road, and slept on the ground beside the car in sleeping bags. Every night they drank large amounts of Castle beer and tried to terrify me with tales of venomous *boomslangs* and spiders. I wrapped a shirt around my head and burrowed down inside my sleeping bag, clutching it tight around my neck.

The trip was a waste of time as far as sales went, because the communities we visited were mostly Afrikaans and not interested in receiving an English-language teaching system. They were poor areas too, without a book shop within a hundred miles, and the people we met didn't have any spare money. I made the only sale of the trip, and Kobus and Willie stopped speaking to me altogether.

A week later, when I got back to Johannesburg, Mum told me she had lost her job. In a stroke of bad luck, she had been spotted by Mr Lawson, the owner of the house that Mum and Dad had been renting after we were evicted. Mum's job at the Consulate involved standing in for the front-desk receptionist when she went on her lunch break. Lawson had come in to apply for a visa to visit the UK and had recognised her. He demanded to see her boss, and told them he was going to sue for breach of contract over the sale of the house. The Consular Officer fired her the same day.

'We represent Her Britannic Majesty's Government,' said the pompous administrator. 'You'll have to leave. We cannot possibly afford even the slightest breath of scandal.'

My earnings from Systems for Education were sporadic, and couldn't be relied upon to pay the rent on time every month.

'You don't have to worry about that,' said Mum cheerfully. 'I'm going to open a shop.'

To my horror, she revealed that she had already signed the lease on a small shop in the Village Market at the end of Pretoria Street.

'But what are you going to sell?' I demanded.

'I've still got a few bits of furniture, and some pictures in the packing cases up on the roof. And I'm going to start going to auctions like I did in Ireland.' Her tone was defensive.

There was nothing left to argue about. We had enough money to pay the next month's rent on the flat, and not much more. But my commission from the sale I had made on the road trip would take at least a month to come through. That night I lay awake on the sofa-bed in the living room and wondered how I could earn a more reliable income. Just as I drifted into sleep I had an idea: I would go to the Carlton Hotel and ask for a job. If they wanted someone with experience, I would tell them I had worked in an hotel in Ireland. It wasn't just the money I wanted, it was the chance to escape from the flat and be part of a more civilised world. It would be like working in *Grand Hotel* (Greta Garbo, Lionel Barrymore, 1932).

Africa's Greatest Hotel

'You've got the right sort of voice,' the personnel officer told me. 'We'll put you in room service.'

Six days a week, and four all-night shifts each month, I sat behind a Perspex window in an office tucked into one corner of the main kitchen at the Carlton Hotel.

In front of me there were four telephones, and beside each one was a little box which magically, it seemed to me, displayed the room number of the incoming caller. The job was straightforward. Pick up the phone – which must never be allowed to ring more than three times – and take the order.

'Good morning, Timothy speaking. How can I help you?'

I had to write out an order slip and then punch it out on the cash register. Then I would pass the order slip – which now had a time stamped upon it – out to the room service waiters. The Carlton had six-hundred bedrooms, and the room service team had eight waiters during the day and four at night. But there was only ever one cashier, and a manager who some-times helped answer the phones if things got too busy.

Sometimes, famous guests would call down and order something. Silvia Kristel, star of the *Emmanuelle* films was one I remember, and Richard Kiel, the giant actor who played the Bond villain 'Jaws' (*The Spy Who Loved Me*, 1977). I also spoke to two of the stars from *Dallas*, Victoria Principal and Patrick Duffy. Apart from being Bobby Ewing in *Dallas*, Duffy was also well known as *The Man from Atlantis*. He stayed in the hotel for more than a week and always said the same thing to me. 'Good mornin', Tim. This is Mr. Duffy in room 1602. I'd like to order some brown bread toast and a pot of coffee.' It felt weird talking to a character from *Dallas*, but I liked the way his Southern accent made my name sound like *Tee-erm*.

I also spoke to Anatoly Karpov, the World Chess Champion. 'Ah, the man who plays chess,' I blurted out when I heard his thick Russian tones.

'Yes,' he replied. 'Do you play tchyess?'

'No. Not really,' I stammered. 'What would you like to order?'

I built up a slightly better relationship with Ilie Năstase, then at the height of his fame as a tennis player. Late one night he ordered champagne and said he was having a party. We had spoken several times, and he suggested I should 'Come up and say hi.' I wasn't supposed to go up to any of the guest rooms, but I couldn't resist the temptation to meet him. He was wearing a yellow Hawaiian shirt and he was flanked by two young, attractive women, his arms clutched around their waists. He had to let go of the women in order to sign the room service bill and I told him I had watched him at Wimbledon many times. He shook my hand, and I left.

Very occasionally, an order slip would go missing, or a waiter would drop his tray and an irate guest would ring to find out what had happened to their meal. If the delay was my fault, I learned that the only way to avoid embarrassment was to answer that caller with a false voice and name. The magic numbers meant I knew which guest was calling before I answered. In a false voice, I could then apologise for 'Timothy's mistake' and offer to rectify it immediately. Occasionally, if I was bored, I would play tricks on the guests by answering in a range of false accents or pretending to be the housekeeping department.

After a time, my need for diversion required more elaborate games. Guests had to call room service in order to obtain a key for the mini-bar. Ordinarily, I would send the key up to the room with one of the waiters, and then we would know to check the bar in that room each day, and bill for any drinks used. But sometimes I would tell the guest that the key was in the room already and they just needed to retrieve it from under the carpet beneath the bedroom window.

'The carpet is nailed down very tightly,' they would report breathlessly.

'Ah, you've got one of the new rooms, sir. I'll send you a key with one of our waiters.'

If I suspected that the guest was particularly gullible I would sometimes tell them to look for the key in the bathroom. There was a metal bottle-opener screwed to the cabinet housing the sink, and I would tell them to put their finger inside the metal bracket and press the button to open the hidden drawer containing the room key.

'Nothing happened when I pressed it!'

'I'm very sorry, sir. I'll send a waiter straight away with a replacement key.'

I didn't play these tricks often, and I was always extremely polite.

Speaking to the guests by telephone taught me that you can't judge what a person will look like just by the sound of their voice. It was even difficult to tell how old someone might be. Over a period of days, sometimes weeks, it was possible to build a relationship with the unseen guests, and constant exposure allowed me to treat the telephone as an intimate tool. It is skill I still possess, I am unhampered by the disembodied nature of the line. On several occasions, but usually late at night, I was invited to go up to guests' rooms; mostly by men, but sometimes by women. Hotel regulations forbade it, but I was never quite brave enough anyway. I had never had a girlfriend and although I enjoyed flirting over the phone the idea of a face-to-face encounter was intimidating.

The Carlton had several permanent residents, and many regular guests whom I got to know because they stayed so often. They loved it when I recognised their voice even before they gave me their name. One of the Carlton's most frequent guests was a flamboyant clothes designer called Mrs Apfelschimmel. She had helped choose some of the hotel furnishings and frequently came in to advise on new curtains and the choice of parasols that were dotted around the pool deck. Late one night she rang to order some champagne, and kept me on the phone far longer than necessary. She kept telling me I was 'a sweet boy with an adorable English accent'. About half an hour later, she rang again.

'Timothy, you know I talk to you every time I stay here, and yet we've never met!' she slurred. 'I need more champagne. And I think you should bring me my order personally this time.'

'Well, I can't really leave the phones,' I said cautiously. 'Perhaps we could meet in the Lobby for a drink tomorrow?'

'No, no. I INSIST that you bring a bottle of champagne to my room.'

Innocent though I might have been, I could tell that Mrs Apfelschimmel wanted more than bubbly. But I played dumb, until eventually, she was forced to make herself very clear.

'Timothy, you have an incredibly sexy voice,' she purred. 'If you bring me the champagne I'll give you a very special surprise.'

I was beginning to get scared. I had seen Mrs Apfelschimmel walking around the hotel. She was slim, suntanned and wore figure-hugging clothes, especially tight black leather trousers that could best show it off. But she was in her mid-fifties, and I was seventeen.

'I'm sorry Mrs Apfelschimmel,' I stammered, 'but I'm not allowed to visit the guest rooms.'

'Timothy, I am a friend of the General Manager. If you don't bring me my champagne, I will telephone him in the morning, and you will be sacked!'

'You're within your rights to do that,' I said as calmly as I could. 'But if I leave the phones then no one else will be able to order anything from room service tonight.'

'Timothy! You have five minutes to get up here with a bottle of champagne. And, by the way, can you guess what I'm wearing tonight?'

'No. I don't think I can.'

'I'm wearing my cowboy boots!'

I despatched a waiter called Philemon with the champagne, and he returned in a state of high excitement. 'Sho! Sho! That white lady, she is crazy! She opened the door without no clothes! Nothing! Only her boots with silver buckles,' he said shaking his head and sucking his teeth. 'Eesh! She is very angry. She says you must go to the room now!'

All of the waiters guffawed loudly as they listened to Philemon's description of what he had seen on the seventeenth floor. All night I watched the magic boxes nervously, but Mrs Apfelschimmel didn't ring again. And the next time she stayed at the hotel she didn't refer to our conversation.

At the end of each shift, I would take a final reading from the cash register and tally up the bills that were charged to the rooms. I also had to pay out any tips added to the bill by the guest from my cash float. Best of all, any bills that had to be charged to the guest's room account had to be placed into a bullet shaped canister and sent down to reception in a pneumatic tube just like the ones in Cleaver's department store in Belfast.

Above the lobby, the main kitchen occupied almost half of the first floor of The Carlton. One floor below, the Koffie Huis had its own kitchen which operated from six a.m. until midnight, and in the basement there was a twenty-four hour staff kitchen, and a cold store as well as a pastry kitchen where all of the hotel's bread was made and baked. On the thirtieth floor there was also a small hot kitchen making hamburgers and simple grilled dishes for the pool-deck, and yet another kitchen that served the Top of the Carlton nightclub. The ballroom, one floor up from the main restaurant level could accommodate 2,000 guests and had a kitchen of its own. But none of them could compete with the main kitchen for noise and drama. This was an empire ruled over by Wolfgang Leyrer, the Executive Chef. When he barked, everyone jumped.

Mr Leyrer was well over six feet tall, and like all of the chefs he wore wooden clogs that boosted his height by another two inches. At our end of the kitchen we didn't need to involve the chefs for the simplest orders. Room service waiters could get their own hot water, coffee, biscuits, milk and sugar, cutlery and linens for the trays and trolleys that went up to the rooms. All other food items had to be ordered from either the cold kitchen or the hot kitchen, and without an order slip nothing left that kitchen. I was allowed to make myself tea in the kitchen and take it back to the office, but Mr Leyrer once caught me drinking a glass of milk.

'You're fined!' came a bellow from the other end of the kitchen. 'Make out a bill for ten rand and send the copy to my office!'

My monthly pay was only three hundred and twenty rand. Milk, I now knew, counted as 'food', and was therefore off-limits except when served in a jug with tea. Ten rand was a significant amount of money, but luckily one of the other cashiers showed me how to print a bill on the cash machine that could be cancelled afterwards without going through the accounts department.

The rent at Mitchell Court was two hundred and forty rand a month, and except for the money Mum could earn at the shop it was our only regular income. I paid the rent and I needed some cash for travelling to and from the hotel. To save money I ate as much as possible at the hotel. The shifts were eight hours long, seven a.m. until three in the afternoon, or three until eleven. Night shift was supposed to finish at seven a.m. but if breakfast was very busy then you were expected to stay for an hour extra to help the next cashier man the phones. Morning shift was the toughest because it was when the room service waiters were working flat out. On that shift you were also taking people's lunch orders, whereas afternoons were generally quiet because very few guests took dinner in their room. During the overnight shift it was possible not to receive any orders between midnight and five a.m., but then by six a.m. all hell broke loose as the breakfast rush began. I didn't mind doing the morning shift because it entitled me to have my own breakfast and lunch in the staff canteen. I would arrive at the hotel by six-thirty, in time to get some tea and toast in the canteen, and then have a proper breakfast around ten when all of the guests had finished. On the afternoon shift, I was just entitled to have dinner.

In the hotel, the Executive Chef was second in power only to the General Manager. Then came the sous-chefs who cooked for the two main restaurants. They were all Europeans, mostly Austrians, Swiss and Germans. The only Africans were one or two commis-chefs in the main kitchen, and the ladies who ran the cold-kitchen producing the desserts, cheese platters and salads for the restaurants and room service.

All drinks had to be ordered from the service bar, which was run by a pair of elderly Portuguese men named José and Fernando. The barmen were a law unto themselves cloistered behind a mesh security barrier to protect the valuable beverages when the kitchen was unattended, but the hotel had its own rigid pecking order. The cold-kitchen chefs were somehow inferior to those in the hot kitchen. Serving staff, white or black, were merely plate-carriers and room service waiters (who were all Africans) were only one rung above the busmen, whose sole responsibility was to clear dirty plates from the side-stands inside the restaurants; removing the empty plates from the table was only done by the waiters.

The main function of the kitchen was to supply the two restaurants that led off it: The Three Ships and El Gaucho. The restaurants occupied the floor above the lobby, and were separated by a central area which was used by the hotel as a gallery and exhibition space. Three Ships waiters were accorded a little bit of respect by the chefs, but not much. Styling itself 'the best restaurant in Africa', The Three Ships was a subtly lit, opulent cocoon. Apart from the hotel guests, important South Africans came to lunch there, including figures from politics and the stock exchange. Like all five-star hotels, The Carlton was exempt from apartheid, and welcomed prominent and wealthy black South Africans. For very important visitors the restaurant had a private room, known as the Captain's Table. In the evenings, a man in a white dinner jacket sat at a grand piano tinkling out a selection of gently arranged show tunes and love songs. Giant glass bowls filled with fresh lilies sat on side tables, and the walls were covered in dark oak panelling decorated with original oil paintings in gilt frames. The diners' plates arrived at the table simultaneously, and the food was concealed under large silver cloches. The waiters always knew which dish to place in front of each diner, and at a signal from the maitre d', the cloches would be whisked away with a graceful flourish to reveal the sumptuously arranged meals beneath. All of the waiters were male, and white. They wore smart midnight-blue jackets with gold braid, and prepared exotic spectacles like Lobster Fra Diavolo in silver chafing dishes at the table. Wine was served in over-sized goblets with long, long stems that were so coveted the guests often tried to steal them.

El Gaucho was different. Themed as a South American steak restaurant, it was as loud and brash as The Three Ships was elegant and stuffy. Buxom waitresses in tightly ruched peasant blouses cooked slabs of prime steak in front of the customers who sat on high chairs around a grille. Every night was party-night in El Gaucho, with a live trio of strolling minstrels complete with bandoleers, playing guitar and maracas.

I liked working as a cashier because I didn't have to wear uniform, just a name tag pinned to my shirt. If I took a break, I could unpin the badge and walk through the public areas of the hotel, mingling with the guests and other staff without anyone paying much attention. Sometimes I went up to the pool-deck and walked around the pool, but my favourite excursion was to the restaurant-level lobby to look at the paintings hanging on the walls. Once they had an elephant exhibition by the wildlife artist David Shepherd, and another time it was work by Sir Peter Scott. I would slip out several times a day to look at one canvas in particular, a large painting of snow geese flying across a vast marshy landscape. It represented a world as far from Johannesburg's city streets as I could imagine.

If I worked the evening shift, Mum made me promise to take a taxi home. After a time I discovered that there were several waitresses at El Gaucho who also lived in Hillbrow. I would have to wait an hour or more for them to finish work, but then we could share a taxi. My favourite was Vivienne, a Swiss girl with porcelain skin and pale blue eyes. She was extremely beautiful and if she was on duty I would wait as long as necessary to share a taxi with her. Quite often she wouldn't take my money, as she knew that she earned much more than me in tips alone. I wanted to ask her out on a date but I knew I couldn't afford it.

There were four of us to cover the three shifts in room service. We worked a six-day week, but the overnight shift, from eleven p.m. until seven thirty a.m. was always covered by the same man, named Solomon. I only ever saw him for a few minutes when we changed shift. One night a week, one of the room service managers worked Solomon's shift, and once a month the daytime cashiers worked three nights in a row so that he could have some normal days off. Apart from me, the other two daytime cashiers were women, Michele and Sally. Sally was Welsh, and suffered badly with her nerves. Sometimes she would stay and talk to me during my shift, even when she was supposed to go home. I learned that she suffered from panic-attacks, claustrophobia and agoraphobia, things I had never heard of before.

There were two ways of leaving our office in the kitchen: either by taking the service lifts down into the basement or by walking out through El Gaucho and taking the escalator down to the Lobby. On a bad day, Sally wouldn't go in the service lift because of her claustrophobia. Even if she could get into the lift she was scared of the basement area which was a maze of windowless corridors. Her best option was to walk through El Gaucho, but getting to the escalators meant crossing an expanse of carpet that she said made her 'feel dizzy'. One night she went to the lavatory and stayed away for three hours.

Meanwhile, back in our office the manager had taken over the phones and couldn't leave them to find out what had happened. Eventually, when the phones finally went quiet for the night he left the office unattended to look for Sally.

'It was awful, Tim,' she told me the next day. 'I just thought about walking across all that carpet and then having to go into El Gaucho and be surrounded by all those people who might stare at me. I was petrified. I could not leave the toilet cubicle.'

After long negotiations through the locked door, the manager was able to persuade her to leave the lavatory. He escorted her back to the office, but after that he never let her go on a break when he was on duty. One day I came in to work and noticed that the swivel chair we used was missing. Without the swivel chair it was difficult to answer the phones and then turn to use the cash register in one fluid movement. 'I'm sorry,' Sally explained, 'but the manager wouldn't let me take a break so I peed in the chair. I just couldn't help it.'

Sally was about forty, which seemed quite old to me at the time. After a few months, I realised that she had started drinking heavily, and was unable to balance her bills and charges at the end of her shift. She would wait for me to come on duty and ask me to do it for her. I didn't mind, because I was fond of her. Like Mum, she had been forced into working for a living comparatively late in life.

'You understand me, Timmy,' she would confide, her breath sweetened with the whiskey miniatures she stashed in her handbag alongside bottles of tranquilisers. 'You're from a good family. We're better than all this riff-raff in South Africa. But you'll see. One day things will take a turn for the better.'

Sally told me she was separated from her South African husband and that they had a young child. She said she wanted to go back to the UK, but her husband had custody of her son. 'That bastard told the judge I was emotionally unstable! Can you believe it?' Then she laughed. 'I suppose I am, but *he* made me that way.'

'I'm a prisoner here,' Sally would say. She had a great sense of humour, but her nerves were a constant debilitation. 'I've got a very good psychiatrist who's helping me a lot,' she told me one day. 'But now, I can't afford to pay his bill so he's taking me to court. And that's giving me more panic attacks! Isn't that brilliant – my psychiatrist is making me crazy!'

After a time, Sally's drinking started to interfere with her job at the Carlton. She was sacked, but later when I was at University, she sometimes visited Mum at the shop and asked how I was doing. Her nerves made it impossible for Sally to hold a steady job. She started working as what she called a 'hostess'. In fact, she worked for an escort agency. Mum tried to persuade her to go back to the UK where she could at least get some social security benefits, and be close to her own mother who still lived in Wales. 'I'm a hooker,' Sally confessed. 'Who would have believed things would turn out this way? But if I go back to the UK, I'll never see my son.'

A couple of years later I saw Sally for the last time. It was late one night on Banket Street. She was wearing a satin skirt that was too tight, and high heels with ankle straps. She had put on weight, and was stumbling unsteadily along the pavement clutching tightly onto the arm of a man in a cheap safari suit. I tucked myself into a doorway as they passed, so that she wouldn't recognise me.

Engelbert and the Malamute

Our Victorian house in Ireland had two sitting rooms. We mostly used the one that we called the playroom because we kept our toys and our board games in there. It was where we all sat to watch the TV. It wasn't scruffy exactly, but none of the playroom furniture matched, and the dogs were allowed in there to snooze in front of the fire. On the other side of the hall was the green room, so-called because the carpet and the three-piece suite were the same colour. Pets were banned from there, and children were only allowed in on special occasions. When Mum gave a dinner party it was where the grown-ups sat with their drinks and little bowls of crisps and nuts before moving to the dining room, and when the vicar called, he was given tea in the green room. It was big enough for several nice pieces of antique furniture, all of Mum's blue oriental china and the walls had space to hang several large pictures. On the back wall there were three oriental scenes that Mum had bought in Malaya and had framed when she got back to Ireland.

I would point them out proudly to my friends when I showed them the green room. They were framed with non-reflective glass and it gave the prints a slightly matte effect, which added to their allure and made them seem extra-special treasures. The scenes were hand-painted on rice paper. One had two fighting elephants wearing elaborate body armour with mahouts and howdahs on their backs, another was of three richly caparisoned horses and the third was of two Balinese dancing girls with pointy hats and curly-toed slippers. The horses were depicted in mid-jump, so that they seemed to be flying, and the dancing girls had long graceful fingers and serene smiles.

'When you grow up, you'll each have one of those pictures,' Mum said. As the eldest, I was allowed first choice and said I would like the elephants.

When Mum set up the Whatnot in Johannesburg, the first thing I noticed was the three black frames hanging on the wall. I also spotted my collection of antique keys, things I had found at auctions in Ireland. They were large iron keys from ancient doors rubbed smooth with age. My stuffed animals from Malaya were also on display. Almost everything came from the packing cases we had brought out from Ireland.

'I just want the shop to look full,' Mum claimed. 'Don't worry, I won't sell anything you really want to keep.'

But that's how it was in The Whatnot. At first, Mum had only our own possessions to sell. Everything went eventually, even my collection of Biggles books and ornamental weapons, including Dad's own regimental sword. The Kit Carson annual lasted more than a year, but my stuffed cobra wrestling with the mongoose and the three batik prints with their non-reflective glass were sold within a few weeks of the shop's opening. Mum had no spare capital, and every month she would have to start again with a virtually clean slate. First, she had to make enough profit to pay the rent, and then to feed us. After that, the next priority was to buy more stock. One month she sold her emerald engagement ring, and a few years later when she was truly desperate she even sold her blue sapphire, the one that she had bought in Colombo on the way to Malaya.

Gradually, people started offering her things that she could buy and resell, and she started going to auctions and house clearances to get more stock. As a retailer, she also built up a network of scrap dealers and jewellers who would sell her stuff at trade or even scrap-metal prices. But quite soon, we all learned that anything, no matter how much sentimental value it possessed, could be sold. Sometimes we hid things that we thought Mum might take to the shop.

For some years, I despised anyone who became too attached to their material possessions. If I wasn't allowed to keep anything, then I didn't see why anyone else should. Friends could never impress me with their cars, clothes or watches. Having hoarded stamps, keys, stuffed animals, silver match-boxes and a host of other things when we lived in Ireland, I lost the desire to collect. I couldn't afford to invest either money, or emotion in 'things'. Now, the only things I will allow myself to acquire are books, but not because they have any resale value. Very occasionally, I will see an object that I would like to buy, but I almost always convince myself that I don't need it in my life unless it has a clear practical purpose. Almost no material object has any sentimental value now.

Mum spent long hours at the shop, and if I was working an early shift I wouldn't see her until the evening. After work one day, I walked into the flat to find Mum sitting drinking tea in the sitting room. 'Don't go into my bedroom,' she chuckled. 'You might get a fright.'

I imagined that the cats or the dogs had caused some damage, or perhaps one of them had died. Naturally, I went to investigate. A shirtless suntanned man with a frothy bib of grey chest hair was hopping on one leg beside Mum's bed as he tried to put on his trousers. I backed out to join Mum in the sitting room.

'That's George the Greek,' she said with an impish smile. 'I invited him back for some tea, and while I was in the kitchen he disappeared. I thought he was in the loo, but after a time I heard him calling out in a hide-and-seek voice: *Pa-mee, I'm in hee-er.*'

'When I went into the bedroom he was stretched out on top of the bed. Stark naked. And,' she said coyly, 'he was very excited. He patted the bed and asked me if I'd like to find out what it is like to have a Greek lover!'

Just then, George emerged fully dressed and said he was leaving.

Afterwards, Mum said she was insulted that he thought she would find a man of his age attractive. But, at the same time, she was highly amused.

'You must have known what he wanted!' I said angrily. 'What possessed you to allow him to come to the flat? You can't be trusted!'

Mum started laughing. 'Oh, don't be so pompous. I'm old enough to look after myself, you don't have to worry about me. I bet none of your friends' mothers have naked Greeks in their bedrooms.'

Mum had a string of admirers at The Whatnot, most of them harmless. My least favourite was Piet, who was doing his National Service in the South African Defence Force. He was a tall, slim man, of about twenty. He had thick, glossy, dark hair and brilliant green eyes that seemed to glow from his deeply tanned face. They reminded me of a snake. When he had time off, he would hang around The Whatnot for hours, and then he started calling at the flat. He and Mum would sit drinking gin and tonic until late at night. She said we should feel sorry for Piet, because his mother was an alcoholic and he'd been beaten by his father.

I never knew why Mum let him visit so much. She seemed to want to look after him. I don't know whether he was interested in Mum because she was the mother he never had, or whether she was flattered that someone so young and handsome seemed to be in love with her. My brother and sister and I would sit in the room watching the TV, trying to ignore him. We never asked him anything or showed any interest in his life. I couldn't bear to look at him because his presence made me so angry. And watching Mum sitting next to him on the sofa made me feel ashamed. He just sat there sipping his drink, smoking cigarettes and talking to Mum in a voice so low we could barely hear what he was saying.

I slept on a sofa-bed in the sitting room, so Piet had to leave when I wanted to go to sleep. After he left, Mum would try to make me feel guilty about how I'd behaved.

'That poor boy hasn't got anyone. He's alone in this big city and we're his only friends.'

'I'm not his friend. I've got nothing to say to him.'

Piet wasn't educated, and I couldn't force myself to be civil to him. I was deeply suspicious of his motives, and he gave me the creeps. Because we lived on such a tight budget, I even resented Mum cooking for him. Piet was part of the life I hated. Going to work was always a relief, and I was glad that I only got one day off each week. Days off were never relaxing because they meant having to deal with the squalor of the flat where all four of us fought for space with six cats and two dogs. On weekdays, my brother would be at school and my sister had started going out to work in a hairdresser's, but if my day off fell on a Sunday we were all at home at the same time.

One Saturday, Piet came home from the shop with Mum when it closed at lunchtime. His presence irritated me so much that I took my brother to the cinema, and we went to the two o'clock showing at the Hillbrow Metro. We saw Jon Voight and Ricky Shroder in *The Champ* (1979). Afterwards we ate hot *shwarmas* at Mi-Vami, the Middle Eastern fast-food restaurant on Kotze Street. Those slivers of lamb drizzled with tahini sauce served inside pockets of hot pitta bread with chopped onion were a special treat that we couldn't afford very often. Back at the flat we found Mum and Piet were halfway through a bottle of gin, and I didn't want to be there too. We went back to the cinema and saw *Jaws 2* (Roy Scheider and Lorraine Gary, 1978). It was early evening when we returned to the flat for the second time, and Piet was gone. Mum was slightly drunk, but she was also in a state of high anxiety.

'Have you seen Piet?' she asked, rushing towards us as we came through the door. She said she had gone to lie down and when she woke up he was gone.

'So what?'

'He's taken something,' she said. 'I have to find him. Stay here while I go and look for him!'

Mum ran down the corridor towards the lifts, but a few minutes later she came back, saying we had to call the police. At first she wouldn't tell us what he'd done, but eventually she revealed that he'd taken her most valuable piece of jewellery. It was an 18-carat gold bracelet that Dad had given her years ago, and on it there was a different charm he had bought for each wedding anniversary. There were the usual things, gold hearts, a cat, a miniature Big Ben, several ornate fish (because Mum's birth-sign was Pisces), but some of them were very unusual. My favourite was a charm in the shape of a lobster pot. By undoing a tiny catch you could flip open the lid of the cage and see the miniature crustacean inside. The bracelet was the most valuable thing that Mum possessed, and along with her engagement ring it was the one thing she always swore she wouldn't sell.

I was angry at Piet, but also with Mum. At that moment I despised her for being taken in by the man. For about an hour, my brother and I went around the streets looking for any sign of Piet, but he was gone. Mum went down to the Vasco Da Gama corner shop and rang the police from the tickey-box. The police said they couldn't help: it wasn't a robbery because there was no violence, and it wasn't a burglary because she had let Piet into her own home. She came back sobbing with rage and frustration.

'I've got to find him,' she cried. She wanted to get a taxi and drive around the city looking for him but we persuaded her there was no point. And we didn't have enough money to get very far anyway. Eventually she calmed down and we made her go to bed to sleep off the gin. She was sure Piet would come back, but she didn't want us there if he did. 'If I could only talk to him,' she sobbed. 'I could make him understand how much the bracelet means to me, and if he needs money so badly, I'll lend it to him.'

Once she was sound asleep, and snoring, we left her in the flat, and went back to the cinema for a third time. This time it was *Moonraker* (Roger Moore, 1979). One day, about six months later, Piet reappeared at the shop. He told Mum he was sorry. He said he was an alcoholic and he'd sold the bracelet to a scrap metal dealer for two hundred rand: less than the value of any one of the twenty-three charms. Then he asked her to lend him some money. She gave him what she had, and we never heard from him again.

———————

Mrs Trubbock soon discovered that Mum didn't work at the Consulate anymore. And it was obvious that 'the Major' wasn't coming back from overseas anytime soon. Meanwhile my own holiday visit had now stretched into several months, and she started asking how long I would be staying in the flat.

Until I arrived, relations with the supervisor had been good but they gradually deteriorated. One day, Mum came home early and found Dollie inside our flat. Unknown to us, she had a spare key and claimed she was checking up on a leaking tap somewhere in the building. Mum changed the lock on the front door and Dollie freaked out. She decided we were not her friends anymore, and there were no more invitations to afternoon tea. I suppose it was my fault in a way, because I wouldn't give her the time of day. She also sensed that I wasn't taken in by her outlandish claims about the life she had led in Rhodesia when she'd supposedly been a vet, a nurse and an optician.

Dollie Trubbock got suspicious when residents of Mitchell Court became friendly with each other. If she spotted people talking in the lobby or outside their own front door she would stand and stare, making it plain that she had noticed their association. She didn't want them trading information, or banding together to make complaints to the landlords about the way she ran the building. Mum didn't know many people in the block, but she introduced me to Esther, a woman who lived on the eighth floor and who hated Trubbock with a passion. A couple of years earlier, Esther had tried to start up a residents group to get Trubbock removed from her job as supervisor, but the landlords hadn't been cooperative. As far as they were concerned Trubbock ran the building with ruthless efficiency.

Esther loved my dog Shandy, and always stopped to stroke her when we met outside. Esther was crazy about animals and had her own dog, a large highly strung malamute with pale blue eyes called Charlie. The dog stayed alone in the flat all day while Esther went to work in a bank at the bottom of Main Street, and every night she took him around the block for his walk. Charlie had a high curling tail that seemed to mirror Esther's own tight perm, and he was her only regular companion. Esther tried to be friendly, and occasionally invited us up to her flat on the eighth floor. One day she asked me if I'd like to see something special. She then produced a programme from an Engelbert Humperdinck concert she'd been to in 1968. She had all of his LPs too.

'Do you like Engelbert Humperdinck?'

Mum gave me a warning look, so I said I did.

'Maybe you'd like to borrow the programme and look at it?'

'That's okay,' I said. 'I wouldn't want anything to happen to it.'

'No, I insist,' she said firmly. 'I know what young people like. You can return it to me in a few days when you've finished with it.'

Then we had to listen to some of Engelbert's music. Charlie sat on the sofa beside Esther, while she went into a misty-eyed trance.

'You'd better make sure you look at Esther's souvenir very carefully,' Mum told me later. 'I don't want to fall out with her.'

The programme was only four pages, and apart from several photographs of Engelbert and his famous mutton-chop whiskers, there wasn't a lot of information to be gleaned. It did leave me with the indelible knowledge that Humperdinck was born in Madras, and that he was one of ten children. But each time we visited Esther she would bring out the programme and I would have to pore over it like it was the Holy Book of Kells. A few years ago I spotted Humperdinck waiting to be interviewed in a BBC radio studio. He was sitting on a sofa leafing through a magazine, and no one was taking much notice of him. We sat opposite each other for some time and I thought about telling him about Esther. I didn't think Engelbert would understand if I told him that whenever I heard 'Please Release Me' on the radio I had a vision of Esther kissing Charlie the malamute.

The only other people we knew were Mum's next-door neighbours, Elsie and Roger Stansfield. 'Have you noticed Mr Stansfield's fantastic complexion,' Mum would say every time we saw them. 'You'd never know he was almost eighty. He told me his secret – he moisturises with Charles of the Ritz night crème every single evening, before he goes to bed. I'm going to get your father to start doing that when he comes back.'

Unsurprisingly, Dad wasn't prepared to wear 'make-up'. 'Too bloody bad if I've got wrinkles,' he would argue. 'Men don't slather cream on their faces, and that's all there is to it.'

Elsie Stansfield was a little bird of a woman, who rarely left the apartment. 'I haven't told Roger yet, but I'm thinking of getting a divorce,' she announced one day when we were invited in for a drink. The Stansfields insisted on serving sherry when they had guests after five p.m. If you stayed until six they would move on to gin or whiskey. Roger wasn't there when we arrived: he had been sent up to Rosebank on the bus to do some shopping in Thrupps, the smart delicatessen that stocked things like imported English teabags and Quaker Oats. 'But, how long have you been married?' Mum asked.

'Fifty-four years,' Elsie replied matter of factly, 'but, you know, I've recently come to realise that Roger and I simply aren't compatible.' Whenever I passed Mr Stansfield in the corridor, I wondered if Elsie had told him about the divorce. She certainly wouldn't find anyone younger looking.

Relations with Mrs Trubbock gradually got worse, and descended into unbridled animosity. Our main crime was that there were too many of us living in the one-bedroom apartment. And we had too many pets. When we first moved into the block, Dollie told Dad that the animals wouldn't be a problem. She said he didn't have to worry about sticking to the letter of the rental agreement.

Our apartment hadn't been designed for a menagerie, even though most of the time we were all out at work, or school and we had a large outside balcony for the cats' litter trays. We walked the dogs around the perimeter walls of the Fort and in a nearby park first thing in the morning and last thing at night. Trubbock only knew about Shandy, because Hennie was hidden inside his bag when we went in and out of the building. And every day he went to the shop with Mum, but Shandy the boxer was left alone quite a lot of the time. No one else ever objected to the animals, but then Shandy started to develop bladder problems. Her back legs would suddenly collapse and she would pee where she fell. She was a clean dog and would never ever have made a mess inside, but the effort of holding it in until we reached the street was sometimes too much. I had to start carrying her from the apartment down to street level but inevitably there were one or two accidents. The obvious solution would be for us to move out, but we didn't have the money for a deposit on anywhere larger. We were prisoners in the apartment.

Once you were on Dollie's hit-list, she would start issuing threats for any contravention of the lease, real or imagined. She could accuse you of being noisy, or decorating your apartment without permission from the landlord. For us, there was only one way to get out of the building without going past Dollie's door. It involved using the fire escape at the end of the outside corridor, and sometimes I would sneak Shandy down there, but the dog didn't like it. Her claws used to scratch and slide on the metal and she got scared on the way down because the staircase had open treads through which she could see the ground far below. Those metal steps on the fire escape also acted like a giant tuning fork which clanged and vibrated when you put your weight on them. If Dollie heard or saw me with the dog she would appear at the balcony in front of her own flat and point her gnarled arthritic fingers at us.

'Get that dog put down or I'll report you!' Her cigarette bobbed up and down between her lips like a diving springboard as she screeched, 'I can have you evicted in seven days!'

Lots of people hated Dollie. There were a hundred apartments in the block and many of them were occupied by elderly widows. 'They're all Jews,' Dollie told Mum. 'They come here to die when their families kick them out of their big houses in the northern suburbs.' And when they died, Dollie was always first in, going through their belongings and taking whatever she fancied before the relatives arrived. She said it was a legal requirement that she kept a spare set of keys to everyone's apartment in case of emergency. According to Mrs Stansfield, Dollie didn't wait until they died, she just stole things anyway, especially when she knew they had no close family or friends nearby to object.

Mum kept looking in the *Star* for a house we could rent, but we knew Trubbock would never refund our deposit. Shandy's incontinence got worse, and I took her to the vet. The nearest one was on Louis Botha Avenue, fifteen minutes away by taxi, and just getting there was difficult enough. He said she had something called anchylosing spondylitis, and it was causing her spine to degenerate. He said there was nothing he could do for her, and I had to decide when she was suffering too much.

A few days later, Mum bought Shandy some raw liver from the supermarket and cooked it with some gravy. 'The poor thing,' said Mum. 'She deserves a special treat.' Afterwards, I walked Shandy in the little park near the Fort so that her bladder would be empty for the bus ride back to the vet. We sat on the back seat so that she didn't get under the other passengers' feet, and so that the driver wouldn't notice if she pissed on the floor. In Ireland she had always sat on the passenger seat in Mum's Mini Clubman, resting her chin on the window ledge and poking her snout into the slip-stream as we drove along the country roads. I took her for long walks along Ballyholme Bay, and further, to chase the rabbits at Ballymacormick Point. I wondered what she made of living in a flat in Hillbrow, surrounded by the noise of the city and with only the short excursions to the dusty patch of grass near the Fort for exercise. And I was ashamed that her last journey was on a noisy, smelly PUTCO bus with a hard floor.

In the surgery I held her on the table while the vet gave her an injection. Like all boxers she had a very expressive face, and as the needle went in she looked directly at me with what seemed like surprise. Then her front legs buckled and she was unconscious. Within two minutes she was dead, and the vet was asking me if I wanted to keep her collar. I went back to Hillbrow on the bus. I felt guilty about the times I had scolded Shandy when she had wet the floor, and I blamed Mrs

Trubbock for making the dog's last few months alive more unpleasant. I started to feel angry.

I can't remember exactly when I decided to begin the screaming campaign. But working shifts at the Carlton gave me the perfect opportunity. My movements were unpredictable and I could carry out my plan at almost any time of the day or night without setting a pattern.

Dollie had two telephones: one was a private line and one was for apartment business. As part of her job, she had once proudly told Mum she was obliged to answer the block telephone in case there was a serious emergency. If she wanted to go out she had to make sure her husband or one of her kids was there to answer it. That's what gave me the idea. All I did was call her up on either one of the two phones and when Dollie answered I screamed into the mouthpiece as loudly as I could. If the fat children, or her harmless husband picked up then I kept silent. I hoped they wouldn't believe it when she said she'd been screamed at. But sometimes I didn't even scream when Dollie answered. So she never knew when it was safe to answer the phone. And because it was her job, she had to pick up.

The secret of success was to do the screaming at irregular intervals. I got the best result when I called around midnight or in the early hours. Dollie was vulnerable then, perhaps freshly awakened from a deep sleep. Four or five a.m. was a good time, as she always got up around six and if I did a good scream she wouldn't be able to go back to sleep. Sometimes I called the same line three or four times in a row. Then I'd call the other line. Or I'd only call once, and not scream. Then I'd call a few minutes later and scream my lungs out.

The best thing about working in the hotel was that when I was on night shift I would often be alone in the kitchen and could scream really loudly without bothering anyone else. I had my own office anyway, but I could also go up to the public phone box on the hotel roof-terrace which was all locked up at night, and here, well away from the guest rooms, I could do some really big screams. In the day I would sometimes go on a break and leave the hotel to find a call box outside on the street, or in a park and scream from there. I learned that even in a call box I could scream very effectively if I cupped my hand around the mouthpiece, especially if there was traffic noise. And in those days, there was no such thing as caller ID – I could vary the pattern in infinite ways.

Dollie played the game well. At first she got mad and swore at me. Then she tried not speaking when she picked up. I'd imagine her holding the receiver well away from her ear every time she answered, just in case it was me, the screamer. If she didn't speak I would call back five, six or more times and maybe only scream on the last call. After a while Dollie started getting her husband or the children to pick up. But they couldn't cover for her twenty-four hours a day, and her job was, after all, to be the apartment caretaker. Her next tactic was to get angry.

'I know who you are!' she would shout down the line. 'Don't worry, I know who you are.'

I never, ever reacted. Loud scream or total silence – that was all I did.

After that, she got abusive.

'My son has a gun, he's gonna take you out if you don't stop this! You fuckin' bastard.'

The son did have a gun, but I was sure she had no idea who was calling. She had so many enemies. Then she got desperate.

'The police are tapping this line, they know who you are!'

Finally, it was pure hysteria and her voice would be strangled with rage as she screamed at the top of her voice: 'Fuck you! Fuck you! Fuck you!'

Dollie's tone got shriller as the days and weeks went on. One night, at about three a.m., and after several months of the screaming campaign, the husband answered the phone. I stayed quiet. Just a little heavy breathing.

'Please,' he half sobbed into the phone. 'Please in God's name won't you stop this, whoever you are. I'm *begging* you to stop. My wife is having a nervous breakdown. She's on tranquilisers from the doctor and she's afraid to leave the apartment in case you are waiting to attack her.'

I felt sorry for the man. He sounded truly miserable and desperate. But then I realised just how effective my campaign had been. I gave them a couple of days' rest and then started calling again. And even after we moved out of the block I kept it going. After all, it would have looked suspicious if I'd stopped.

No one in the family knew I was doing the screaming, though pretty soon everyone in the block knew that someone was making Dollie's life hell. But I never heard anyone say they were sorry.

False Passports and Chicken Pies

After nine months at the Carlton I had to make a decision. Mum and Dad were insisting that I took up my place at university in Belfast. Leaving Mum behind in the flat, at the mercy of Trubbock, didn't seem like an option.

'Timmy, if you don't finish your education. I'll never forgive myself. Look at me, I've had no choice in life because I didn't have any qualifications. You must go back, or I'll have yet another thing to feel guilty about.'

Once again I left for Ireland, and life with Dad. And yet again I was separated from Mum, our only contact through letters. At Queen's University, I lived a different, more normal life. Dad rented a small house in a village on the coast, taking me into Belfast each morning on his way to work and collecting me each evening. It was an isolated place, just a few houses with gardens that led down to a rocky foreshore. There were no streetlights, and if I left my bedroom curtains open at night there was a lighthouse beam that would blink every three seconds from a small offshore island. During the day, I could climb down onto the rocks that were slick with

bladder wrack and dulse. Blood red beadlet anemones, win-
kles dark and shining with brine and horse mussels treacher-
ous to the hands lined the tidal zone. The rock gullies formed
natural pools and when the water was clear, I would sit and
stare into the depths for hours mesmerised by the waving
strands of shoe lace-thin mermaid's tresses. By Easter, it felt
warm enough to try swimming and I could jump from high
into the cool dark water. Even on windless days, the tide
sucked against the rocks like a greedy nursling.

At home, there was little to distract me from my studies.
Each evening, I fell into the habit of typing up each day's
lecture notes, reinforcing whatever knowledge I had absorbed.
It made revision easy, but – ironically, given my attitude to
school – it quickly earned me the reputation of being a swot.
Unlike many of the other students, who had come straight
from school, I found being at university an easy option. After
working for almost a year, I didn't find attending a few
lectures and writing essays made unreasonable demands on
my time. I was able to play sport, go to the movies at least
once a week and enjoy myself. The letters from Johannesburg
kept coming, and Mum wrote to say that she was moving out
of the flat. She didn't need to pay a deposit in advance because
one of her fellow traders at the Flea Market was leaving
Johannesburg and he had offered to sublet the small house he
was renting.

Dad scraped enough money together to go out to Johannesburg to help her move. Later, I learned that he too had
taken his revenge on Mrs Trubbock, although instead of using
the telephone he had taken to firing marbles at her bedroom
window with a catapult.

Mum never told me how difficult things sometimes got in Johannesburg, except for saying that she was trying to make enough money to come back to Ireland. Only occasionally did she hint that she was miserable. 'I'm glad we can't see too far into the future,' she once wrote. 'Here I am, a faithful wife and loving mother, and I've ended up in the dregs of Hillbrow, and yet I can't bear the thought of coming back to those grey skies and small minds in Ireland.'

For four years, I travelled to and from Belfast and Johannesburg each summer for my ten-week summer vacation, and usually at Christmas too. Mum sometimes bought the tickets from travel agents she had befriended. Usually she bought the tickets on credit and during the visit I worked to pay for them.

The Carlton Hotel welcomed me back, and gave me a job during my first summer vacation following my return from Ireland. I then discovered that working as a waiter was far more lucrative than my old desk-bound job in room service. In addition to my monthly salary, I earned enough in tips to pay for all my bus rides and food, while the rest could be saved up until it was time to go back to Ireland. For two long summers and two Christmases I also worked at the Münchener Haus, a Bavarian restaurant in Braamfontein with its own three piece *sakkie-sakkie* band. The musicians dressed in lederhosen, knee-socks and Tyrolean felt hats decorated with pheasant feathers. We served beer in wooden casks with a brass tap and regular customers had their own *steins* with conical pewter lids. The atmosphere was very Bavarian, though unlike one of the other German restaurants in Johannesburg at the time, the Münchener House didn't hold parties to celebrate Hitler's birthday. On the dance floor the mixed German and Afrikaans clientele could dance the *lang-arm*, with its rapid two-step rhythm halfway between a waltz and country and western. On Friday nights an older crowd came for the dancing, and there was something poignant about the stiff-armed way they slid around the wooden dance-floor to the accompaniment of tunes that relied heavily on the concertina. I made good money at the restaurant, and I would leave it all behind for Mum when I went back to college.

My Africa was a secret world, that I couldn't discuss with my friends at university, or even my relatives in Ireland and England. When I returned to Johannesburg they imagined a South African idyll, where white people sat beside swimming pools and were attended by black servants. I chose to let them think that was how we lived. I didn't want to discuss the days when we were at the margins of hunger, or the fact that Mum wore the same pair of sandals for years on end and sometimes slept in her old sheepskin coat to keep warm during the winter. Each October, at the start of the new term my friends would be talking about their shared experiences of the summer, working for a few weeks to pay for an Inter-rail trip across Europe. I listened to their tales of ferry rides between the Greek islands, and their hazardous experiences on hired mopeds with envy. Those shared student holidays and summer romances were denied to me, because I had to return to Africa to see my mother.

I started to resent both Mum and Dad for putting me in this limbo-land between Africa and Ireland. And once reunited with her, I had to acclimatise once again to the world of The Whatnot, of living in a tumbledown house and hiding from debtors or the law. It always took me a few days to get used to it, but gradually I would learn to be part of the family again. But then, by the end of the vacations when the time came to return to the safe, orderly world of university I would dread our parting.

For Mum's sake I always made a determined effort not to cry when we said goodbye. Just before we left the house for the airport, I would sneak into the kitchen and swig down a large mug of neat gin. No matter how little money we had, the gin and the tea were about the only things that never seemed to run out. By the time we were on the airport bus, the alcohol had kicked in and I would be able to maintain my composure successfully. What I didn't know was that Mum was taking her own precautions to stop me getting too upset. For a few days before I had to leave she would be slipping Valium into my morning cup of tea. To maximise my earnings, I generally worked until just a day or two before I took the flight back to Ireland. Working in the restaurants meant that I often didn't get home until one or two in the morning, by which time Mum was generally asleep. In the mornings she got up early to go to the shop, and I wouldn't leave the house until about eleven. I would make sure to call in at the shop to see her for an hour or so, and that was our main contact except for my days off. When I got back from the restaurant late at night, there was always a glass of milk and a biscuit beside the bed, which Mum said 'would help me sleep soundly.'

Mum often said she felt guilty that I lived so far away from her, and that she worried about how I looked after myself while I was at university. She said she needed 'to fatten me up' while I was home. I drank the milk, not because I needed it, but to make her feel better. I didn't know it at the time, but the milk was laced with tranquilisers too, and in conjunction with my last-minute gin-slugging ritual, I was able to get through the departure gate without making an emotional scene.

Years later she told me what she'd been doing and, as she predicted, I was angry. 'How dare you drug me?'

'I had to do it,' she smirked. 'When you were studying so hard – filling your head up with all those weird ideas at Queen's, you were very highly strung. You *needed* to relax. It was for your own good, you know.'

———————

When I was in my second year at Queen's, Dad lost his job in Belfast. He had been using his office telephone to ring Mum in Johannesburg, and when his employers found out they sacked him without any warning. She didn't have a phone at home, but there was a public tickey-box on the wall near the shop. If we wanted Mum to answer it, we would let it ring three times, then hang up, and redial. At first, Dad had been ringing her once or twice a month to check that she was alright, but when it seemed like the phone calls were going unnoticed, he became reckless and started ringing every week, staying on the line for at least half an hour. Within a few days of losing his job, Dad had decided to leave Ireland and go to London, where he said he had contacts in the security services who would help him out. He left me what money he had – a few hundred pounds – and told me he would send more when he had it. Once again, Dad owed the landlord money, and he told me not to tell anyone anything about his movements. The money never came, and in the dead of night I had to move out of the house he had rented. I had no choice but to stay with my aunt again.

For a few years I would receive postcards from Dad sent from the Middle East, mostly from Saudi Arabia and the Emirates. He didn't tell me what he was doing exactly, but occasionally he would say he was training bodyguards or acting as a broker. What he was broking was never clear. Once he was involved in a deal to sell a jet to an Arab sheikh and somehow it meant going to Seychelles and Mauritius. Sometimes he brought back diamonds to sell in Hatton Garden, and he made several trips to Antwerp. For a time he shared an office in Mayfair with some men who shared military backgrounds, but I never knew exactly what they all did. Dad said it was better that I didn't know too much, an arrangement that I was happy to keep. He wore smart suits again, but he carried a pen that could shoot a bullet. Really. He was like one of the mysterious characters in Alistair MacLean's *Puppet on a Chain* (Sven-Bertil Taube, 1971).

Whenever Dad resurfaced in London, he might ring me with high hopes of a big deal that he couldn't discuss over the telephone. His life in London was precarious, and for a time he lived in a cheap hotel on Baker Street. I visited him there once, and was shocked to find him in a tiny room just big enough for a bed and a TV mounted high up on the wall. He had to share a bathroom and most of the other residents were on the dole. Once, in a telephone conversation, I suggested that he might be better off in Johannesburg. 'I'm never going back there,' he said angrily. 'The whole place is run by stupid bloody Dutchmen and Jews. And they'll never give me a job because I'm not one of them!'

One day I got a letter from my grandmother in London asking me if I knew where Dad was, because she said the police had been looking for him. I found out later that one of his schemes involved providing false passports to people who could pay cash, and he was using her flat as the delivery address. He had a couple of passports of his own in different names. They proved useful in South Africa, where shops and banks accepted a British passport as a main proof of identity. At various times, thanks to Dad's aliases we were able to rent a house, open a spare bank account and, at one time, buy a new car on hire purchase. Mum couldn't afford the monthly payments of course, so the car was repossessed a few months later in the dead of night. Mum was outraged when they took the car, because she had been careful to hide it in a friend's driveway. 'Those swine from the bank – they must have been following me to find out where the car was!' she fumed. 'How *sneaky*.'

Secrecy came naturally into our lives. Perhaps it was because of Dad's military background, or our generally precarious relationship with debt collectors and landlords. For seven years in Ireland, we had lived in one house. During the same period in Africa, Mum moved six times. Once, when I was with her in Africa I asked her why she didn't come back to Britain. Life seemed so uncertain there, and the constant worrying about money was extremely stressful.

'Maybe I'm a fool,' she said. 'But no matter how bad things get out here, when I wake up in the morning and see the sun shining it cheers me up. All of those years in Ireland I was wrapped in a grey blanket of rain and drizzle. You don't notice it when you're young, but as you get older it becomes more important.'

'That's pathetic,' I said. 'The Irish weather doesn't stop me doing anything.'

'Pathetic it may be, but you're young and fit. I was the same at your age, I played tennis and went sailing. But here the weather never gets me down, even though I do struggle to survive. Sometimes I wish I could just pack up the shop and walk away and come back to live with you. Being separated from you has been the worst thing in my whole life. But if I came back, I'd be a housewife again, and I know I'd get ill.'

I never questioned the fact that Dad and Mum would eventually live together again. They both said they loved each other, and it seemed like a battle of wills was keeping them on separate continents. 'If only we could find a way of making some real money,' they would both say independently, 'then we could get the family all together in one place.'

It took me a few years to understand that Mum craved independence more than anything. Running the shop was a constant struggle, but it was hers. She was accountable to no one. She wanted the family to be together but she wasn't prepared to go back to being a housewife in order to achieve it. That would have been a sure route to depression, and she believed, to inevitable obesity. To her, a return to the domesticity of life in Ireland represented little more than a sentence to a slow death.

I don't know when my mother was born. I can narrow it down to a probable period spanning eight or nine years, but pinning down the precise year of her birth is not easy. Over the years I have found three passports containing different years for her birth, and other official documents also disagree, sometimes by as much as ten years. If I wanted to, I suppose I could track down her official birth certificate, or even ask one of my surviving aunts and uncles to tell me her age. Instead, I choose to leave it alone.

'What bloody business is it of theirs?' Mum would rage, at any suggestion that anyone needed to know her age. To my father, institutionalised by life spent at boarding school from the age of four, followed by more than twenty years in the Army, her attitude was perplexing, infuriating, and sometimes alarming. For many years I thought I could rise above it, but I now know that I have inherited my mother's inability to reveal my true age to strangers, and wherever possible I will lie on documents and even to friends. But in these data-obsessed times, it's not so easy to falsify dates on official documents. I can get away with it in some cases, but inevitably things get harder when banks and credit card companies ask for my date of birth 'for security reasons'. Sometimes it's easiest to compromise and stick to one false date for important stuff. I have mostly been reduced to just two choices when I get to the part of the form where I have to give my date of birth, but whenever I do get to use the incorrect information it's a small victory that pleases me. I think it's a shame that we can't all be like the original Hollywood stars whose obituaries were vague about their true age.

When I was about twelve, Dad came home from work one day to find that Mum had filled out a government census form. She hadn't told him she was doing it but he was supposed to sign the form before they sent it back to the government. As he was about to seal the official envelope he glanced at the section on 'family details'. He discovered that she was claiming to be the mother of eight children, with fictitious names and ages provided. Naturally, her own birth-date was also fictitious.

'You can't do this!' he raged.

'Why not?'

'Because I'll be sent to prison!'

Mum's response was to laugh and decry the government as 'a bunch of snooping bureaucrats'. As the arguing intensified, I heard her tell Dad that he was 'a craven lackey of the State'. It was the first time I'd heard the word 'lackey', and I rather liked it. Defeating the system was in Mum's eyes her God-given duty as an Irishwoman. Northern Irish people do that, they choose whether they want to be British or Irish depending on the situation.

Mum's attempts to keep her own age a secret sometimes led to arguments. On my tenth birthday, I had been given a silver matchbox to add to a collection I had been building up. Called *Vesta* boxes, they were made between about 1890 and 1930 and came in lots of different designs. I had one in the shape of a pig; one was an elephant's head complete with ivory tusks and several were made into circular boxes slim enough to fit into an old-fashioned waistcoat pocket. I started collecting them because Grandpop had given me his own, a memento presented to him at a regimental football tournament in 1926. I could date the little containers by their hallmarks, and I loved the silken feel of silver polished smooth by frequent handling. Most of them had a serrated strip along the bottom edge against which the matches could be struck. We were sitting in the green room eating a birthday tea of cake and chocolate fingers as I unwrapped my presents. Everything was calm enough until Granny took a look at my new matchbox and remarked: 'You remember the old wax matches don't you, Pam?'

'Wax matches?'

'Yes, you know, that's what we used before the War.'

'How would I remember before the War, I was much too young.'

'No you weren't.'

Mum delivered a death stare, and the conversation developed into an argument that cast a definite shadow over the birthday tea. I had been ill in bed and this had stopped me having a proper party, so luckily there were no other adults or children present. Afterwards, when Granny had gone home, Mum returned to the topic, clearly fearful that I had somehow gathered an impression that she might have been old enough to remember events before the War. In fact, I never gave any thought to her age, but it struck me as distinctly odd that my mother and her mother could disagree about when she had been born.

'Granny's going senile! Absolutely *senile*,' Mum declared. 'How could she be so stupid. Wax matches! She's mixing me up with Uncle Herbert. He's *much* older than me.'

I never found out what those wax matches were really like. But for years afterwards my mother occasionally referred to the time 'Granny had been so confused'.

In this way, we grew up knowing that dates of birth were not to be bandied about freely. My sister started lying about her age very young. Like most teenage girls she did the usual thing of pretending to be older than she was in order to date boys. But as she reached her mid-twenties she saw the sense in going the other way. Eventually, she met the man whom she considered the love of her life. They arranged to go on a foreign holiday together, and she became afraid that while travelling together he might see her passport and discover her real age. Although she was only twenty-five, she was claiming to be twenty-two. She was more concerned that he would end the relationship because she had lied, than because he was shocked by her biological age. Mum was consulted, and with the aid of a scalpel and some black ink the passport was altered. This was in the era before laminated pages, and machine-readable technology made forgery more difficult for the general public. Then they soaked her passport in cold tea and crumpled the pages a little. The trick with the tea came from a book Mum had once read about the forgery techniques of British prisoners at Colditz Castle during the war.

My sister's holiday passed uneventfully but shortly afterwards she went to Germany. The German border police proved more assiduous in their duties, and challenged the authenticity of the passport. Caro claimed that it had fallen into the sink, but they said they had seen that trick before, and she had better get a new passport or find herself arrested the next time she tried to leave the country.

Dad had a different philosophy when it came to the subject of age. He liked to pretend to be older than he was. Mum had her own theory about why he did it: that even as a young man he felt guilty about not having been quite old enough to have seen active service in the Second World War. All of his superiors in the Army had been in the war, and he liked to give the impression that he had shared in some of their experiences. But, even within the family he would pretend to remember things that had happened during his father's youth, rather than his own. He would reminisce about places he hadn't been to for forty years and we children would quickly wheedle a more accurate time-frame out of him.

Mum would smirk during these interrogations, and laugh when he was caught out. But when it came to her own place in events we'd often watch her carrying out a swift piece of mental arithmetic, making doubly sure that she wasn't admitting to being present at a time and place which might lead to us narrowing down her own true age.

———————

About once or twice each year, Dad would come back to South Africa. For many years, he was more like a visiting uncle than a father. Sometimes he stayed for a couple of weeks, at other times it could be three or four months depending on how his foreign contracts were going.

It was difficult for outsiders to accept that Mum and Dad still loved each other. Mum had her admirers, as she called them, but I don't believe she ever had affairs, or that she and Dad were unfaithful to each other. She never had time alone with anyone, and whatever Dad's faults – he was incapable of lying. When Dad came back to Johannesburg, they would go through a honeymoon period of about a week. Mum was very glad to see him, and they would sit holding hands. He called her 'Kiddo' when they were like that. If Dad had been working he would have cash, and the exchange rate meant that a little bit of sterling went a long way. We would be able to go to the supermarket and buy things we couldn't normally afford. But his visits usually meant trouble, especially when the money ran out. Living on her own, Mum was used to making her own decisions, and running her shop the way she wanted to, and she didn't like it when he interfered. And, like me, Dad got jealous of the people who clustered around The Whatnot.

————————

After a year or so in the market, Mum was able to move from the tiny shop she first rented to a larger space with a big double window where she could display more stock. This shop had a small alcove at the back with a sink and Mum curtained it off to make it into a private space. When I worked at the Three Ships and the Münchener House I worked a split-shift that gave me three hours off between lunch and dinner. It took about half an hour to walk back to the shop, and I could then snatch half an hour's sleep in the back room before it was time to go back to the restaurant. Having a bigger shop meant that more people could congregate around Mum at closing time. Ollie the Jeweller was a regular, frequently coming round to see Mum throughout the day and often supplying the drinks if she didn't have any in the shop. He asked Mum for advice every time he made a decision, whether it was about hiring and firing his salon staff, or how to conduct his relationship with his fiancée. He was one of those who had discovered that Mum could read tea leaves. He would beg her for a reading if there was anything especially difficult happening in his life, and she agreed to read his cup so long as he promised never to tell other people that she could do it. Inevitably the secret leaked out little by little, and there were soon half a dozen customers and market people who relied on Mum's readings. 'It's a curse,' Mum would say. 'But somehow I do see things, and I just wish I could channel that energy more efficiently and put it to good use myself.'

Mum's clairvoyance made me uneasy, and I despised the people who seemed to need it as a crutch to get them through their lives. I couldn't decide whether I disliked her fortune-telling because it seemed somehow low-class and anti-intellectual, or simply because it frightened me. Her belief in the presence of the paranormal was unshakeable, and yet it went against everything she wanted me to achieve through education.

One night, Ollie the Jeweller stayed in the shop until almost ten o'clock. My brother and I wanted to go home but Mum was being supplied with gin and tonic by Ollie. It was during a period when Mum had begun to drink too much. She was a quiet drinker, using the alcohol to numb the reality of her daily struggle to make ends meet. We knew that after a few steady hours consuming gin and tonic (never anything else), she would go to sleep. That night she became less and less interested in going home and cooking us any supper. It looked like we would be falling back on our default meal: Mamma's Chicken Pie. These glutinous, salt-laden pieces of pastry were the cheapest ready-meal available from Chequer's supermarket near the shop, and they came in little tinfoil dishes in packets of four. They were so cheap they must have been made from offal, but the gravy inside the little round pies was tasty and we were hungry enough to enjoy them. I went out to buy the pies and when I returned, Ollie had sunk into a decidedly maudlin frame of mind. Mum was sufficiently drunk that she was impersonating a nodding dog, and not really listening to what he had to say. He spoke extremely slowly, taking care with his words in the way only the very inebriated can.

'I should never have been a jeweller,' Ollie lamented. 'It's brought me nothing but trouble. I'm not educated like you, Tim,' he said, turning to me as a fresh victim for his story. 'You must study hard and get a good job so you can help your mother.'

I wasn't in the mood for career advice from Ollie, but he wasn't finished. 'You know, Tim, there's a lot of bad people in the world. Do you know that? When I was only sixteen I was offered an apprenticeship to a jewellery designer in Munich. He was queer, but I didn't know about that stuff, I was just a boy. He said he would employ me if I came to a jewellery fair in Amsterdam. I leapt at the chance to go with him, because I'd never been abroad in my life. Do you understand? Do you?'

Mum still wasn't listening, although Ollie had now shifted his attention back to her, his face only a foot or so away.

'That bastard, he made me share a room "to save on expenses", *that's what he told me*. Anyway, that first night he brought some wine into our room and we had a couple of bottles. Then he attacked me and tried to have sex. Can you imagine it? Can you? An older man putting his hands on you when you didn't want it?

'I fought him off,' Ollie continued, deadpan. 'And then I hit him on the head with a bottle. And I kept hitting him until he was dead. The blood was all over me. It was everywhere.'

Ollie sat staring at the floor after he finished his story, and I had no doubt he was telling the truth. Mum didn't react to this confession other than to shake her head sympathetically. My brother and I exchanged glances, while Ollie sat quietly for a moment. 'That's why I ended up here,' he said. 'I went straight back home the next day, and told my mother. She got me on a plane the next night to South Africa. I've been here for nine years on a tourist visa. They'll deport me if they find me, but I daren't go back to Germany. That's why you must always look after your mother. Without our mothers we're nothing. Nothing. Do you understand me?'

I found Ollie's story shocking, but I was desperate to get Mum back to the house and sober her up with one of Mamma's Chicken Pies.

Stealing Water

The house on Natal Street had a tin roof that had once been covered with red rust-proof paint. By the time we lived there, the tin was dotted with bald patches where the paint had been colonised with lichen that lifted and bubbled and frayed the surface, now faded to palest pink under the African sun. The house was a square single-storey box with a patch of lawn to the front and a walled yard at the rear, and a single garage to one side. In Yeoville, and neighbouring Bellevue and Observatory there were dozens of houses like it. Middle class white South Africans had lived here in the 1950s before the flight to the greener, more spacious northern suburbs. By the 1970s Yeoville was more trendy than respectable, and Rockey Street, the main thoroughfare, was lined with all-night bars and clubs where you could find several varieties of music and drugs. In the surrounding streets, the old houses were often shared by younger single people, living in what the South Africans liked to call 'communes', giving the district a Bohemian feel.

Some of the houses in Yeoville were showing their age, but I never saw anything so dilapidated as ours. A low chain-link fence protected a small scrubby front garden overgrown with tall grass that turned pale yellow in the dry winter. Arriving from the airport, after finishing my degree, I was shocked that Mum was living there. I knew she was watching me to gauge my reaction to the latest in a line of progressively more dilapidated dwellings.

'Can't we at least cut the grass?' I asked weakly, trying not to show how depressed I felt.

'No, don't you touch it!' Mum ordered as she locked the gate behind us. 'It's better left that way, so that no one can be sure if anyone's living here.'

The house had a front porch supported by two white concrete columns that gave shade to a peeling green front door with an ornamental wire grille protecting a central stained-glass panel. Mum had nailed a wooden board to the rear of the glass to stop any light showing through from the hall.

Natal Street was a shabby fortress. Mum kept two automatic pistols in the house: a Beretta and a Browning, both fenced to her by customers. The Beretta was stashed in the chimney breast for emergencies, and the Browning was in her bedside table. She rarely took them out of the house, but if she sent Will to the scrap dealers with a consignment of jewellery on his own, he took one for protection. When I queried the wisdom of allowing a twelve year old to carry an illegal weapon, she shrugged: 'Your father showed him how to strip it down and take care of it, and Will's *very* responsible. Anyway, would you rather I sent him into the roughest parts of town without any back-up?'

It was an unwritten rule that we never, ever answered the door, and no one was allowed to have our address. If anyone we knew ever offered to give us a lift home, we made them drop us outside some apartments a few blocks away. We would then wait until they had driven off before we walked to Natal Street. The house was so utterly shaming in its appearance that I asked taxi drivers to leave me outside a neighbour's house when I came back from the restaurant late at night. We kept the gate locked at all times with a thick iron chain and two heavy-duty brass padlocks, and in the front windows Mum had hung curtains so thick that even at night you couldn't tell if the lights were on or off. Keeping the house in darkness had a dual purpose. If any debt collector ever tracked her down, they couldn't be sure if anyone was at home. More importantly, Mum didn't want the municipal electric company to realise that we had power. She was regularly disconnected for arrears on the monthly account, but she had worked out how to restore the supply by lifting a manhole cover on the pavement a few yards from the house. Sometimes we came home to find the supply had been cut, but she would go out with a torch and a pair of pliers to snip the wire ties that they fixed on the junction box leading to our house.

When I was at home, I tried to make sure that the electricity bill got paid. Customers like us who were repeatedly in arrears had to go down to a small office in the middle of the city and pay the municipality in cash. Water was a bigger problem. The water company had more patience than the electric, and even in South Africa they weren't supposed to cut off the water supply until it was a last resort. But after six months they did, and even Mum couldn't reconnect the water supply herself. She had tried, but you needed a special wrench for the stopcock under a manhole cover in the middle of the road to get to the supply.

The house on Natal Street had a small back yard with an outside toilet that would have once upon a time been intended for the maid. The pan was cracked and stained and it didn't have a seat. The cubicle was built hard up against the back wall of the yard, and on the other side of the wall stood the maid's quarters for the house that backed onto ours. Mum had rigged up a piece of hosepipe that collected a trickle of water from the neighbour's supply, but it was only about a gallon or two per day and we didn't think it was safe for drinking. Mum had collected an assortment of large plastic barrels that could be used for storing water, but they had to be filled. Back at the shop, there was a little back room with a sink where we could replenish smaller containers. That water was safe to drink, so each evening we carried as many bottles as we could manage back to Natal Street. It was a two-mile walk from the shop, so we couldn't carry more than a few litres each.

For some of the time at Natal Street we had an old VW Beetle that we could use to carry the bigger barrels. After midnight, when I got back from the restaurant Mum and I would go out looking for garden taps that we could reach in people's front gardens, but we had to watch out for dogs. We also found a garage forecourt where we could fill up with water. On Sunday nights the garage was closed and unattended, so that was the day we had to get our main supply. Because the Beetle only had two doors it was difficult lifting the filled barrels back onto the rear seat, and one person on their own couldn't do it.

The problem with the Beetle was that it wasn't taxed or roadworthy, so driving it in the daytime when there was a greater chance of meeting traffic cops was always hair-raising. Everyone was on alert for the telltale white helmet of a motorcycle cop, or the khaki peaked cap of an officer on street patrol. When we left the Beetle parked on the street, we invariably got a ticket. I had managed to get the vehicle registered in my name, and I hoped that we could get it fixed up and legal so that Mum would have a car when I wasn't there. She had bought the car from a friend of John the Hippie who had gone back to the UK, and I discovered that he hadn't got the proper documents we needed to get it taxed. Providing my real name was a rare mistake, but it had to match the one on my driving license. The traffic department had my details on the temporary registration permit. One night the police turned up at Natal Street and Mum had to open the door. They had a warrant for my arrest because the Beetle had so many outstanding fines. That night I had taken the car to work, but Mum told them I was studying abroad. She said I had loaned the car to a friend who had been very irresponsible, and he was driving it around Johannesburg without getting the paperwork in order. The policeman was quite pleasant, she told me afterwards, and showed her that there were several thousand rand worth of fines outstanding. Mum invited the officer into the house, and plied him with gin. Caro my sister, was skulking in the back bedroom, but Mum decided she could be useful. 'Doll yourself up,' she instructed. 'And then come out and give the traffic cop the glad eye.'

'Agh! I know what these young kids are like,' the policeman said with a sigh. 'Your son has learned a very important lesson: sometimes you mustn't trust your friends when it comes to legal affairs.'

'Whatever can we do?' Mum asked innocently. 'I'm very worried that my son could be arrested because of this other boy.'

'You mustn't worry lady,' said the cop. 'I'll take your son's name off the records. But you make sure he doesn't make the same mistake again. And when we catch his friend he's going to be in big trouble.'

There and then, the traffic cop saluted Mum, and proceeded to tear up the bulging file of tickets and the arrest warrant on her doorstep. 'Yah, kids today,' he intoned gravely. 'They bring us parents a lot of trouble!'

For a time, the traffic cop became a persistent visitor to the shop, and Caro was under strict instructions to keep him sweet. Fortunately, he was married and didn't pose too much of a threat but he sometimes took her out in his patrol car to have a coffee break. He invited Mum and Caro out to his house one weekend but they decided they couldn't go because their only transport would have been the illegal Beetle.

A little while later, there was a front-page story in the *Citizen* newspaper about a man who had amassed around two thousand rand worth of parking fines. Our tally in the Beetle was at least triple that and we were all amazed to read the caption describing the man as 'Jo'burg's most persistent traffic offender.'

'That's typical of these reporters – they don't do their research properly,' said Mum with some irritation. 'We've had a lot more tickets than him!'

Mum was arrested twice that I know of. The first time was when I was working at the Carlton. It was six a.m., and we were awoken by fists banging heavily on the front door. Mum answered and was confronted by two uniformed policemen who said they were investigating the theft of some animal hides from a tannery in Krugersdorp. They had already arrested two African men, who had told the police that Mum had bought two lion skins from them. She was given five minutes to get dressed and the policemen told me that they were taking her to their headquarters at John Vorster Square. The police station was notorious for the torture of terrorist suspects, several of whom had been thrown from its upper floor windows.

Mum wasn't in any such danger, but going to collect her at the station later that day was intimidating. She seemed unconcerned. 'Well, I did buy skins,' she told me calmly. 'But the skins I bought have a number tattooed into the ear. That means they have been released for sale with a permit, and I've got a copy of the permit to prove my innocence.'

A few days later, Mum was contacted at the shop by a lawyer representing the accused. She was no longer under suspicion, but they needed her as a defence witness when the case came to trial. The problem was that the case was to be heard in Nelspruit, in the Eastern Transvaal, half a day's drive away. The Beetle wouldn't make it that far, and the trip would involve several nights away from home. The court would only pay her expenses by public transport, an unrealistic option that would involve two days on a train. The only solution was to hire a car, something that would make a serious dent in our monthly budget. Mum said that Wally the

Willie-toucher might be able to give her a good deal. Mum gave Wally his nickname because he always wore extremely tight linen trousers and would frequently rub one hand across his crotch and try to pluck at the hem of his underwear to adjust his genitals. It was a nervous tick, and his actions weren't generally visible to his clients since he mostly dealt with them by telephone. Wally ran a small travel agency from a booth at the Market, and catered exclusively to gay clientele. After a bit of haggling, and crotch rubbing, Wally got us a very good rate on a bright yellow Austin Mini. The car was normally used by the owner of the hire company, and not given out to tourists because it had the words 'Budget Hire – the cheapest deals in town', painted in large scarlet letters along both sides, and across the bonnet.

I took four days off work to drive Mum to Nelspruit. My brother Will was taken out of school, and we all piled into the Mini for the long journey. It was the first time Mum had left Johannesburg, or spent the night away from home since we had arrived in South Africa five years earlier. 'Let's treat this as a holiday,' she said as we left the city. She was as excited as a child going on a school trip, even though I knew she was worried about leaving the shop. Mrs Corrigan, an elderly Irishwoman who sometimes worked for her, was going to be in charge while we were away. Mum couldn't afford to employ anyone full-time, but Mrs Corrigan would stand behind the counter for an hour or two while Mum went to an auction or into the city centre to collect stock from the scrap-metal dealers.

'It's better than not opening at all,' said Mum, though she wasn't entirely sure. John the Hippie was keeping an eye on things too, and the old lady was to hand over the keys to him each evening for safe-keeping.

When we reached Nelspruit Mum reported to the court-room and we were told that she would have to appear sometime during the morning the next day. We drove around the outskirts of Nelspruit for some time looking for an hotel we could afford. Eventually, we found a motel that was closed for the winter season, but Mum persuaded the caretaker to let us have a room. The mattresses were damp and mouldy and the bath was full of spiders and cobwebs, and we had to drive into town to find something to eat.

The next day, we couldn't really follow any of what was going on in court as the proceedings were all in Afrikaans, except for some of the witness statements which were trans-lated into Sotho, and of course Mum's own testimony which was in English. She was in the witness box for only a few minutes, and simply identified the two accused men as those who had sold her the animal skins, for which they had produced a legal permit. As a result of her evidence, the men were acquitted. A few weeks later they appeared at The Whatnot and presented Mum with an ivory bangle. 'You have saved our families from going hungry,' one of the men said with a deep bow.

After the trial there was time to get back to Johannesburg the same day, but Mum had other ideas. 'Do you realise we're not very far from the Kruger Park?' she said to me as we left the Courthouse. 'I've *always* wanted to go there. You know, we've been in Africa all this time and never seen any wild animals. We've got to go!'

None of us understood how the park operated, but I had heard that guests at the Carlton on their way to the park had to book accommodation quite far in advance. I didn't really want to go, fearing it would be expensive and that we would look out of place in the Mini with it's garish advertising slogans. But Mum wasn't to be dissuaded, and it seemed foolish not to take the chance of seeing something more of South Africa.

At around three in the afternoon we presented ourselves at the Malelane Gate and paid a day visitor's fee. As I suspected, the ticket said we had to be out of the park by five p.m., at least an hour before it started to get dark. And inside the vast game reserve – famously the size of Israel – there are strict speed limits, making the distances seem even longer. We had no guide book, just a simple map issued with our day ticket, though it didn't mark all of the dirt tracks that looped away from the main roads inside the park. When I suggested that we shouldn't drive too far away from the exit gate, Mum told me to stop being a kill-joy. 'Don't be like your father, Timothy. He always spoils everything by worrying. We're here now, let's just enjoy the experience and see where we end up.'

'But we haven't got anywhere to stay – what if we get locked inside the park?'

'I'm not going to discuss it,' she admonished. 'This is my one chance to see something of this country instead of being stuck in that shop in the bowels of the earth, seven days a week. Stop spoiling it.'

As the light faded from the sky, I realised we were miles from the nearest exit. Mum was unperturbed. 'They're bound to have someone on duty at the gate. We'll just tell them that our engine overheated, and we had to wait for it to cool down.'

I started breaking the speed limit in an effort to get to the exit gate, but it was soon pitch dark and I had to slow down in case we hit an animal. The Mini's engine sounded as loud as a jumbo jet in the stillness of the night. I hunched over the wheel, as if I could urge the little car to get to the perimeter of the park more quickly. There were no other headlights visible, and nothing but the African bush all around us. And at the bottom of the entrance ticket it stated clearly that driving after dark was strictly prohibited. At the time, the South African tourism industry wasn't nearly as sophisticated as it is now, and because the Kruger Park formed a border with neighbouring Mozambique it was also a sensitive security area. Terrorists from the communist neighbour were known to infiltrate the park, and anyone moving around after dark could be a poacher, a terrorist or simply a desperate refugee trying to get into the country. I began to be afraid. 'This is an adventure!' Mum chortled in the seat beside me. 'Enjoy it.'

There was something ahead in the road, and as we got closer we saw that it was a large male lion. His head was level with the top of the Mini and he was walking slowly but purposefully down the very centre of the dirt road. We trailed behind him for about twenty minutes and then I tried to get past. He moved to the side a little and I slowed to a crawl to stay beside him. I opened my window an inch or two and we listened to his breathing. As he walked he emitted low rumbling growls, occasionally barking out his presence to any other lions in the area. He plodded along, with his muscular shoulders rolling and his great black mane just inches from the window. We stayed with him for half an hour, captivated by his solid strength and aura of ultimate self-assurance.

Soon afterwards I spotted headlights some way behind us. Fearing it might be a game warden I started driving faster, a little above the speed limit. It was no good, after about ten minutes we were overtaken by a large four by four with spotlights mounted on the cab roof. It slewed across the dirt road in front of us, blocking our path. An irate man in a game ranger's uniform jumped down from the cab, brandishing a rifle. As I wound down my window he started babbling a stream of angry sounding Afrikaans.

'Hello,' I said, ignoring his tirade. 'Can you help us find the way out, we seem to be lost.'

'English!' he exploded. 'I might have known! I could have shot you – don't you know it's illegal to be in the park after dark. Which camp are you staying in?'

'We're not staying anywhere,' I replied. 'We're just trying to find an exit gate.'

'Follow me,' he shouted, practically foaming at the mouth. 'You're under arrest. You'll face a heavy fine for this!'

'I told you this would happen!' I ranted at Mum as we followed the ranger's truck through the darkness.

'Take no notice of him, Timmy,' she said calmly. 'He's just a minion – and you've already shown that you're not going to be intimidated by his uncouth display of temper. You must make sure these people understand that you're their superior in every way – try to sound as English as possible: just do your George Sanders voice (*All About Eve*, 1950) and they'll think you're aristocracy.'

An hour later we reached the main camp at Skukusa, where we were made to sit in an anteroom while the ranger reported to his boss. We could hear the ranger shouting about the 'Engels' through the door. Then, Mum was summoned inside to face the Head Game Warden. My brother and I sat outside like naughty schoolchildren, and I began to wonder what would happen to us. After a time, Mum emerged with the Head Warden. 'You must meet my son,' she said beaming. 'He's always wanted to be a game ranger haven't you?'

'Oh, er . . . yes,' I said weakly, as he shook my hand manfully.

'And, I'll see you all tomorrow morning at breakfast,' said the Warden. 'Have a very good holiday.'

We were shown to a rondavel, where we spent the next two nights. 'Such a charming man,' said Mum. 'I noticed a copy of his autobiography on the desk as I walked in. I told him I'd read it, and what an amazing story it was – I got it from the library years ago. He used to be a big game hunter and then his wife was killed in an accident. He decided he was being punished for killing all those innocent animals, and since then he's devoted his life to conserving nature instead.'

'But what about the fine for driving in the park after dark?'

'Timothy, I told you not to worry about that. The Head Warden is a gentleman. He didn't even mention it.'

We drove around the park in the yellow Mini for two days, and afterwards Mum had the satisfaction of telling her friends at the Market that she'd been 'in the Kruger, for a holiday'.

Mrs Corrigan was from County Wexford and made much of the Irish heritage she shared with Mum. She was a tall bony woman, always neatly turned out in a black cardigan, brown tweed knee-length skirt and a high-necked white blouse fastened at the neck with a circular Celtic brooch. She had pale grey eyes, like a wolf, and thin lips that she would pucker into a tight small circle when she was agitated. Her politics were staunchly Irish Republican and she would often drop comments to gauge where Mum's political allegiances lay. Mum refused to be drawn, and simply tried to change the subject when the conversation turned to Irish affairs. Mrs Corrigan had a permanently distracted air, but would sometimes sail into the shop in a state of high excitement.

'Isn't it terrible what the English did?' she would cry by way of a morning greeting.

'What's happened?'

'In Ireland. It's terrible isn't it.'

The first time she did it, we assumed something dreadful had been in the news about the Troubles.

'Oh yes, indeed,' Mrs Corrigan would continue, shaking her head from side to side. 'It's terrible. What Cromwell has done to the Irish. And in Drogheda, that terrible massacre. Wasn't it awful? Terrible. *Terrible*.'

'That was three hundred years ago,' Mum would say as diplomatically as she could. 'I can't be getting worked up about things that happened so long ago.'

'Yes, yes. But it was a terrible thing all the same. Don't you think?'

Mrs Corrigan was an unusual sort of Republican because she had a great love of the British Royal Family. 'Oh, that

Princess Diana, she's a beautiful, *beautiful* girl, don't you think? But my favourite is the Prince Andrew, sure and he's a handsome man. And a Navy officer, too. Wouldn't it be lovely to be a young girl again and be chasin' after the likes o'him.'

One of the things Mum put up for a sale in the shop was a pair of long-sleeved evening gloves. She had once worn them to a function at Hillsborough Castle in Northern Ireland at which the Queen Mother had been present. Mrs Corrigan loved those gloves.

'Imagine that!' she would murmur reverently, holding them to her cheeks like newborn kittens. 'Your own dear mother was there with the Queen herself. And she shook her hand with these very gloves. To think these beautiful gloves have been touched by a queen.'

Mrs Corrigan eventually had to be given the sack for taking money from the till. And the last thing she did in the shop was to steal the white gloves.

Gold Coins, Roulette Wheels
and a Witch Doctor

Carl the Cat-Burglar walked into the shop one day and offered to sell Mum some gold jewellery. He said it was stuff that had belonged to his grandmother. Lots of people came to the shop with that kind of story, and Mum bought a gold chain and a couple of rings. But then a week later he came into the shop again. This time he had an antique man's watch and some more gold chains. She was suspicious, and wary in case he was a plant – someone working for the police to find out which shopkeepers would 'fence' stolen property. Mum did everything by intuition, but it was good quality stuff and she could sell it easily for a high profit. And she needed the money.

Mum's business licence allowed her to buy secondhand gold and silver, as long as she kept a clear record of the sales and purchases in a ledger. Like all jewellers and pawnbrokers, she was supposed to check the seller's ID and take down their name and address. She gave Carl half the cash he wanted for the gold, and told him she would have to keep the items for twenty-one days before she sold them. If the police didn't issue a stolen goods description within that time she was legally entitled to sell the gold, and Carl could then collect the balance. Mum kept their deals on that basis for several months, because she was certain the merchandise he sold was hot.

'I would never, ever tell the police that I sold it to you,' Carl told her one day. 'But you tell me what sells quickest, and that's what we'll deliver.'

And so it continued. Mum knew that Carl the Cat Burglar was part of a gang, but she never met any of the others. 'I feel sorry for that boy,' she would say when I said I didn't trust him. 'And I make sure there are never any witnesses when he comes into the shop. He knows he must never even speak to me when there are other customers or dealers in here.'

Carl usually came to the shop first thing in the morning, when Mum was opening up and things were quiet. One day he arrived in a bad mood. 'Last night, we did three big houses in Parkview,' he blurted out. 'You know, where all those rich Jews live. But you won't believe how little stuff they've got. Sure, the main lounge has got nice carpets and antiques, but when you go round the other rooms they're almost empty. It's all for show – they haven't got half as much money as they like to make out! I'm not doing Jew's houses anymore.'

Mum made up false names and addresses for her ledger when she bought from Carl the Cat Burglar. And usually, she only recorded a fraction of the jewellery he brought in for sale. She didn't take any of the stuff he brought in large quantities, and she sold most of it the same day to the scrap dealers who could melt it down quickly. It was a lucrative arrangement, but she knew it couldn't last. One day Carl brought in a stash of fifteen Krugerrands, bullion coins made of one ounce of pure gold. Each one was worth more than a month's rent on the shop and the house, and Mum couldn't afford to buy them for anything like their true value. But Carl refused to take them anywhere else.

'You can pay me when you get the money,' he said. 'It doesn't matter how long I wait. I trust you.'

The coins would be easy to trace, especially as they were an entire collection stolen from one owner. Mum hoped to ease them into the market one by one, but it would take time, and she would have to find buyers who wanted pure gold as an investment. Luckily, South Africa's political and economic isolation made lots of people put their savings into gold, which was more secure than local currency, but she could only sell them to people she knew, and most of them didn't have that kind of money. So, Mum took the coins home and hid them in a wooden trunk under my brother's bed. She had other stuff from Carl in the trunk, including some silver cutlery engraved with the owner's monogram, and some heavy 18-carat gold bracelets. It was all too hot to sell through the shop, but far too good to trade in for scrap.

A few weeks later, two uniformed policemen arrived at the shop as Mum was opening up for the day. They were fresh-faced, clean-cut young men in their trademark pale blue trousers and peaked caps. At first they didn't say anything, but looked around the shop for a long time, picking things up and inspecting the price tags as though they were browsing. Then, one of them asked if she had any gold for sale. Mum unlocked the glass display cabinet she kept near to her desk to show them what pieces of jewellery she had, but then they asked to see her second-hand jewellery ledger. She always kept enough records of transactions to make a legitimate show.

'Where's the stuff that you buy from Carl?'

The question came without warning, but Mum said she didn't know anyone by that name. She didn't believe that Carl would have implicated her, but the police seemed to have good information. The questions continued, and it was clear that Carl, or someone in his gang, had given the police detailed information.

'Lady, we want the Krugerrands,' one of the officers said aggressively. He leaned over the desk so that she felt his breath on her face. 'We know he sold them here.'

John the Hippie saw that the police were in The Whatnot, and when I arrived later that morning he intercepted me on the street. 'Don't go to the shop, man. They've got Pam trapped in there and things are getting very heavy.'

The police locked themselves into The Whatnot with Mum and they kept her there from ten in the morning until seven that night. John and I took turns to saunter past the shop as if we were just browsers in the arcade. Through the window I could see Mum sitting at her desk with one or other of the two cops standing over her. She didn't show a flicker of recognition when I walked by, but I could see she was scared. They had ransacked the drawers and gone through the back room but hadn't found anything that linked Mum to Carl. We learned later that Carl and the three other men in his gang had been caught breaking into a house in Sandton. In custody, they were badly beaten, but Carl never revealed Mum's name. It was one of the other gang members who spilled the beans.

John the Hippie started to panic. 'If she's charged, we'll have to get her out on bail. Then we can somehow get her across the border into Botswana. You'll all have to go.'

'What, in your Beetle?' Despite my fear, I couldn't resist the jibe.

We started making plans, and then I remembered the loot hidden in the wooden trunk back at the house. And John's untrustworthy VW was the only way to get there quickly. We drove back to Natal Street, circling the block and driving past the house slowly several times to see if the police were watching the house. It seemed safe, so I ran in and retrieved the Krugerrands, stuffing them into a Checkers Supermarket bag with some tins of dog food. I had the idea of opening the cans and stuffing the coins into the meat as a hiding place. John was agitated, running his hands back and forwards across his forehead and grinding his cheeks with his knuckles in a nervous twitch.

'If we get caught with the gold we'll all go down for years.'

'Shut up, John!' I said, almost without thinking. 'Take me to Gerry the Forger's house.'

Gerry was an Irish artist of some talent who lived with his wife and four wild daughters in an old bungalow in Bez Valley. He produced oil paintings of South African landscapes which he sold at several of the open-air Saturday markets that were at that time becoming fashionable in Johannesburg. Gerry's real talent was in forgery, especially when it came to the work of some of the lesser seventeenth century Dutch Masters. His forgeries were produced to commission for a couple of European dealers, and although it paid well, it was a slow and painstaking process. By his own admission, he was no stranger to hiding from the law.

'This is for Pam,' I said in a hurried doorstep exchange. 'It needs to be kept well out of sight. The police are in the shop.'

'Sure. No problem,' he said with a wink, as I handed it over. Gerry didn't even ask what was in the bag.

John the Hippie and I spent the rest of the day drinking chocolate milkshakes in the Wimpy Bar. If the police took Mum away, at least we would see them do it. Every hour or so, one of us would go down into the market and check that she was still alright. We enlisted other shopkeepers to take turns walking past the shop window too.

My brother was safe at school during the morning and the early part of the afternoon. But when he got home, there was a police car outside. Two cops followed him to the front door, telling him they needed to search the house. First, they went through the cupboards, the kitchen units and through all the old wooden packing cases stored in the back yard. Finally, having lifted up the sofa and emptied out Mum's clothes drawers onto the bed, they arrived in his bedroom.

'What is it you're looking for?' he asked sitting on the bed, still in his school uniform. The trunk was inches from his feet. He didn't know that I had retrieved the Krugerrands, but the monogrammed cutlery and some pieces of gold jewellery were still inside.

'Stolen property.'

'Well, you haven't looked through my toys, yet,' said Will with a smile. He gave the wooden trunk a tap with his heel. Afterwards, he said his heart had almost stopped when he made the bluff, but the policemen ignored him.

'We're wasting our time, they wouldn't hide it in the house,' said one of the men. They left, threatening to return.

Back at the shop, Mum maintained her composure. She never wavered from her claim that she didn't know Carl, and that she would never buy gold without keeping the necessary records. That evening, the officers finally left, and I rushed down to the shop. Several of the other Market People were there ahead of us, and Scots John started dishing out the gin and tonic.

'I thought I was going to faint,' Mum gasped. 'They've been trying to trip me up all day, making out they knew I had those cursed Krugerrands.'

None of the Market People needed to know exactly what the police were looking for, or why. They all had their own secrets, and the police were a common enemy.

That night, my brother and I collected the plastic bag from Gerry the Forger. This time, we didn't have John the Hippie's car, because we didn't want any witnesses when we disposed of the Kruggerands. On foot, at around two o'clock in the morning we reached an area of rough scrubland on Observatory Ridge, overlooking the city. Below us, a steep slope studded with red shale and a few stunted trees stretched downwards into the dark. Ahead, the city glittered with thousands of street lights, and here and there the tips of the skyscrapers flashed their red aircraft warning signals into the night sky, but the rumbling traffic had all but stilled for the night. We pulled the Krugerrands from their protective plastic wallets and hurled them into the darkness one by one. The coins disappeared into the long grass without a sound. It was more money than we had ever handled in our lives, but the risk of Mum being caught with them was too terrible to contemplate.

Later, we learned that Carl, who was then twenty-two, had kept his promise. He never told the police about Mum. He, along with two other members of his gang were sentenced to fourteen years in Kroonstadt gaol. The sentence seemed harsh, but apparently Carl was out on parole for similar crimes when he had committed these robberies.

———

At university in Ireland, friends often asked if Johannesburg was truly dangerous. 'I don't think of it that way,' I would answer truthfully. 'But, even in Northern Ireland, most people don't know anyone at first hand who's been murdered. In Johannesburg I've known five.' The first victim was Katina, a beautiful Swedish woman who worked with me at the Carlton. She had honey-coloured skin and the darkest blue eyes I had ever seen. Katina lived in Yeoville, but she frequently talked about moving out to Midrand, an area on the way to Pretoria where many of the residents kept horses. She wanted her own horse, and to return to a rural space, somewhere more similar to the place she had grown up in Sweden.

Katina and I would share a table in the staff canteen at lunchtime, and talk about our shared love of horses. She said I could come out to Midrand to go riding one day. Only a few weeks after she moved to the country she was killed. Katina had employed a man to look after her horse when she was at work. One night he got drunk, and broke into the house and raped her. Then he tied her to the bed and set it on fire to destroy the evidence. It was the kind of raw, futile killing that the Johannesburg newspapers barely reported.

Mervyn was the next friend to die. He was a gay jeweller who came into the shop several times a month to see if Mum had any gold chains he could buy. He liked Gucci link chains, nothing too chunky.

'I've got fine bones,' he would shriek. 'I don't want to look too macho.'

'I don't think that's your problem,' Mum would laugh, and he would shriek even louder. Mervyn was the kind of regular customer who Mum could always count on to buy something if she was desperate. One night he stayed with us in the shop for a drink, and said he would be back the next day to collect a signet ring that Mum was having repaired for him. On the way home he took a taxi, and invited the driver up to his apartment for sex. We don't know exactly what happened, but Mervyn didn't return to the shop the next day, or for several days afterwards. One of his friends came in later that week to tell Mum that Mervyn hadn't turned up for work either. The police broke into his apartment and found that he'd been tied up and tortured before being fatally stabbed. The killer made him reveal the combination to his safe, and his jewellery collection was gone.

————————

At one end of Anderson Street there was a wholesale African curio shop selling zebra tail fly whisks and springbok skin rugs, elephant hair bracelets and hippopotamuses carved from soapstone. There were ivory cigarette boxes and malachite chess pieces carved to resemble African warriors, drums draped in silver-backed jackal skin and elegantly twisted kudu horns. It was stuff for tourists to take home as souvenirs, and the shop supplied the hotels and resorts around Johannesburg, as well as retailers in the smart shopping malls in the suburbs. Upstairs, there was a different kind of Africa for sale. It was a dark dusty world where Sarah the *sangoma* sold herbal cures, powdered buffalo horn, dried monkey skulls, hyena teeth and mysterious liquids in brown bottles. This was the *muti* shop, and in a small inner-sanctum Sarah herself would cast the bones for her customers. The sangoma sat behind a metal office desk on an old swivel chair. The chair had once been covered in a rich golden-brown fabric, but her forearms had worn away the material and the stuffing was now visible. There was nothing remarkable about Sarah's appearance, and she wore a two-piece ladies suit, with a plain blouse underneath. Her hands were bony, with misshapen knuckle joints betraying her age, and she had a gap between her front teeth that allowed her to make dramatic and slightly sinister sucking noises when she was muttering her incantations. Once or twice a month, more often if finances were especially dire, Mum would take a taxi ride down to Anderson Street to consult Sarah. Like all good seers, Sarah didn't claim to have a clear vision of what her clients should or should not do. All she would say was whether or not the omens were propitious.

After I had finished my degree at Queen's, I didn't know what to do with my life. I had a place at Cambridge, but I was undecided about whether to become an academic or stay in Africa and look for work. 'Sarah will help you decide,' Mum decreed.

I was disgusted at the idea. My brother had told me about Mum's visits to Sarah. I knew that after one consultation, she had persuaded John the Hippie to take her to the northern edge of Johannesburg to collect water from the Jukskei River. According to the witch doctor's instructions, Mum had to visit the river during the time of the full moon. 'She said that the moon had a purifying effect on the water,' Mum confessed sheepishly.

'It would need to,' I muttered acidly. 'That river has cholera in it from the raw sewage running into it from Alexandra township.'

'I'm not drinking it!' Mum blustered. 'I just have to keep it in the shop to ward off the bad spirits. And I'm not supposed to talk about it, that weakens the power of the *muti*.'

'Jesus Christ! You're out of your mind – there's no way I'm going to see a witch doctor.'

'You're just like your father. You close your mind to things you don't understand. Well, let me tell you Timothy, you don't know everything, even if you think you do.'

Resentfully, I went along to Anderson Street. And there in the little office beside the muti shop I found myself sitting in front of Sarah. I found Mum's faith in this alternative world-view infuriating: it was a peasant mentality, where Old Moore's Almanac and magazine horoscopes held sway over lesser minds. I was angry that her circumstances forced her into that world, and the idea that she had put herself in real danger by wading around on the banks of the polluted river in the dark horrified me. My university education, which Mum was determined I should continue, was gradually driving a rift between us, and making me reject so much about her world.

Sarah passed me an animal skin bag and told me to shake it while I thought about the problems I needed to solve. Then I had to open the bag and shake out the collection of objects inside. On the grey metal table-top I saw animal bones, a round stone and something with small feathers attached to it. 'You have many worries,' Sarah said after half a minute of staring at the runes. 'And you have to decide where in the world you want to live. It does not matter which place you choose, because you will meet a woman who will help you. Her family is very wealthy.'

This prediction made no sense, and much of Sarah's diagnosis of my problems was couched in generalities that might apply to anyone. At the end of the consultation, she smiled. 'You must wait many years before you know what you want to do. But you will make many, many, many journeys in aeroplanes, and one day you will start to write stories that will be made into books.'

When I got back to the shop I had to recount in detail what Sarah had predicted. Mum was triumphant. 'You see, now you don't have to worry. Everything will turn out alright.'

Dad and I shared a disdain for fortune telling. For him it was as irrelevant as religion. From early childhood I had heard my parents arguing about the existence of God. Given the opportunity he would start ranting about what he believed, and didn't believe in. To Mum's dismay he rejected the idea that good or bad behaviour would be rewarded or punished in the afterlife.

'When you die, you die. And that's all there is to it.'

'You're wicked,' Mum would rebuke him. 'And I don't want you filling the children's heads with your views. You can keep them to yourself.'

Dad never went to visit the witch doctor, and Mum didn't discuss her visits with him. It would have led to a bitter row.

Only one thing got him more worked up than arguments about religion: gambling.

Uncle Alfie was a professional gambler. I only met him once when he was alive, a skinny little man not at all like his brother, my grandfather. When I was twelve, Uncle Alfie reappeared in Ireland after living in America for many years, and was the talk of the family because he had survived purely on the proceeds of placing bets on horses. His other claim to family fame was that at the age of seventy-six he didn't have a grey hair in his head. No one ever actually said it was because he dyed his hair with something that looked about as subtle as boot polish. A couple of years later, when he died, I remember going to his wake and staring at this little wizened face in the coffin with a shock of jet black hair above it.

Dad said gambling was a mug's game, but Mum said he only thought that because he was a boring Welsh Methodist. When it was convenient, she was happy to cite his mother's religion as an influence, even though he proudly professed to being an atheist. Meanwhile, she laid claim to an inherent Irish right to placing a bet. In Ireland the dispute never seemed more than a bit of banter, especially as the only time it came up was when the whole family would put a bet on the Grand National or the Derby. My grandparents always had a small bet, and from the age of about eight I was allowed to join in, but Mum was the one who would bet a whole pound to win on single horses. Then Dad was the one who had to go down to the bookies to place her bet because Mum said respectable women in Ireland didn't do that. When I got older, she used me to place her bets during my lunch break from school. She would wait outside in her red Mini Clubman while I went in and filled out the betting slip according to her instructions. She would have to wait for the newspaper results the next day to see if she had won, but sometimes we'd go home and watch the afternoon races on ITV. Obviously, Dad was never allowed find out about our trips to the bookies.

One of the cultural shocks of moving to Africa was losing the annual ritual of the Grand National. There was barely any television service at all when we first arrived there, and due to apartheid sanctions, certainly no chance of seeing foreign sport. Gambling, like images of nipples, was illegal, except at the government controlled horse racing tracks. But then came Sun City. In 1979, the opening of the gambling resort just two hours drive from Johannesburg was extremely exciting for South Africans hemmed in by government regulations in almost every area of their lives. Until Sun City opened, South Africans had to go to Swaziland for their gambling, but that was a five-hour drive from Johannesburg on dangerous roads. Through the political expedient of establishing the *bantustans*, the so-called homelands for black South Africans, the apartheid government tried to convince the outside world that places like Bophututswana were independent nations. Sun City, a holiday resort with a large casino operation was opened up in 'Bop' and South Africans flooded to it, quickly dubbing it Sin City.

Sun City wasn't especially sinful, though it did have cabaret shows with topless dancers, and of course the casino. There was also a big lake for watersports, lots of swimming pools and a tropical aviary. After a few years they started laying on buses from Johannesburg, and if you bought a ticket they gave you vouchers for the restaurants and a few 'free' chips for the casino.

From time to time we would go there, when Mum was 'feeling lucky'. More accurately, we went when she was especially desperate. And, if Sarah the witch doctor said the omens were good, then a visit to the casino was definitely an option. One weekend Mum announced that we were going to drive to Sun City. For the first time in years, we had a car. It was an elderly Mitsubishi Colt Gallant, a red beast with sunken seats and faded paintwork. When I went out with friends I had to park the car out of sight. As one of my girlfriends once said, 'Your car is very Soweto, isn't it?' But the Colt was indestructible and the engine had done over 350,000 kilometres when it finally died. Unlike most of our previous cars, it even had road tax, so we could drive it in daylight without fear of the traffic cops waving us down.

On Sunday morning we set off for Sun City and arrived just before lunch. It was a blistering hot day. We bought tokens for the pool lockers, and stored our clothes in them before going for a swim. Then we had lunch in one of the cheaper restaurants. Dad ate his lunch, and started drinking beer. With each drink his mood worsened. I knew it was because he didn't want to be there, and didn't want to waste what little cash we had on gambling. We spent the afternoon by the pool, and watched people waterskiing and racing jetskis across the artifical lake. We didn't have money to spend on things like that, but swimming was free. When the sun went down it was time to hit the tables. He said he wasn't coming into the casino, and that he'd wait for us in the car. Mum wasn't going to let him spoil the day. 'Don't be such a martyr,' she remonstrated. 'It's only a little "flutter". If we make back what we've spent, at least we've had a nice day out.'

'And what if you don't?' he growled back. 'How much is this all going to cost? You're just putting money into these shysters' pockets.'

Mum had a lot of self-discipline. She set herself a limit of two hundred rand for the night, and if she lost it she simply stopped playing. She usually stuck to the cheap tables for roulette, where the minimum bet was one rand, and with judicious betting on odds and evens could parlay her two hundred rand into three or four hundred after a few hours. Caro, Will and I all had the same amount. I preferred roulette, but they would also play blackjack, where the odds on winning were more favourable. We all enjoyed the excitement of the roulette wheels and the social atmosphere around the table as people reached over each other to put down their chips on their chosen numbers. Blackjack tables tended to be more serious, as players watched each others' cards to try and calculate the odds of the dealer having a better hand.

That night, I got hooked on roulette. I had played a few times over the years, and sometimes won small amounts, but mostly I lost. There's not much point in gambling if you don't need the money. But when you haven't got much cash, the idea of getting something for nothing is intoxicating. This night seemed different. Within an hour I had turned my two hundred rand into over eight hundred. It was more than all of us had spent on the entire day's entertainment, including the petrol for the journey. And I thought I had developed a system. Unfortunately, it was part probability and part psychic power. And like many compulsive gamblers I believed that there was something called Luck. Luck could defeat the odds if it was running your way.

Perched on a high stool in the cigarette smoke-filled atmosphere above the table I kept a meticulous score card, logging the spins of the roulette wheel and waited for statistical blips in the number of times the evens bets came up (roughly 50:50). On a roulette table you can bet that an individual number from one to thirty-six will come up – a simple thirty-five-to-one probability. You can also bet on whether the number will be 'red' or 'black' – a rough 50:50 probability (excluding the '0' which is neutral). Because '0' is neither 'odd' nor 'even' it doesn't count in the evens bets: and so reduces the odds from a straight 50:50 to a 48.65% chance of being right. You can also split your bet on adjacent numbers, halving the odds, or even on blocks of four, six or twelve numbers thus reducing the odds further. These bets then reduce the payouts accordingly. Mathematically, the odds are the same every time the wheel spins, but if red came up three times in a row I would double my bet on the next spin being black, and vice versa. If it still came up red a fourth or fifth time, my tactic was to double my stake. It worked beautifully until the croupier spun seven red numbers in a row. Unfortunately, I had been so sure that I was on a winning streak that I had graduated to a table where the minimum bet on evens was ten rand. In minutes, I was cleaned out. I felt sick. I had lost the equivalent of a whole month's pay after three hours of intense gambling.

Back at the cheap tables, Mum and my siblings were winning, but not the spectacular amounts that I had gained on the more expensive table. It was almost time to stop, but I asked them to lend me their winnings to recoup my losses. At first they wouldn't cooperate. I begged and pleaded until they handed over their cash. I told them about my system, and how they had to trust me, and be brave. And then I lost it all. Will and Caroline were angry with me but Mum said there was nothing we could do about it. 'Just don't tell your father,' she said calmly as we headed outside from the brightly lit casino. 'He'll have a fit.'

Dad was asleep in the passenger seat of the Colt. The beer had worked its magic and he had slumped against the front passenger window, mouth agape and snoring loudly. His principles had forced him to stay in the car for all the time we'd been in the casino. And we hadn't left him with any money at all in case he found a bar. As we piled in for the long drive home he awoke, wiping away a trail of spittle from around his mouth and looking groggy. 'What time is it?' he asked sullenly. It was almost midnight. None of us dared say anything for fear of giving away our disappointment. And for Mum, the idea that he had been proved right was worse than losing the money. But the inevitable question came soon enough.

'Well, how did you do?'

'Some of us won, some of us lost,' Mum said in a neutral way. She was hunkered down in the back seat directly behind Dad with Caro and Will squashed against her. In the darkness of the car it was impossible to read her expression.

'How much?'

'Oh, we've pretty much broken even,' she said casually. 'But we've had a good day out.'

I drove through the darkness with a knot in my stomach. The roads were unlit and there was very little traffic at that time of night. Dad didn't speak and Mum and the others sat in the back pretending to sleep. After about an hour Dad asked me if I had my headlights on full beam. I had, but the lights didn't seem very effective. Gradually, as we drove, the beam became weaker and weaker. Eventually I was forced to drive extremely slowly because the headlights only illuminated the road for about six feet ahead. We had just reached the very outskirts of the city when the lights died out altogether. And then the car engine stopped. At least we weren't out on a country road, but we were still at least a half hour drive from home.

'If the worst comes to the worst we can get a taxi from here,' Dad said as we stared at the silent engine in the dim light of a street lamp. He was uncharacteristically calm about the roadside drama, and had sobered up on the long drive. None of us said anything, because we couldn't let him find out that we didn't have the taxi fare to get us a hundred yards, let alone all the way home. If Dad found out we had lost all of our cash we'd never hear the end of it. Even worse, Mum might have to acknowledge that he was right to disapprove of gambling. In a situation like this we maintained solidarity with her.

Hardly any traffic passed by, but after a time a large BMW saloon pulled up beside us and a smartly dressed Japanese couple asked if we needed help. 'There's a hospital up the road,' they said. 'We could take you there and you could use the telephone.'

Caro and I took a ride up to the hospital, which turned out to be a small private clinic with just one bored receptionist on duty. Grudgingly, she said we could telephone the AA. When we got through, they asked us for our membership number and we told them it was our mother who had broken down and we didn't know her details. The operator said she would send a breakdown truck, but we'd have to show our membership card in order to get help. We decided to deal with that problem later.

The Japanese Samaritans took us back to the Colt and we waited for the breakdown truck. When it turned up, we told Dad to stay in the car and Mum got out to do the talking. She told him she had left her membership card at home, but I'm not sure he cared. He diagnosed a broken fan-belt and produced a spare from the back of his truck. After the engine was running, Dad decided it was time to get involved. 'Don't forget to give the man a nice tip,' he called out grandly. Mum rummaged in her bag and found that she had exactly two rand in small change left in her purse, barely enough to buy a cup of coffee. She imperiously handed it over to the mechanic as if it were indeed a generous tip. 'That was lucky,' Dad said as we drove off. 'It would have been dangerous to get stuck all the way out here in the middle of the night, and expensive to get a taxi all the way home.'

On the Film Set

After leaving Cambridge I went back to Johannesburg to be with the family. Once again, I found work at the Carlton, this time as a waiter at the Three Ships. By 1985 things had become more relaxed since I first worked at the hotel, and I was one of just three white waiters in the restaurant. Within a few weeks the other two left, and I was the only white member of the serving staff. My colleagues all lived in Soweto and seemed bemused that I had come from England to work with them.

'We need a white man who will work *with* us, and not just order us around,' Herbie Tshabalala told me after a few days. 'Because you will be useful. When the Boere come in and don't leave a tip, you can go to them and ask them to give it. They will not be rude to a white man. Ay, ay, ay. We can never do such things!'

One night I reported for duty, and was called into the manager's office. Jurgen was an Austrian, a ladies' man who drove a scarlet Porsche. He was ultra-smooth, fluent in English, German and French and quite handsome in an obvious tall blond fashion. If there were attractive women in the room he would insist on showing them to their table and sometimes take the order himself. The waiters laughed at him behind his back, and loved impersonating him.

'There's trouble,' Jurgen said. 'And I need your help. We may have to close the main restaurant tonight because your black brothers are threatening to strike. They won't tell me what the problem is, but I'm counting on you to back me up and stay on duty.'

Returning to the kitchen, I found Mike Dlamini, the Head Waiter, sitting with the other eight men in the corner of the kitchen. He told me that the restaurant was hosting a large table of black businessmen from the USA who were in South Africa on a fact-finding mission. The waiters were refusing to serve them.

'Why?' I asked.

'Because,' Mike said implacably. 'They're *niggers*.'

'What do you mean?' I stuttered.

'Well, we know that in America black people are just niggers. We've seen it in the movies. But we're Africans. We're not going to serve them, and have them acting all important. Who do they think they are?'

'That's right!' Francis, the sommelier chipped in. 'They can't even speak any African languages. We're not going to say "Yes, sir. No, sir," to them.'

'But if we go on strike we'll lose a day's pay,' Mike added. 'But you my friend can help us out.'

'If you strike, then I will too,' I said.

'No. That's not what we want. We want you to tell the manager that you will serve them in the private function room – and we'll all work the main restaurant.'

So that's how it was. Jurgen and I served the black Americans in the private room, while the African staff stayed in the main restaurant.

The weeks passed in a cycle of split shifts. From eleven in the morning until two-thirty in the afternoon from Monday to Friday, I served lunch at the Three Ships. My world was polishing glasses and cutlery, laying tables, folding napkins, carrying food and pouring wine. From seven p.m. until midnight, much later at weekends, it was dinner. Dinner service was more interesting because I was allowed to make crêpes Suzettes and flaming liqueur drinks that had to be poured from a ladle that we were taught to raise high in the air so that the liquid formed a blazing arc. It looked very dramatic, and the sense of theatre was amplified by our double-breasted Naval style cream jackets, complete with brass buttons and gold braid. On Mondays, we closed. Just as I had done six years earlier, I used the bus to get into town in the mornings and home in the afternoons. At night I would take a taxi, but just for the journey from the Carlton to Hillbrow. Then I would make a thirty-minute walk back to Natal Street, which reduced the taxi fare by half. Once I left the main thoroughfares of Hillbrow, I rarely saw another soul, but everyone thought it was a dangerous habit, and Mum made me promise not to do it.

I disobeyed, because walking in the night air allowed me to wind down from the buzz of the noisy Carlton kitchens and the plush splendour of the Three Ships. I relished being alone on the empty streets, and would try to remember normal things from life back in Britain, wondering what my friends were doing while I tramped back to the ramshackle house on Natal Street. Just knowing that they had more comfortable lives was reassuring, even if it made me envious at times. I wished that we could rejoin that life, and have running water and be free of the constant pressure of worrying about money. But at the same time I knew that we had gained something that my friends and relatives didn't have: we would never again take any kind of material comfort for granted. By the time I reached the house, I was calm enough to sleep.

Sometimes, I would spot Marco the Maltese taxi-driver in a side street near the hotel. He wasn't allowed to wait on the official rank at the front of the Carlton, because his cab was too shabby. And Marco himself looked like a tramp. He was a squat man with a leather cap pulled down low on his forehead. Sitting on a tattered cushion, his seat was pulled as far forward as it would go. Marco's cab smelled of fried chicken and strong cigarettes, and his hands gripped the wheel in black leather fingerless gloves. Marco had a terrible permanent cough that made his chest rattle as he breathed. One night I got into conversation with him and he asked me lots of questions about why my family had moved to Africa. I gave him a brief version of the events that had led to me working as a waiter at the Carlton.

'Business,' he coughed, spraying phlegm into a cupped hand. 'I lost everything fifteen years ago. My wife left me and went back to Malta to her family. She took my daughter too, and I'll never see them again.'

Whenever Marco saw me he would honk the horn, and I would take his cab. His English was poor, but he sensed a common bond. One night, after I got out of the cab and started walking he followed, drawing up beside me after a couple of blocks.

'Where you are going?'

'It's not far,' I lied. 'I just want some air, and it's good to walk a little way before I go home to bed.'

'No, no, no. Not good. Very *bad* to walk here at night. I take you.'

From then on he always switched off his meter when we got to the outskirts of Hillbrow, but insisted on taking me all the way to the corner of Natal Street. Marco disappeared from the rank a few months later, and another driver told me he had died.

Life at home was as difficult as ever. We lurched from crisis to crisis. Dad had returned to Africa on a permanent basis, mainly because he had developed cataracts in both eyes, and couldn't work. For months he refused to consult a doctor, partly because of the cost, and partly out of fear. We needed to save up to pay for an operation to get plastic lenses inserted in his eyes, a treatment that appealed to him because it could be carried out under a local anaesthetic. 'You're not putting me under,' he barked at the ophthalmologist. Privately, we knew he was scared at the prospect of the operation, and he felt that having it done while conscious would somehow allow him to monitor proceedings. It was also considerably cheaper than having a general anaesthetic. In the meantime, he had to wait until we got the money together, a matter of several months. His deteriorating eyesight made him irritable, and a lot of time had to be spent placating him. We also had to try to stop him driving, something he wasn't prepared to give up no matter the danger. His moods were so unpredictable that Mum didn't like him coming into the shop, because she said he frightened away the customers and the other dealers.

———————

Mrs Van der Meulen was a regular visitor to The Whatnot. She owned a small swap-shop on the outskirts of Johannesburg, dealing in porcelain and items of crockery that her mainly Afrikaans clients bought as ornaments. Her customers had a taste for the sentimental; china doves, porcelain Hansel and Gretel figurines holding hands and picture frames inscribed with trite verse. Although she dealt in rubbish, Mrs Van der Meulen was a shrewd businesswoman and would pore over items in The Whatnot for hours before committing herself to buying anything.

One day she came to the shop to view some boxes of odds and ends that Mum had bought at auction. None of it was good enough for her own customers, but Mum thought Mrs Van der Meulen would buy it for her swap-shop.

Dad sat in a chair near Mum's office desk and watched Mrs Van der Meulen deliberating over the kitsch. He had been drinking beer at lunchtime, and his mood was sullen. We spotted the danger signals. His hands were locked behind his head and his legs stretched wide apart. It was what my brother called 'aggressive open-crotch display', a phrase he parroted at Dad after learning it from a book about body language.

'Poor Mrs Van der Meulen didn't know where to look,' Mum told us afterwards. Mum knew that Dad didn't like the woman, and he barely spoke to her when she visited. But then

Mum started negotiating a price for the assembled bric-a-brac.

'Oh, I don't think I could pay that much,' Mrs Van der Meulen began, when Dad suddenly sprang to life.

'You bloody thieving Afrikaans bitch!' he shouted. 'Get the hell out of here. If you don't want to pay a fair price for all this fucking china crap you can go to hell!'

'Stuart!' Mum said as we all stared at him with horror. 'How dare you speak to Mrs Van der Meulen like that?'

It was too late, Dad had gone into a rabid phase. 'I'll speak to her any way I please. Bloody old cow!'

Mrs Van der Meulen was grey with fright. She started gathering her belongings and heading for the door. But Dad wasn't finished, berating her as she went.

'You bloody Dutchmen – you're worse than the Jews. Get the hell back to Krugersdorp where you belong!'

Mum was in tears by the time Mrs Van der Meulen had left the Market. We all knew there was no reasoning with Dad when he flipped out of control like that. Instead, we tried to comfort Mum that evening, ignoring Dad completely, knowing that he was in a dangerous mood. 'I've been doing business with that woman for five years,' Mum sobbed quietly. 'He doesn't know how difficult it is to sell things, all he cares about is telling people what he thinks of them. I've never, *ever* been so humiliated in all my life.'

I didn't imagine that Mum would ever be able to face talking to Mrs Van der Meulen again. But a few days later, when Dad wasn't around, Mum rang her up.

'Hello Mrs Van der Meulen, this is Pam. How are you?'

I didn't hear Mrs Van der Meulen's reply, but Mum carried on the conversation in a very casual tone.

'I'm so sorry that you had to witness my husband during one of his attacks,' she continued. 'We realised after you had left that he hadn't taken his medication that morning. You know, ever since his war-wound he has to take very strong drugs otherwise he gets these episodes where he doesn't know what he's saying.'

Mrs Van der Meulen was clearly taken in, because Mum carried on elaborating, all the while sounding as if she was totally unfazed by the dreadful things he'd said. 'We're all used to his terrible temper when he has an attack, but it must have been frightening for you. You know he gets these *terrible* headaches – ever since he was in Korea. Yes . . . shrapnel in the skull . . . you can't *imagine* the pain he goes through: sometimes he's on his knees on the floor holding his head in his hands. And the doctors say he doesn't remember anything that he's said or done afterwards.'

By the end of the conversation, Mrs Van der Meulen was in tears with sympathy. 'Aagh shame, the poor man,' she said. 'I never knew what you had to cope with. And all because he was a soldier, serving his country.'

The claim that Dad had amnesia after one of his 'attacks' was the master stroke, and not far from the truth since Dad didn't remember things he'd said when he was drunk. Mum's lie allowed him to see Mrs Van der Meulen again without embarrassment, although she never lingered in the shop when he was around.

Sometimes Dad's belligerence came in useful. One day, two men arrived at the shop claiming that Mum owed them money. Maybe she did, maybe she didn't. But Mum wasn't there and Dad didn't like the look of them. I was on my break between shifts at the restaurant and trying to have a snooze in the back room of the shop. One of the men said they'd come back later, and that Mum had better have their money or there would be trouble. That was a mistake.

'Fuck off out of here,' I heard Dad say. 'And don't come back here making threats you can't carry through.'

As the altercation gathered steam I decided to get up and show some moral support. Dad was almost sixty, and he was on his own. By the time I emerged from behind the curtain, one of the men was brandishing a knife. Dad moved from behind the desk with surprising speed, and before I could even speak he had kicked the knifeman in the groin. As he went down, Dad hit him under the chin with a rolled up newspaper he had been reading when they came into the shop. I was about seven the first time Dad had shown me what a useful weapon a newspaper could be: 'hit them under the nose with that,' he said, 'it's as good as an iron bar.' On this occasion the man hit the ground and lay still, and Dad had his foot on his throat. The other man took his chance, jumping onto Dad's back and wrapping his arm around his neck. It was all happening so fast I didn't know what to do. A display table went crashing to the ground. Quite deliberately, and with surprising forethought Dad carried his assailant out of the shop and flipped him over his head onto the ground where he lay, winded. Dad said afterwards that his instinct was to throw the man through the shop window, but he realised that would cost us money. It was uncharacteristically sensible of him. Within seconds, Markus from the Sex-Shop and Scots

John were in the corridor, Markus armed with a pepper spray and John brandishing a machete.

The two men staggered to their feet and started backing out of the Market.

'Let them go, son,' said Scots John. 'They're afeard o'ye!'

'I'm going to kill them,' Dad said with total calm.

Markus stepped in front of Dad and spoke to the two hapless thugs. 'He *will* kill you, and if you ever come back here again I'll bear witness that it was self-defence. Do you understand?'

That night, I relived the adventure with Mum as we sat up drinking tea after Dad had gone to bed. I had contributed nothing to the debacle, and wouldn't have known where to start when faced with a man brandishing a knife.

'I knew something must have happened the moment I walked into the shop,' she said. 'Your father looked happier than I've seen him for months, and somehow much younger. It really does him good to have a fight. That's what he was trained for.'

That was when she started referring to him as Rambo (from *First Blood*, Sylvester Stallone, Bryan Dennehy, 1982).

———

Things got better when Dad had his cataracts fixed. It wasn't just me that worked to save up the money, we all did. Caro had left home and moved to Germany to live with her boyfriend, and she would send money when she could. My brother had left school – mainly to avoid being conscripted into the South African army – and ran his own market stall on

Saturdays, selling jewellery that he bought from Mum's contacts in the scrap metal trade.

One night we were watching television when there was an interview with a British film producer. He said he was hoping to make a feature film in South Africa, and that it would be a big-budget affair.

'You should ring him up,' Mum said. 'Offer to help him with the film, you'd be good at that sort of thing.'

When Mum had an idea, it was foolish to argue. The next morning, I rang the TV studio and asked for contact details for the film producer, Mark Cassidy. Armed with the number of his hotel, I made the call. He agreed to meet me, and said he would consider giving me a job. No one else on the crew had been recruited, and Mark said he would tell his business partners that I was a useful contact with local knowledge. A few weeks later, I was working as the producer's assistant. I was nominally in charge of ensuring that Mark knew everything that was happening on and off the set, but my main duty was reporting to Mark at his rented house each night after dinner to play tennis on the floodlit court. We often played until midnight, the only way Mark knew to unwind after a day wrestling with the stresses and strains of handling the budget. It was a good arrangement, and the tennis games allowed me to persuade Mark to give Dad a contract to supply the film company with security guards. Then my brother was employed as a stand-in for the leading man, and when filming actually began, Mum was even employed as an extra. She loved it, and for several years afterwards she became a regular on film and TV sets around Johannesburg.

The film was an adaptation of *Hold My Hand I'm Dying*, a novel by the Rhodesian author John Gordon Davis. Like many films made in South Africa in the 1980s it was part-financed through generous tax incentives from the government. For its time, *Hold My Hand* had a big budget, and making the film was an adventure. The crew provided as much excitement as the film itself, and we had car-hijackings, drug overdoses, love affairs, gunplay and knife-fights before the cameras had even rolled. The actual plot revolves around the friendship between Joe Mahoney, a British colonial official and his African friend, Samson, who saves Joe's life when he is attacked by a crocodile. Years later, Joe returns to Rhodesia during the guerrilla war and Samson goes to work with him on his farm. The guerrillas force Samson to set fire to the farm, but he only carries out the attack when he knows Joe and his wife aren't at home. Sadly, Samson is caught in the act by the police and sentenced to death for terrorism. In spite of Joe's pleas, Samson will not tell the court that he was coerced into violence because the guerrillas are holding his family to ransom. He is hanged.

One of the exciting things about making the film was that Mark had been able to recruit Oliver Reed (*Women in Love*, 1967) for a cameo role. On the day that he was due to arrive in Johannesburg a driver was sent to the airport to collect the star and deliver him to his suite at the Johannesburg Sun and Towers. What Mark didn't know was that Oliver Reed had been to Johannesburg before. 'Take me to the Carlton,' he ordered the driver.

Several hours passed, and I was told to find out why Oliver Reed had not arrived safely at the Sun and Towers. After a morning of fruitless enquiries Mark started to panic, fearing that Reed had been hijacked en route from the airport, or had been involved in a car crash.

'Come on, Tim,' he said, at lunchtime, 'let's drive out to the airport and see if we can find out what's happened.'

As we hurtled down the stairs from the production office, the receptionist ran after me. 'Tim, wait, your mother is on the phone.'

'I can't stop now!' I shouted over my shoulder.

'No – see what she wants,' said Mark. 'I can wait two minutes.'

I wasn't in the mood for chit-chat, and barked angrily into the phone that I couldn't talk as we were in the middle of a crisis. 'What's wrong?' Mum asked.

'We've lost Oliver Reed,' I said self-importantly. 'And I have to go and look for him.'

'Just calm down,' she said. 'I might be able to help you with that.'

'What do you mean?'

'Well, your father and I had just popped into the Carlton for a cold drink, and we spotted him in the Clock Bar.'

'What! I'm coming straight over – Mark's with me.'

'There's no rush,' Mum laughed. 'He and your father are at the bar, and I don't think they'll be leaving anytime soon.'

Mark decided that it wasn't a good idea for him to meet our star in the hotel bar, and I was despatched to make sure Reed made it back to his own hotel in one piece. When I arrived, Dad and Oliver Reed were holding court. It seemed they had played for the same rugby team in Wales.

'So,' Reed bellowed as Dad introduced me. 'This is your son who doesn't drink beer, and doesn't play rugby.'

The danger signs were plain to see. Reed and Dad were several beers past the point of reason. 'What's wrong with you, lad?' Reed said placing a meaty hand on my shoulder. 'Are you a poof?' He turned to Dad. 'He's not a bloody poof, your son, is he?'

'I don't think he is,' Dad replied. 'He just doesn't like rugby. And it's a great shame.'

'Well, maybe he likes wrestling. Do you, boy? Do you like wrestling? Come on, let's give it a try—'

'I'm not much of a wrestler,' I squeaked, backing out of the bar in a hurry. The last thing I saw from the safety of the doorway was Dad and Reed arm wrestling on the bar. Fortunately, when Reed eventually appeared on set he was a model of professionalism, and I kept out of his way.

Hold My Hand I'm Dying provided me with more than a year's work, and the financial security to leave Natal Street and rent us a house with running water, *and* electricity. After more than a decade of adventures centred around The Whatnot, it looked as if the crazy times were about to end. I had dipped in and out of that world, maintaining that secretive second life while studying at not one, but two universities. Now, with Mum and Dad together, and at least able to pay the rent, I decided to return to London. I wanted a career that had better prospects than working as a waiter.

My experience in Johannesburg led to a few more jobs in the film industry, and then I applied to the BBC. My CV ended up on the desk of the Head of the African section of the BBC

World Service. Her name was Dorothy Grenfell Williams, and she called me in for an interview. Things started formally enough, but then she told me she was a film buff. She was fascinated by my experiences on *Hold My Hand I'm Dying*, and we talked about old movies for over two hours. At the end of the afternoon she offered me a job as a producer in news and current affairs. My actual qualifications seemed irrelevant.

'You can soon learn all the radio stuff,' she guffawed. 'What I need here is *interesting* people who won't bore me!'

Dad was thrilled when I got the job at the BBC, although Mum was less enthusiastic. She worried that my career would prevent me returning to South Africa on a permanent basis. In her view, having the whole family together in one country was all that really mattered.

Working at the BBC gave me a good salary, more than I needed as a single bachelor living in a shared flat in Shepherd's Bush. I sent regular monthly bank transfers back to Johannesburg. Mum and Dad weren't living in the lap of luxury, but things were nothing like as tough as they had been. And occasionally, when they could tune in the short-wave radio successfully, they could even listen to me broadcasting from London.

Whenever I telephoned home, Mum told me that they were managing fine. Once the film was finished, she had returned to running the shop full-time. Dad got occasional security jobs, but his age was starting to count against him. One day she told me that she was giving up the lease on the shop. 'I've done as much as I can with the business,' she claimed. 'And another dealer has offered to buy all my stock at a good price.'

It took me a few months to understand that Mum was unwell. She claimed that she was suffering from various things: a bladder infection, gastric flu, and colic. In South Africa, the outlook for patients without expensive medical insurance was, and still is, bleak. And when Mum couldn't find the answer to an ailment in her Pears Medical Encyclopaedia, the only affordable option was Old Doctor Rabby. His real name was Saul Rabinowitz but everyone called him Rabby. He practised out of a tin-roofed house on Doris Street, and he was eighty-four.

Mum and Dad liked the fact that he was nearby, and although he was old, he was conveniently located, and cheap. South African doctors are among the best in the world, and in the private clinics the standards of care were exceptional. But without medical insurance, the cost of a consultation was prohibitive. Old Doctor Rabby, as he liked to be known, relied on sixty years experience rather than technology. His stethoscope was his main, and virtually only, tool of the trade, and he never charged more than a flat fifty-rand consultation fee. I saw him myself a few times, and he was a wise man, as close as you could find to the avuncular TV character in *Dr. Finlay's Casebook* (Bill Simpson, 1962). Doctor Rabby didn't actually have a housekeeper called Janet, but he did have Mrs Rabinowitz who answered the door in a pinny, and showed you into the waiting room – her lounge. Rabby was a great clinician, but he had a habit of falling asleep in the middle of a consultation.

'I thought he'd had a stroke the first time it happened,' Mum warned me when I went to see him once with flu. 'Don't worry if he suddenly goes very quiet, and falls backward in his chair. Leave him for a minute and then tap him gently on the knee – he always comes around eventually and remembers exactly what's wrong with you. Then he'll write you a prescription.'

Mum didn't tell anyone how ill she had been feeling, and by telephone she would simply tell me of various self-diagnosed ailments. I knew she had been confined to bed at times with what she said was a bladder infection, that made it painful to walk. By the time she went to Doctor Rabby he was fairly certain she had cancer.

'You have a large mass in your abdomen and you need to see a surgeon,' he said in his slow, deliberate manner. 'If it's not too late.'

Goodbye

Doctor Hetherington, the obstetric surgeon, wore thin-rimmed half-moon spectacles and was reassuringly suave and upper class. He had immaculately manicured hands and wore handmade dark grey suits with a college tie. His mild Capetonian accent added to his charm, and Mum flirted outrageously with him, insisting on calling him Mr Heatherington, adopting the British form of address for surgeons.

As we left the consulting rooms she jokingly quoted a line from a TV comedy show we had watched together years earlier: 'I wouldn't mind his boots under me bed.'

Doctor Heatherington's diagnosis was not amusing, or charming. He confirmed that she had an ovarian tumour, and said it had to be removed urgently. In private, he told me that the operation would provide Mum with a temporary respite from discomfort, but all the signs pointed to a malignancy that had progressed past the point of salvage. It was November, and Mum at first refused to go under the knife.

'If I die on the table,' she said quietly, as we sat in his consulting room, 'it'll ruin everyone's Christmas. Let's wait until the New Year.'

'My dear lady,' he said with a startled expression. 'At this stage, you must only think about yourself. You must be in a great deal of pain, and if we leave it any longer it will simply get worse.'

To the surgeon's consternation, Mum ordered Dad not to visit her immediately before the operation. 'I don't want him here,' she said. 'He'll go to pieces, and then he'll fall out with the doctors and nurses. I can't be dealing with him as well as everything else.'

'I'm afraid the tumour was very large,' Heatherington told me after seven hours in the theatre. 'With most patients I wouldn't have bothered battling to remove a growth of that size, but I think your mother has a very strong spirit. I think she deserves a chance to fight it. Do we agree?'

At first, they said Mum was unlikely to leave intensive care, and then they said she would never leave the hospital. Will, Caro and I took turns at sitting with her, and, although we didn't have the money to pay for it, she was given a private room. Late one night, the ward sister told me it was because they thought Mum was going to die quite soon. But gradually, agonisingly slowly, she regained her strength. Doctor Heatherington was a daily visitor, peering at her chart through his glasses for a few seconds before conversing about everything except her condition. Mum had the sensitivity to leave her medical dictionary at home, and on her bedside table she contented herself with the Oxford Dictionary of Art and a biography of Amy Earhart, both thick tomes that impressed the surgeon.

Mum always read voraciously, and even when she had no money she would often cross Pretoria Street after closing up The Whatnot to spend the evening in Exclusive Books. For an hour or more, she would stand in there, her worn out sheepskin coat covering her flimsy threadbare green dress reading great chunks from novels and biographies that she couldn't afford to buy.

'If I had to choose between clothes and books, I would always use my last penny on a book,' she claimed. It frustrated me when she said she was uneducated, because she read at least two books a week her entire life. Yet when she was dangerously ill she chose not to question the doctors about the disease, or its likely progression. That was my job.

'I don't think your mother wants to know too much in the way of detail,' Doctor Heatherington told me. 'Some people prefer to deal with their illness in that way. Are we correct?'

On Christmas Eve, she begged to be allowed to come home from hospital for a day. He said I could collect her, but that she was to return the following morning.

We ate a family Christmas dinner together, for what I was sure was the last time. Mum was a shrunken bird-like figure at one end of the table, barely strong enough to lift a fork to her lips. But she brushed her hair and put her make-up on, laughing and joining in with the celebrations, forcing us to enjoy the day. On Boxing Day morning, she called me to her bedside. 'Ring the hospital,' she said. 'And tell them I'm not coming back. This is where I belong, and I feel much better here, with all of you, than I ever can in hospital.'

For weeks I was expecting her to die at any moment. But she didn't. Instead, she got stronger, and refused to return to the hospital. The surgeon referred her to an oncologist, and I persuaded her to go for the appointment. The new doctor was a very different species to Doctor Heatherington. Brusque and sneering, he didn't like to be asked too many questions. And to make matters worse, he had bright red hair. 'I can't take a doctor with ginger hair seriously,' Mum decreed with raised eyebrows after meeting him. 'He's certainly not a gentleman, not like Mr Heatherington.'

The oncologist was a leading authority in his field, and highly respected. He muttered something about an intensive course of radiation and chemotherapy, and swept out of the room trailed by a posse of junior doctors. After a few minutes, one of the female doctors returned alone. She seemed embarrassed, almost nervous.

'You won't remember me,' she said to Mum. 'But you have an unusual surname, and I realise that we've met before. It must have been about twelve years ago.'

The doctor took out a purse from her jacket pocket and extracted a tiny photograph that had been trimmed to fit inside a cellophane window in the lid. The picture showed a tabby-point Siamese cat, and Mum immediately recognised the distinctive colouring. For a short time, when we were living in Mitchell Court, she had managed to make some money by selling kittens. The cat in the photograph was one of Mae-Ling's offspring. The doctor talked to Mum about her cat, which was still thriving, and then she beckoned me into the corridor.

'I shouldn't say this,' she said cautiously. 'But if it was my mother, I wouldn't let her undergo the treatment the professor recommends. It's a very gruelling regime, and she's already very weak.' The doctor paused for a moment, unwilling to state the obvious. 'Do you see?'

And so we left the hospital. Over a period of several months Mum regained her strength and gradually put on weight. As far as Mum made out, the operation had been a complete success.

'I never thought I'd be happy to be gaining weight instead of losing it,' she said to me one day. 'As long as I don't get thinner, I must be getting better, don't you think?'

For over two years, Mum was able to live a normal life. We didn't discuss the specifics of her illness, and she never, ever called it 'cancer'. The only time she acknowledged the nature of the disease was in a telephone conversation once I had returned to London.

'I need you to find someone for me,' she said. 'I've read a magazine interview with the actress Moira Lister, (Rex Harrison, Ingrid Bergman, *The Yellow Rolls Royce*, 1964). It says she's had cancer and she beat it with positive thinking, something called visualisation. I'd like to talk to her about that, and maybe I could try it. Can you find her for me?'

I tracked down a number for the actress, and made the call. I didn't know where to begin explaining what I wanted, but she was a kind and generous listener. The next day she telephoned Mum at home and they discussed their experiences.

Mum didn't go back to a hospital, or to any other doctor until two days before she died. When she was in discomfort, she simply didn't talk about it. Meanwhile, Doctor Rabby was content to supply her with painkillers, giving the prescriptions to Dad without Mum having to go to the surgery.

She swallowed them like Smarties, and after a few months she announced that she was strong enough to visit me in London. It was the first time she had left Johannesburg to return to Britain since we had emigrated. 'I can never repay you for what you've done,' Mum told me repeatedly while she was in London, a visit that lasted three months. 'All my children have been wonderful.'

I assumed that we were on borrowed time, and enjoyed showing her all the good things about the city. We went often to the cinema, to exhibitions and to the theatre. At the National Gallery we saw the original paintings she knew from *Masterpiece the Art Auction Game*. At the Royal Ballet we saw productions of *Manon*, and *Giselle* and went to the Coliseum to watch the visiting Kirov. She conceded that the dancers were, indeed, amazing athletes. 'I understand why you have to be here,' she said one night as we travelled home in a taxi. She was still using her battered old sheepskin coat. 'Johannesburg is such a one-horse town compared to London. It must have been very boring for you all those years, having to keep coming out there to see me.'

Having Mum living with me felt strange. I lost my independence. She insisted on cooking me dinner each night, and ironing my clothes. One day I came home from work to find an enormous yucca plant on the dining room table. 'You need some greenery in here,' she said. It wasn't an appealing specimen, but I knew she was trying to turn the flat where I lived alone into something more like a real home.

'I can never make up for all those years you had to manage on your own,' she would say when I protested. In the evenings she would go to bed early but wanted me to sit on the bed and talk for a while. More often than not we sat up until midnight drinking endless cups of tea and gossiping. 'You don't have to stay at home with your old mother,' she would joke. 'It must be boring for you, stuck here with me. You should be out on the town, giving the girls a whirl.'

Mum's hopes of marrying me off to produce grandchildren were never quelled. During her visit, I despatched Mum to see her siblings. The first visit was to her eldest brother, Uncle Herbert, a journey that she made alone on the train from Paddington to Cheltenham. As I walked her to the platform she looked in dismay at the Standard Class carriage. 'Timothy, you *surely* don't expect me to travel Second Class on a train? You were never, ever brought up to go anything but First Class on the railways.'

'First Class is three times the price!' I protested. 'Hardly anyone goes First Class these days. It's not like it was in the 1960s – the last time you were *actually* on a train in England.'

'I am not just anyone,' Mum announced grandly. 'And I can't believe that you *want* your mother to go Second Class.'

In spite of everything that had happened in Africa, it seemed that going Second Class, as she insisted on calling it, was not admissible. There was just time for me to run to the booking office and change the ticket.

My BBC job had provided the money for Mum's treatment, and allowed Mum and Dad to live a more comfortable life in Johannesburg. My salary had even purchased her air ticket to London. But, at the end of her visit Mum asked me to return to Africa as soon as I could. 'I know how you love it here,' she said. 'But I'd rather you were closer to home. I can't keep shuttling between you and your father. He needs me too.'

'But what about my job?' I protested. 'I can't give up the BBC.'

'Well, you've been there over three years,' she said dismissively. 'And frankly, I never thought you'd end up working in an office. There's more to life.'

It was about nine months later that Dad warned me that he thought Mum was getting weaker. Commuting between London and Johannesburg wasn't an option, but under the circumstances the BBC gave me permission to work in South Africa for a year. With the end of apartheid in sight, and the old regime crumbling fast there was no shortage of reporting work to be done, alongside the coverage being provided by the mainstream correspondents.

Each night I returned to the small house in Bedfordview, where Mum and Dad now lived, and we watched a large number of movies on video. One of her favourites was *Amadeus* (Tom Hulce, F. Murray Abraham, 1984), which she watched five or six times. In the day, Mum snoozed and read when she had the energy. Her three little dogs kept her company, sleeping on the bed until they heard Dad approaching, when they would slink to the floor with their ears flat against their heads. Towards the end, even watching films was too tiring and Mum inevitably dozed off halfway through. 'Have I seen this?' she asked me one night as the opening credits rolled. And then she started laughing, 'That was Irish logic, wasn't it? Tomorrow I won't remember whether I've seen it or not, and I could watch the beginning all over again – I'm no better than a goldfish!'

Goodbye

I remember a small and hurried conversation as Mum lay propped up on a heap of pillows in her hospital bed. It was a sunny morning, and I was anxious not to be late for a meeting that really didn't matter. I knew that the meeting was unimportant, but I was using it as an excuse to leave, something to take me away from the pain of staying with my mother on that clear fresh day. Her bed was by the window, a bright place where she could see the African sun. I felt too cowardly to face up to a final goodbye, to take a last look into her face and walk away. I kissed her and said I would return in the afternoon. In fact I got no further than the end of the corridor, and returned a few minutes later, conquering my fear and my dread to stand beside the bed, holding her hand and talking to her, repeating small trivial things that were simply a reason to stay a little longer. Neither of us needed to make grand statements, but we both knew that time was short.

'Don't be late,' she said. 'Don't put yourself in a rush.'

'It doesn't matter,' I mumbled, staring out of the window and seeing the morning rush hour traffic on a fast road far below. The window sealed us in, making us look at the outside world as if on a TV screen with the volume turned down. 'It's a beautiful day isn't it? You know I never get tired of that blue sky, it always cheers me up.'

'It'll be hot later, but it's still fresh now.'

'You look nice,' she told me with a squeeze of her hand. 'Handsome. There's a very nice nurse on this ward today, and I've found out she's not married.'

I remember her hand: the skin slack and cool, not softened and fresh as I had always known it, but toneless and wasted. Nearly lifeless, but still her hand. Her fingers around mine and the soft familiar glint of her wedding ring shining against her skin.

'I don't think I want to meet any nurses today. I don't feel nice, certainly not handsome.'

'You look handsome to me,' she replied.

I couldn't talk. As usual, she broke the silence. Reassuring me and making light of her own situation. 'Go on, Timmy, you go now – don't make yourself late.'

No one else ever called me that, not since we had left home. People there weren't embarrassed to say 'Timmy', but outside Ireland people couldn't seem to cope with it, imagining it fit only for very young boys. Hearing it now, the familiar, familial version of my name was unbearable. It stopped me speaking, words frozen hard in my throat. If I tried to get them out I would break down.

'Go before you have to speed to get there,' she said. 'I don't want you speeding.'

'It doesn't matter if I don't go. No one will miss me at the meeting.'

'You've got work to do.'

'It's not important.'

She squeezed my hand again. 'It *is* important,' she said with a mischievous smile. 'Don't forget what the witch doctor said. You have to write those books, remember?'

Years had passed since that day in Sarah's musty little office above Anderson Street. I had barely thought of it since, but Mum's world was different. It was where intuition, premonition and looking into the future were as valid as any branch of science. Her jibe had the desired effect, spurring me to leave with a flash of ire, and a reminder, if I needed it, that my education did not provide me with the answers to everything.

When I returned to the hospital that evening, Mum had slipped into a coma. The night dragged by, measured in countless Styrofoam cups of tea from a vending machine that hummed and whirred in the unearthly fluorescent corridor outside the ward. When she died in the early hours of the morning, we were all with her: Dad, Caro, Will and me, taking turns to hold her hand.

Afterwards, a young doctor offered his condolences. 'I'm sorry,' he said. 'Your mother was a strong person, she had lived a long time with her illness.'

'Can we have some Valium?' I asked. 'Two tablets each would be good – we're kind of used to it.'

'I'm not allowed to prescribe medicine for relatives,' he replied. 'You'll need to go to your own doctor.'

But he relented. And so we left, and went to a friend's house where we all sat by the pool. Later, when the tranquilisers had worn off, I immersed myself in the water, still cool at the beginning of the highveldt summer. It was getting dark and I stayed there, floating like a crocodile with only my eyes and nose above the water as the pool and the night became one.

A week later we held the funeral. Some of the Market People came, and one or two of my friends from the Carlton. Mum's youngest brother came too, the one she called Golden Boy because he was Granny's favourite. A vicar gave the sermon, and spoke about Mum's life from notes provided during an interview with me. Afterwards, my uncle took me to one side. 'That was a fine service,' he said. 'But, where on earth did the vicar get your mother's date of birth from? He was quite a bit off.'

'Oh, was he really?' I said, moving away before he could dwell on the facts. 'He must have been confused.'

A House by the River

Two years after Mum died, Dad came to London for a visit. I thought he was coming to see me, and my fiancée Jessica. I wanted her to meet him on neutral ground before I took her to South Africa, and I thought he would enjoy visiting her in Oxford where she lived, and where he had been a student. The girlfriends I had taken home to meet Mum had never been serious relationships, even though she always got her hopes up that one of them would provide her with a grandchild.

Things didn't go according to plan. Dad was travelling with his own girlfriend, a woman he'd met in Johannesburg. They were sitting at a table at a café at Heathrow when I went to meet him. I had no idea that they were travelling together, and at first assumed she was someone he'd met on the plane, and that she too was waiting for someone to pick her up from the early morning arrival. Only when Katherine excused herself to go to the lavatory did Dad reveal that they were a couple. She was a decade younger than him, and he said they were hiring a car to tour around the south of England. She had friends to visit too, and for that first night Dad came back to my flat in central London. I was glad that we had the evening alone together, but I was trying to adjust to the idea that he had a girlfriend. Dad was clearly too embarrassed to talk about it, but I was annoyed that he hadn't told me about her. I felt sorry that he was so frightened of telling me he'd formed a new relationship.

'So,' I said as casually as possible. 'What's the story with this woman Katherine?'

'No story,' he stammered. 'She's, um, a girlfriend. That's all.' His words spilled out too fast, and he was blushing, fiddling with the unpacking. 'Look, you don't have to worry, she's not a replacement for your mother. I'll never find anyone like her again.'

'I'm not *worried*,' I said. 'And I don't want you to be lonely.'

'Well, there you are,' he recovered himself. 'She's my girlfriend and that's all there is to it.'

'He's frightened of you,' Mum would tell me when I argued with Dad. 'You're the only person in the whole world who can intimidate him. It's because he's so afraid you'll turn against him. And you never lose your temper with him, he really can't deal with that.'

If Dad was afraid of hurting my feelings, it didn't show. That night while unpacking, Dad uncovered a small grey cardboard box tucked among the neatly folded clothes. It was Mum's ashes, in the same simple container we had collected from the crematorium the day after the funeral.

'Why did you bring them?' I asked. We had never properly discussed what we would do with the ashes.

'She didn't want to be left in Africa,' he said brusquely. 'She was terrified of being left out there, because she thought you kids would all come back to the UK.'

'What are you going to do?'

'Well, your mother always loved the sea. I'd like to scatter them at the coast.'

'Where?'

'I don't know yet.' His voice was unsteady, not because he was upset at the idea, but because he was expecting me to object. He was moving things pointlessly from one end of his suitcase to the other, staring fixedly at the underwear and neatly folded shirts.

Extravagant ideas for a memorial gathering flashed through my head. I imagined hiring a boat and getting my aunts and uncles to come with us so that they could say goodbye. I wondered about getting a priest to conduct some kind of ceremony.

'How about taking them back to the mountains in Newcastle?' I suggested. 'And then we could get her sisters to come, maybe Uncle Herbert too.'

'That's too complicated, I haven't got time for all that. And your mother hated Ireland anyway.'

Part of me was angry. I wanted her to be somewhere that meant something to me, somewhere that we would all regard as a spiritual home. 'Maybe I should keep the ashes,' I suggested, 'until we can all be together one day, and do it properly.'

'Well, we'll talk about that.'

I didn't think much more about it, and over the next few days Dad went visiting around the south of England while I was at work. The night he returned, I cooked dinner. While we were eating, he suddenly announced that he'd been to Dover. I imagined he might have been showing Katherine the White Cliffs. 'What was in Dover?'

'Well, your mother grew up not far away at Folkestone, so that's where I've scattered her ashes.'

I swallowed hard, and couldn't speak for a moment. Inside, I was angry and upset. But I was also aware there was nothing I could do. Carrying on with the conversation calmly took all of the self-control I could muster.

'I thought we were all going to do it together. Or at least I could have come with you?'

'Well, who knows when that could be arranged,' he snapped. He was on the verge of losing his temper, the way he always did when he couldn't justify his actions.

'I think Will and Caro will be upset.'

'Too bad if they are – that's their business. I know she was *your* mother, but she was *my* wife. And sometimes husbands know best. It was my job to do it, and it's done now so there's nothing to argue about.'

I had to struggle not to start crying. 'Where exactly did you put the ashes?'

'I walked along the sea wall and tipped them out at the end. You know your mother loved the sea.'

'What, at the ferry port?'

'Yes, well, she always loved boats.'

'I'm not sure she found P&O car ferries terribly romantic.' Sarcasm was my only weapon. That was how crass he could be. It was like a disease with him.

The next time I visited Johannesburg I took Jessica with me. As we walked into the house with our luggage I had warned her that the three poodles, Mum's dogs, would come bouncing out to greet us. There was no sign of them, and I walked through to the sitting room to see if they had been shut out in the small garden. Then Dad came out of the kitchen with some drinks for us.

'Where are the dogs?' I asked.

'They've gone.'

'Gone where?'

'To the vet, I had to have them put down,' he announced without a flicker of remorse. 'Yes, Kiki was really on her last legs. And the other two were just a nuisance.'

'But, they were Mum's dogs,' I began, trying to control my emotions in front of Jessica.

'Yes. I know they were. But I'm the one who had to look after them and clean up after them.'

I was dumbstruck, but he continued, his voice rising angrily. 'People keep on about the dogs, and how they love them but no one actually offers to look after them. No, I'm the one who has to feed them twice a day and take them to the vet.'

'Did you ask Caro or Will to have them?'

'No, I didn't! If they loved the dogs so much they should have bloody well come and got them.'

In 1997, Dad remarried. It was a happy occasion, and I was glad that he had again found companionship, and love. Carole, his new South African wife, seemed to know how to handle him and his ire, although in many ways he had already calmed down considerably. He was in vigorous health, and he had a regular income from a contract to supply and train security guards for a large office block in Johannesburg.

Life for all of us settled into a more recognisably normal pattern. Mum's death had been a great loss, but I no longer felt torn between London and Johannesburg. I could start to live my own life. But, once a year, Jessica and I would take our own children to Johannesburg to see 'Grandpa'. He lived some distance from the city in a quiet village in a house with a large garden leading down to a river. He and his wife had several dogs, including 'Mac', a black Scottie that Dad chose as a puppy. He planted roses and drank sundowners on the stoep beside the swimming pool. It was the South African life he had imagined for us all when we left Ireland more than twenty years earlier.

Dad still had flashes of temper, but we all learned to ignore them, and steer clear of the topics that inflamed him. He was active, but he suffered from gout and high blood-pressure. Obstinately, he refused to reduce the amount of salt he put onto his food. 'I've been eating salt for seventy years,' he would say angrily if we challenged him, 'and I like it. So don't tell me what I can and can't eat.'

Quite suddenly, he developed angina. It became so severe that he underwent an angioplasty, a procedure to widen one of the coronary arteries. It cured the angina immediately, and for a time he was back to an active life. A few years later he agreed to have knee replacement surgery. 'It's the same bloody knee that's always given me gip,' he told me on the telephone. One of the few childhood stories I knew about him was that as a baby, Dad had been injured by a nanny employed privately by his mother. When he was only a year old the nanny had tugged on his right leg with great force to make him lie down in his pram, and ruptured the cartilage. The nanny was sacked and the cartilage surgically removed. Dad was always warned that the injury would make him prone to arthritis. He also blamed a succession of rugby injuries for a weakness in the joint, and a bad fall during parachute training for the SAS.

'It's all catching up with me,' he joked before the operation. 'It's time I was taken out and shot.'

———————

The operation led to complications and for several months he went back and forth to the hospital, complaining about 'useless bloody doctors'.

My push-me-pull-you relationship with South Africa had not quite ended. A few months later a phone call from Carole alerted me that Dad was weaker than he made out to me by phone, suffering from uncontrolled internal bleeding and recurrent infections. I flew out to Johannesburg to see if I could help. He was in a private clinic where all of the nursing staff, and the other patients, were Afrikaans speaking. They found him a novelty because he didn't speak their language, and jokingly called him *The English Patient* (Ralph Fiennes, 1996). On his part there was no longer any talk of 'stupid Dutchmen'.

'I wish I'd never agreed to this treatment,' he moaned from his bed. He was propped up on a bank of pillows, too thin and very pale. He ignored the food the hospital brought him and I made trips to a nearby shopping mall to buy strawberry-flavoured energy drinks, the only thing he said he enjoyed. 'I'm nearly eighty, well past my "three score years and ten". There's no point in fighting nature.'

'Actually, you're seventy-four,' I corrected him.

He managed a rueful grin. 'Well, maybe, but I feel older than that.'

In the family we had always made fun of his ruthless self-reliance. It was partly why we called him Rambo. Devoid of self-pity, he always reduced every situation to its simplest, crudest form. In his world view, this final sequence of illnesses was only to be expected. Sitting beside his hospital bed I tried to encourage him to muster the energy to recover. He shook his head at me. 'Tim, you can't beat old age, and that's all there is to it. I've just got to face up to it.'

'Mum would never have let you away with a remark like that.'

I said it to goad him, to remind him of how she hated any mention of old age, or the inevitably of its symptoms.

'No,' he said with another quiet smile, and a slow nod. 'I know she wouldn't. But she was stronger than I am. She always was.'

It was by no means clear that he might die, and after a week the doctors told me he was getting stronger. It was time for me to return to my own family in London. 'I'll stay a few days longer, if you want me to,' I said on a final afternoon visit.

'No, you need to get back and get on with your own life now,' he said.

We were alone in the hospital room for just a few moments. I tried to make myself believe that it wasn't the last time I would see him, that he would rally and I would return with his grandchildren for at least one more visit. Sensing my difficulty, he made a rare effort to be positive.

'Go on, I'm alright. You don't need to worry about me any more. I never thought I would find another woman who could love me as much as your mother did, but I've been very, very lucky. You know,' he said without a trace of irony, 'this is the best country in the world. It's been good to me.'

There was no point in reminding him of the years he had refused to acknowledge anything positive about South Africa. A few weeks later, he died at home in the house overlooking the Klip River. His ashes are scattered near the tall rose bushes he and his second wife had planted in the middle of the open grass leading down to the mud brown water. The roses are in orderly contrast to the shaggy, weeping willows at the river's edge and the tall eucalyptus trees with the peeling bark that shield the house from the road. At dusk, half a dozen large Hadeda ibises stalk the lawn plucking earthworms from the ground with their long curved beaks. Their loud barking cry is a very African sound to me, both brave and grand, lonely and futile.

South Africa feels like a home to me now, and I often crave its bright clear light, its open spaces and even the outline of the skyscrapers on the approach to the city from Johannesburg airport. The highveldt thunderstorms are as comforting as a heartbeat, and the flat colours of the parched land in winter are more precious than gold.

The old commercial centre of Johannesburg is a different place now, and many of the shining tower blocks that seemed so impressive when I was a teenager stand empty and dilapidated. As the city has Africanised, the big money and the international finance houses have moved northwards to Sandton, Midrand and beyond. The Carlton Hotel is still there, but it is an empty shell, the doors barred and locked.

The Whatnot, and most of the Market People are gone now too. For so many years I hated them. I was ashamed of knowing them, and I kept them secret from almost everyone I knew. My friends at university and at the BBC didn't know Babette the Tart, or Carl the Cat Burglar, Gerry the Forger and John the Hippie. And they didn't share their houses with Russian lodgers or survive on a diet of Mamma's Chicken Pies and Valium. I never talked about it. Perhaps that was how I protected myself. Living with Mum and joining in with what she called her 'adventures' was as unreal as walking onto a film set, and the Market People were just characters in a scene.

Recently

I am staying with Mum's younger sister in her crumbling house by the sea. Her toy-boy is long gone, and she lives alone in a house big enough for her children and grandchildren to stay in when they visit. It is a solid Victorian building, but there are holes in the roof, and from my bed on the top floor I can see pigeons nesting in the tiles. It always feels colder inside the house than outside, due to the penetrating damp that has taken over the walls since the central heating was turned off seventeen years ago. Light switches fizz alarmingly when you flick them, and there are curling brown mushrooms growing on the ceiling in the hall. After rain, the carpet inside the front porch squelches underfoot. The only heating comes from a small coal fire in the large living room, but my aunt only lights it when she has visitors. She seems immune to the conditions, and winter and summer sleeps with her bedroom window open to the sea air coming straight in across Belfast Lough.

Late into the night we talk about family history, and the things that happened in her youth. We laugh about Granny and her unsuccessful attempts to cultivate the elderly members of the Newcastle Bridge Club in the hope of an inheritance. My aunt laments the fact Mum died in Africa. Auntie Viv loves Ireland, and she could never understand her sister's desperation to leave. She tells me about her own colonial life in Hong Kong, at about the same time we were living in Malaya. 'Oh it was great, we had servants and life was one big party. But I knew I always wanted to come home.'

'Something strange happened recently,' she tells me, giving the fire a poke to produce a last small flame. 'A man rang me and said his name was George. He said he had once been my boyfriend, and that he wanted to apologise for disappearing from my life without an explanation. I didn't know what he was talking about – I thought he was a crank – I didn't even remember ever going out with someone called *George*.'

Somewhere, something stirred in my own memory. I am sitting on Mum's bed on a Saturday morning. She is telling me a story about my aunt, and a boyfriend of whom the family disapproved. 'He was some kind of an artist,' Mum said. 'And he wore sandals with socks, and he had a beard.'

In the family military dynasty such things were decidedly uncool. I remembered Dad joining in with the tale, a general condemnation of my aunt's choice of boyfriends over the years. Mum said that her father, Grandpop, was always terrified that Viv would end up getting pregnant by some 'unsuitable man'.

'But you did have a boyfriend called George,' I say cautiously, not wanting to admit just how much I know about her youth. 'He was an artist and Mum told me he wasn't very clean.'

'Well, that's the extraordinary thing – I didn't remember him at first,' Viv continued. 'He said we had gone out on a few dates when I was sharing a flat on the Malone Road in Belfast with your mother. It was when she and your father were first going out. Anyway, this man George remembered your mother and described the location of the flat very accurately, so I listened to what he had to say.'

'Don't worry, I'm not some kind of a stalker,' he reassured her. 'I'm happily married and I'm a grandfather myself now. But I really wanted to trace you, and tell you that I never forgot about you even though I never saw you again. And I want to explain why. As I left the flat that night to walk back to my digs, I noticed a car following me slowly along the road. When I got to the corner, the car pulled up beside me and a man asked if my name was George. Then he got out and dragged me into the car. There was another man in the back seat and they pushed me down onto the floor and put a gun to my head. They had balaclavas over their faces and I thought I was going to die. Then they said that if I ever saw you again, or contacted you they would come back and I would disappear. They had English accents, so I thought maybe they were soldiers.'

'Isn't that weird,' my aunt mused, giggling youthfully as she stared into the dying fire. 'But after he put down the phone I started to remember things. It was all so long ago . . . but then I began to think that maybe it was all true. And the only person who could have organised something like that would have been your father. Don't you think it *had* to be him?'

'He never mentioned anything like that,' I said truthfully. For a moment my instinct was to deny Dad's involvement.

Then, deep down, I knew for certain that he wouldn't have wanted me to defend him.

'Yes, it does sound *exactly* like the kind of thing he would have done,' I paused. 'But only if Mum had asked him to do it.'